CAUSES AND CONSEQUENCES IN INTERNATIONAL RELATIONS
A Conceptual Study

Michael Nicholson

P
London a

PINTER
A Cassell Imprint
Wellington House, 125 Strand, London WC2R 0BB
Cassell, 215 Park Avenue South, New York NY 10003

First published in Great Britain 1996

British Library Cataloguing in Publication Data
A catalogue record for this book is available from the British Library

ISBN   1 85567 242 1 (hb)
       1 85567 243 X (pb)

Typeset by Keystroke, Jacaranda Lodge, Wolverhampton
Printed and bound in Great Britain by Biddles Limited, Guildford and King's Lynn

CONTENTS

To Christine

Preface

In the academic discipline of International Relations today there is a basic division over what can be done in the discipline and how it can be done. If an individual were the victim of such a split it would be regarded as an acute case of schizophrenia. The disagreements are not about how the international system operates but on the nature of the very things that we can say about the system, if indeed we can say anything very much at all. Many scholars are struggling to develop the study of International Relations as a social science. According to this view, we can have theories about how the international system works which, in general form, resemble those in the natural sciences. Economics is usually cited as being the most successful social science in this respect, this view being particularly popular among economists. Crucially these theories are justified by whether they fit with the facts or not. This is not a fringe area of study but is a central part of International Relations as it is practised today particularly, though by no means exclusively, in the United States. However, a significant and perhaps growing number of scholars argue that what these would-be social scientists are doing is nonsense. Social science, at least as modelled on the natural sciences, is a chimera. The mathematical models and statistical tests of which the social scientists are so proud are idle vanities with no relationship to anything but themselves. There has always been a school of thought which held this point of view about the social sciences. Charles Taylor and Peter Winch have long argued it. However, its advocates have become more vociferous and more extreme with the increasing popularity of post-modernism. From another wing, theorists of the classical school have always been critical of this school of thought, regarding it as an American fad. The first group of critics have a clear and consistent point of view, though one which I shall argue is wrong. The classical theorists are harder to classify.

Though the world groans under the weight of the books on the philosophy of the social sciences, there are comparatively few on International Relations as such. Charles Reynolds has written a sequence of books critical of the empiricist endeavour. The excellent book by Hollis and Smith, one a philosopher and one an International Relations specialist, outlined the field in a balanced way, though I have many points of disagreement with them. My own earlier book, *The Scientific Analysis of Social Behaviour: A Defence of Empiricism in Social Science* (Pinter, 1983), was an avowed attempt to justify the empiricist approach in International Relations. While this present book overlaps my earlier one to some extent, it develops further, and also modifies, some of the ideas discussed there and, to a lesser extent, in my later book *Rationality and the Analysis of International Conflict* (Cambridge University Press, 1992).

The first three chapters are largely expository of standard positions, though I hope the sections on the relationship between explanation and prediction might be of interest to more seasoned scholars also. These chapters are intended to be useful to those who come fresh to the philosophy of the social sciences. The rest of the book is a justification of the view that we can acquire systematic knowledge of the behaviour of the international system with an examination of the presuppositions of such a view. The established scholar can skim the first three chapters. Some of the later chapters have significant expository elements in them, enough to make the argument clear to the newcomer to either the philosophy of the social sciences or to international relations. I hope readers will come from different academic backgrounds. Therefore I have provided a glossary to save too much interruption in the main part of the text.

I am indebted to Allan Hayes, formerly of Leicester University, Hidemi Suganami of Keele University and Andrew Williamson of Sussex University for the care with which they have read this manuscript even though they may not approve of the final version any more than they may have approved of the earlier one. Though they have not seen this particular version of this manuscript, I have discussed the issues involved with Tony de Reuck, formerly of the University of Surrey and Keith Webb of the University of Kent over many years. Their imprints are here in many places though I would have difficulty in saying precisely where as my ideas have moved around over the years. As ever, I am indebted to Christine Nicholson, not only for careful reading of the successive drafts of this manuscript, but for a long-term broadening of my intellectual horizons which has made possible this sort of examination of fundamentals.

Michael Nicholson
Brighton, 1995

1
Introduction

The nature of international relations
International relations, as a scholarly discipline, is concerned with the study of such basic aspects of human behaviour as war and peace, imperialism, the discrepancies of wealth between societies, and other such topics. More specifically, scholars in the discipline look at the relationship between arms races and war, alliances and war and the interaction between language and national identity. It asks questions such as why and in what circumstances do people fight wars? What caused World War I? Why do states come together and integrate, such that some of the activities which were earlier done separately are now done together under the auspices of such organizations as the European Union? Why do others, such as Yugoslavia, break up? Are religious beliefs important when we try to explain such phenomena or are they merely a cover for the desires and interests of states (or, more properly, of the rulers or governments of states)? Similarly, does the growth of multinational corporations reduce the powers of the state or does it merely mask them, with corporations acting as surreptitious agents of the state? Conversely, are states themselves nothing but the pawns of social classes or religious groups which are the real holders of power and the determinants of international behaviour? How significant, then, is the state as an actor in the international scene? We can go on to ask why and under what circumstances do empires grow? Why did the British Empire, so vast as to be the largest ever known as recently as 1945, decline to a few scattered islands within a quarter of a century? How has behaviour altered in the face of nuclear weapons? Is war more or less likely as a consequence of weapons of mass destruction?

It would be hard to deny that these are important questions deserving of answers if answers are at all possible. They touch on some of the basic moral issues which have always faced the world and continue to face it today. Practitioners of the discipline are not modest in their concerns, though they are, or ought to be, modest about their successes in providing useful insights on the problems. To date, these have been few and ambiguous. For example, there is very little we can confidently assert as knowledge about the causes of war, one of the central problems of the discipline. This is unfortunate, as these problems are among the most fundamental to be faced by human beings, while our ability to tackle them has been meagre so far. An improvement of human behaviour in these respects is much to be desired.

A crucial problem which besets the discipline, and, indeed, the whole of the social sciences, is that there are basic disagreements about how even to approach the problem. Disagreements in a natural science are, for the most part, due to lack of data, or lack of a theory which is sufficiently well substantiated for it to be generally accepted. Thus, at the time of writing, there are disagreements about the mechanisms used by migrating birds to navigate the huge distances which many of them do. However, scientists in the area know what would constitute an answer to the question and are in general agreement about the characteristics of an answer. The disagreements come because there are two or more competing theories but there is no doubt what a theory should consist of. Of particular importance, scientists could specify what evidence would convince them that their favoured theory was wrong such that they would be compelled to accept a previously unfavoured rival theory. A big enough research programme would probably solve the problem. This is not the case in international relations. It is not just that there is the lack of a theory established by generally accepted criteria. There are fundamental disagreements about what such criteria consist of. This is a totally different type of disagreement from the internal disagreements about which is the best theory. (There are those too, of course, among those who agree on the more fundamental issues.) Clearly this is a serious problem.

In very broad-brush terms there are three schools of thought as to how we should approach such questions. The first is the social scientific school, whose members hold that it is possible to develop a social science of international relations in terms of which questions such as the above can be answered. They are sometimes, if mis-leadingly, known as 'behaviouralists', in view of their interest in behaviour (somewhat broadly construed).[1] They take economics as a general model while the economists in their turn take the natural sciences as their model. The second group I shall call the classical theorists.[2] They are sceptical of the extension of the social sciences to the analysis of such subjects. They believe one can, nevertheless, analyse such phenomena in terms of theories. How-ever, such qualities as 'judgement' come into the assessment of truth rather than the somewhat narrow, and stricter, concepts of testing which the social scientists adopt. The third group are a newer brand, culminating, at least so far, in the post-modernists. Their origins are to be found in the work of many earlier writers, notably Peter Winch (1958), and they form part of a clear tradition. There are several post-modernist analyses of international relations, though earlier the discipline had been relatively neglected within this tradition. Its adherents doubt the nature of what most of the social scientific school would regard as social knowledge.

The aim of this book is to add to the discussion of two central questions: are generalizations possible in international relations and, if so, what are the rational grounds for believing in such generalizations? The second question is a useful one only if there is an affirmative answer to the first. I am not neutral in the debate. I am defending the social scientific approach, arguing that it is genuinely contributing cumulative knowledge to the understanding of the conditions which lead to war and peace. However, I want to give a clear and I hope sympathetic portrait of the serious arguments against it. Implicit in my argument is the view that understanding a problem is normally a prerequisite for modifying it, while the problems of international relations, and centrally war, are aspects of behaviour which urgently need modifying. Explicit is the view that it is possible to have a theory of social behaviour, and in particular of international behaviour, which is in some sense of the word objective – objective, that is, in the sense of being separate from the moral views, or even of the prejudices and other subjective views, of the commentators. Though the argument will be abstract and conceptual, it is of great practical significance. We desperately need answers to questions such as why there are wars. However, if we cannot recognize an answer when we see one, or doubt we can have such an answer even in principle, then we are in serious trouble.

The methodological dilemma

A central argument about the nature of our knowledge of social behaviour involves the issues of 'explanation' and 'understanding'. Broadly, those from the social scientific school argue that one can explain social events in terms of theories in much the same general sense as one can explain events in the inanimate world. We can have theories in terms of which we can talk of causes and effects, and which are testable by confrontation with the facts. Others, inspired by ideas of Wittgenstein that have been interpreted in terms of the social sciences by Peter Winch, argue that the role of the social observer is to empathize with actors and understand social behaviour in terms of the actors themselves. Winch holds that empathy and understanding make generalization impossible. If generalization is impossible, then theories in the normally understood sense are not possible either, from which it follows that explanation in such terms is likewise impossible. Winch is also pessimistic as to how far one can go in understanding societies very different from one's own. Others, following Weber, hold that these two modes are not as inconsistent as Winch alleges, and that some degree of understanding does not preclude generalization and hence explanation. In substance, this last point of view is the one I shall argue for.

A view rather like that of Winch is held by some historians and philosophers of history, and in particular R. G. Collingwood (1946). Collingwood wrote before Winch (and is referred to by Winch as being within the same general school of thought) and before the publication of Wittgenstein's *Philosophical Investigations*, which was a central influence on Winch's thought. Collingwood's view, that the job of the historian is to understand events as the actors involved understood them, is very close to Winch's position. Collingwood's scepticism about how far one can go in such understanding is, if anything, even more extreme than Winch's. In its more optimistic forms, this mode leads to the view that social events are explained *sui generis*. Narrative history is written in this mode. Following it through in a more pessimistic vein, one might conclude that it is hardly possible to say anything at all, a view we shall come across again in Chapter 6. Some would argue that, even though generalizations may exist, in the social world they are very weak and insecure and we might as well ignore any systematic search for them. Though we perhaps do engage in social explanation and relate events to generalizations, we use our common sense in formulating these generalizations, giving them no great status. We formulate them or abandon them as seems convenient. Fundamentally, the facts are seen to speak for themselves.

Unsurprisingly, the different methodological principles lead to different ways of studying international relations. Some overlap, and there is a fair degree of methodological confusion which I shall try to untangle.

Adherents of the social scientific approach are relatively clear about their general methodological position even if there are numerous disagreements internally. They are trying to produce testable and replicable propositions about international behaviour which are of their very nature generalizations. The replicability comes from agreement about procedures, so that two people, perhaps with very different political and moral views, looking at the same problem about the behaviour of the international system will come to the same conclusions. There are two central but interrelated modes: the development of theory (a term which I shall discuss in much greater detail later), and the systematic collection of data. Systematic collection of data usually, though not always, means statistical data. The important assumption behind it is that is possible to classify phenomena together as being 'similar'. This is an issue we shall return to. By now a lot of data of this sort have been gathered, particularly on the period from 1815 onwards (Cioffi-Revilla, 1990).

The development and application of social science methods to international relations were not universally welcomed when they became a significant feature of the discipline in the 1950s and 1960s. Most scholars of international relations at that time were originally trained in disciplines such as history or, sometimes, law.[3] The thought that their discipline was being invaded by statisticians and calculators was not appealing. Further, the 'behaviouralists' rather grandly assumed away a number of epistemological problems as was then the custom among social scientists at a time when a rather extreme form of positivism was widely held. However, few of the classical scholars tackled the epistemological difficulties that should have troubled them too. Judging from the frequency of favourable citations, Hedley Bull in 1969 spoke for many in his 'International theory: the case for a classical approach'. It was a witty defence of common sense but one which evaded the genuine and serious epistemological problems involved in his own work and that of many others who adopted a similar methodological approach.

The so-called classical school of international relations theorists of Morgenthau (1948), Bull (1977), Wight (1966, 1979, 1991) and others is hard to place methodologically, though probably they would feel a position close to the historical 'weak generalization' school of thought congenial. Despite their objection to social scientific methodology, their analyses often depend on generalization and one is left wondering just how consistent their position is. Morgenthau exemplifies the methodological and epistemological confusions in claiming at one time to be developing a theory based on 'objective laws that have their roots in human nature' (Morgenthau, 1960, p. 4). These laws are apparently close to being deterministic, as they are 'impervious to our preferences, men will challenge them only at the risk of failure'. Quite why they should not be susceptible to the standard methodologies of the social sciences is unclear. However, shortly after Morgenthau urges us to 'retrace and anticipate, as it were, the steps a statesman . . . has taken' and then to 'look over his shoulder when he writes his dispatches; we listen in on his conversations with other statesmen; we read and anticipate his very thoughts' (p. 5). Such a view would endear him to Collingwood. However, these two approaches are not easy to reconcile. Some clarity on the issue would have been helpful.

Confusingly, the classical theorists such as Morgenthau and Bull deplore the methods of the social sciences but still wish to retain a theoretical approach where theory rests on some concept of generalization. Concepts such as power are used, especially in such constructs as the balance of power. They see themselves as in the tradition of the older classics such as Hobbes and Hume. Their position is anomalous. They make the crucial step of accepting the legitimacy of generalizations without accepting the methodological consequences. The acceptance of generalization has led some writers to characterize Morgenthau, at least, as a positivist* though this seems to be stretching the application of the term beyond reasonable limits. The positivists (or, as I would prefer, 'empiricists') are very self-conscious about the proper procedures required for making truth claims. It is one of their major virtues. It is precisely on this issue that Morgenthau and the other classicists are lax. I shall argue later that, once one has accepted the legitimacy of generalization, whether statistical methods are used or not becomes an issue of methodological convenience. It is not a profound issue of principle as some seem to think. The failure of some of the leading classicists to appreciate these methodological points has led to a great deal of confusion. One of the great misfortunes of the discipline of international relations has been the failure of those in the classical school to analyse the epistemological problems which face them.[4]

The later part of the 1980s saw the rise of post-modernism in international relations as in all the other social sciences. The position of the milder post-modernists is quite close to that of Winch, though some, while holding that empathy with and understanding of people is the central goal of the social observer, are more pessimistic about its feasibility (Ashley and Walker, 1990b). Among some there is a near-total rejection of the idea of any sort of shareable knowledge, a view enhanced by the obscure style in which some of them choose to write. Post-modernism has raised some interesting questions which need addressing, though the answers the post-modernists provide are, in my view, almost always wrong.

The non-behavioural approaches, both as they were then and largely as they have remained, are less clearly defined from a methodological and epistemological point of view than those of the social scientific school. In a rather over-simplified way we can distinguish between approaches which look upon events as being *sui generis* and those of the so-called classical theorists. Practitioners of the first are rarely self-reflective about their methodology, seeing it as self-evidently legitimate. This is a view which would be generally accepted even by the behaviouralists, who would argue, nevertheless, that there were some hidden epistemological premises which were not the less real for being unrecognized. A great deal of the analysis of current events in the international scene is likewise carried out with little concern for its theoretical underpinning though, as time and space are limited, there is no particular reason why it should concern itself with theory. One may quite properly discuss a particular instance of, say, an international crisis without conscious reference to theory because in this case one wants to emphasize the particular. This is very different from denying overtly the legitimacy of the discussion's dependence on generalization. Both positions can be coherently defended even if, in a practical instance, the differences may be subtle and not very obvious.

Basically, the argument of this book suggests that the scholars of the 1960s and earlier – Richardson (1960a, b, 1993), Deutsch (1963, 1964), Singer (1968, 1980, 1993) and so on – were and are on the right lines. There are many eager successors. A continuing development along the same path is necessary if we are to get more to grips with international behaviour and in particular international violence. The argument will be essentially philosophical in that it is primarily a discussion of concepts. I discuss the underlying nature of social behaviour, using facts and theories as illustrations and not as ways of deciding the argument.

There are two underlying disagreements with other schools of thought. The first is fundamental: some serious and coherent arguments can be made that the nature of social behaviour is such that it is not amenable to scientific methods as commonly understood. However, I believe these arguments to be mistaken. They apply not just to international relations but to all the social sciences. I shall discuss them throughout the book. The second is a disagreement with the classical school of theorists. While pouring scorn on the behaviouralists they themselves use generalizations and so are themselves open to the most serious critique of the behavioural position. Other disagreements with the classicists are comparative details. I shall also return to this argument, but less frequently, as I believe it to be largely the result of a misunderstanding.

The contrast between classicists and their descendants and behaviouralists is less clear than was once the case. It was not that classical work could not be fitted into a perfectly respectable epistemology so much as that the classicists did not realize what it was and were apt to attack those who did in terms which would have invalidated their own approach. This is less true now. The passions are spent. The debate is more over the degree of usefulness of certain methodologies, such as formal and statistical methods. It involves less heat than when it was believed that there was a fundamental disagreement over the epistemological bases of those methodologies. More central today is the debate over how far it is possible to understand human behaviour in terms recognizable to the actor, how relevant it is to do so and whether doing so precludes some sort of scientific analysis of international relations.

The desire for science

By, perhaps, the eighteenth century, the general mode of scientific explanation as far as natural phenomena were concerned had acquired sufficient status as to give it some sort of privileged position as a general mode of explanation. When explanations of physical events provided by the natural sciences conflicted with those provided by religious works, the scientific explanation became the dominant one. Whatever doubts there may be about scientific explanation, and we shall discuss these further below, science not only gave a coherent account of the world but also provided the basis of technology. By the end of the eighteenth century the development of technology had become spectacular and undeniable. Scientific explanations had been very successful when offered in mechanics and chemistry, where, for the most part, these had not involved any religious conflicts, such documents as the Bible and the Koran, perhaps fortunately, being silent on those subjects. This success meant that people were apt to look more charitably on scientific explanations where there was some conflict with the religious authorities such as over geological matters and the theory of evolution. 'It works' is always a powerful argument.

Given the technology which has evolved from the scientific methods in natural sciences, it is understandable that the same sort of approach should be looked at with a degree of envy by the social scientists. If some sorts of diseases can be cured or alleviated by scientific medicine, which manifestly they can, it is natural to wonder whether various forms of obviously malign social behaviour can be alleviated also by a technology based on an equivalent analysis of social behaviour. The way we run societies could be improved enormously – we could stop having wars, for example. We seem totally unable to arrange this. However, if we had a science of social behaviour which adequately explained why wars were fought, then it might be possible to have a technology of social behaviour which would make the elimination of wars more of a possibility. The pursuance of a science of social behaviour is a proper and laudable goal. If we can find a theory of aspects of social behaviour – whether this is of full employment or war – then the possibilities of improving the human lot are enormous. It might not be possible, but at least it would seem right to try.

Unfortunately there does not seem to be a neat proof that such an endeavour is either possible or impossible. If we could show that such a theory were by its nature impossible then we could abandon the search and save a lot of trouble. If we could show that it were possible, then we could go ahead and look for it with some hope of finding something. All we can do is formulate the conditions which are required for a theory of international relations (or any other social science). That is, how would human beings have to behave if it is to be possible to describe their behaviour in a scientific manner? Do they behave in such ways either always or sometimes? Would the answer to this last question be a genuinely empirical statement, which can tested against our observations of how people in fact behave?

Science consists of two principal characteristics: systematic observation and theorization. It is the two together which give it its power. By systematic observation I mean looking at either all the cases which are available, or some selection of them based on some systematically random method such that we do not bias our observations either in favour of or against some hypothesis. For example, we should avoid taking cases just because they are spectacular or are well known for some reason. The mundane is theoretically just as important. Systematic observation enables us to say whether generalizations are in fact the case or not on the basis of the existing evidence. However, science and the dependent technology require not only systematic observation but also theorization. Precisely what we mean by this is discussed in detail in Chapter 2. In general, however, a theory involves the relationship between lots of generalizations and not just single ones in isolation. Thus we can design an effective submarine because we have a theory of the pressure of water, of how various metals resist such pressures and of the shapes in which they should be moulded to resist water pressure most effectively. These are not *ad hoc* generalizations but parts of theories. No doubt there has been in the past a great deal of 'inductive technology'. Boats were probably built by simply observing which designs worked well long before there was any theory of the mechanics of boats. The more systematically boat builders observed past efforts, the better would their designs be. No doubt people in fact generalized excessively from spectacular shipwrecks but the shrewd boat builder would look at all cases of both failure and success. Such a boat builder would be half-way to science. However, the predictive element would be missing. One might make some tentative guesses as to how a new design would behave but on the whole it would be guess work.

Is international relations a social science?

If a social science in the sense of deductive theory about the world is impossible, as many argue, then the question in the title of this section is redundant. It is not a social science because nothing is. However, let us assume for the sake of argument that some aspects of social behaviour are analysable by the methods of the social sciences. Given this, can international relations be developed as a social science? It would seem to be an odd sort of question to ask as the obvious answer would seem to be yes. However, some scholars, notably classical theorists, appear to hold the view that this is not so. I use the cautious phrasing as the assertions are implicit rather than explicit. Thus clear statements about international relations are made while silence is maintained on other social sciences at points where one would expect them to be repudiated if that is in fact what people believe.

The exemplar of social scientific methods is economics. The concerns which troubled Peter Winch about the nature of social explanation leave most economists unmoved. The few post-modernists essentially go unheard. Blaug (1992) considers the views fleetingly and rightly points out that their adoption would mean the end of most of modern macro-economics (and more of micro-economics than he seems to allow as well). However, he argues about the *verstehen* (understanding) doctrine that 'There must be something wrong with a methodological principle that has such devastating implications' (the 'devastating implications' being the demise of macro-economics due to methodological impropriety). But why? Perhaps it is the case that macro-economics is impossible. Blaug (1992), along with most economists, assumes that it must be possible and we must find a way of justifying it. I broadly agree with Blaug's general position but we must still leave open the possibility that the scientific monism which we both espouse might be untenable. The position must be argued for. Broadly, economists of all schools of thought aim to produce testable theory in a deductive form and believe they are doing this. Mathematical economics in particular has the imprimatur of Karl Popper (1959), whose attitude to the social sciences is at times ambivalent. If we take Winch seriously then all this is pretence. His strictures apply just as much to economics as to any other forms of social behaviour. Economic behaviour should not be specially privileged. This seems to be largely disregarded both by economists and the philosophers of the social sciences who espouse the understanding point of view in social theory.

If social scientific economics is legitimate, then why not international relations? Both are accounts of how human beings behave in groups. They account for different forms of behaviour and different types of groups but ultimately it is human behaviour in human groups. I can see no reason to make a distinction. My claim is that if economics can be formulated in the standard social science mode, then so can international relations. However, if a social science is in general impossible then economics likewise is impossible, at least in the deductive, testable form in which it has traditionally been practised.

There is one route which could distinguish international relations from other social disciplines. If we go to Hegel and other thinkers who espouse an organic theory of the state or the nation, then we can argue that states are something totally different with no resemblance to the organizations which are studied elsewhere in the social sciences. International relations would be the study of states alone and a separate study altogether from any other aspect of social behaviour. Such a view would be a 'holist' view in which the state is seen as a whole unit and not just an amalgamation of its constituent parts. However, this needs developing further as holism does not necessarily equate with a Hegelian view of the state.

First, let us elaborate the concept of holism and the related concept of reductionism. In economics and organizational theory, a social group such as a business firm is often considered to be a collection of individuals interacting. It is defined as just those individuals and does not have an existence above and beyond these individuals. This does not preclude a holistic analysis as distinct from a reductionist analysis of the firm. A reductionist analysis of the firm is one where the whole structure is regarded as reducible to the activities of its parts and where the whole is, in some sense, a direct summation of the parts. A holistic view is one where one needs to interpret the activities of the parts in relation to the whole in order to understand the behaviour of the group. In this sense a firm could be regarded as analogous to a human body where the behaviour of the body is not just the sum of the actions of the liver, the heart, the kidneys and so on. However, whether one's social analysis is holistic in this sense or not, the firm is still the collection of the individuals. Many views of the state are individualistic in the same way, holding that the state is in principle the same sort of organization as a business firm in that it is a collection of individuals albeit related to each other in very complex, interdependent ways.

An organic theory of the state is one where there is a notion of something additional to the state which is above and apart from the individuals who are its members. It is qualitatively different from a business firm in that it is not just the sum total of the individuals involved. Even in holistic analyses of organizations such as a firm, the holism resides in the interactions between the individuals who are its members and not in some concept of an existence over and beyond the membership.[5] It is possible for the interests of the state (or nation[6]) to be different from that of any or all of the individuals who are members of it, which quickly leads to the view that an individual's rights *vis-à-vis* the state are negligible or non-existent. This view is not very fashionable now, though it was once. (Its espousal by Adolf Hitler did nothing for its social standing, though there are ominous intimations that this might change.) It is, of course, a purely metaphysical theory as there is no way of establishing the view one way or the other. It leads one to argue that the prime entities in international relations are qualitatively dissimilar from those in economics or any of the other social sciences. It is not a view, however, which seems to have been held by classical theorists. They seem to have accepted essentially an individualistic view of the state but they have been unwilling to follow through the consequences of this point of view and accept the validity of the social scientific method for the analysis of international relations.

A religious argument also might be used to distinguish certain forms of social behaviour, analysable by social scientific methods, from those which are not. Thus, some might argue that the course of human development was the fulfilment of the triumph of Christianity, Islam or whatever was the favoured religion. It would be consistent to argue that those aspects of social behaviour which were largely separate from the development of the religion, such as the behaviour of business firms, could be analysed by social scientific methods, but that those which touched on religion were of a separate genus. Such arguments have little currency, as those who might be tempted to argue for such a position seem uninterested in the philosophy of the social science, for the moment at least. However, such views could be made into a consistent, if in my view misguided, philosophy of international relations. With the possible exception of Martin Wight, the classical international relations theorists did not make, and probably would not have wanted to make, such an argument, and my criticism of them still stands.

International relations in an intellectual context
Histories of international relations abound but usually as if it were some isolated discipline detached from any other intellectual

context and in particular from the rest of the social sciences (Olson and Groom, 1991; Hollis and Smith, 1991). This reflects an earlier detachment from the rest of the social sciences and a still reluctant attachment in many quarters even today. The purely philosophical arguments can be made without a history but it is helpful to tie the subject in with the developments in the social sciences. It has been a consistent weakness of international relations to fail to see its place in the broader perspective of the social sciences but as somehow isolated and oddly separated from some of the broader debates in intellectual life.

International relations as a recognized discipline is relatively new. The first chair in Britain was founded just after World War I and in response to it. The discipline was seen essentially as an aspect of history, though lawyers played a significant role. This was largely true in both Britain and the United States. The discipline developed during the 1930s in what was predominantly an idealist mode; that is, many practitioners were explicitly working along lines which assumed that world peace would be preserved by strengthening the League of Nations and collective security. They held a somewhat optimistic view about the nature of human beings. Optimism about the human condition took a sharp knock with World War II and the realists, headed by E. H. Carr in 1939 and Hans Morgenthau in 1948, took centre stage, arguing that the struggle for power was the dominant feature of international politics. The substantive arguments were immensely important, relating to a world which looked as though it might well destroy itself, and it is not surprising that some of the central scholars in the discipline did not interest themselves directly in methodological questions. There is always a problem as to how much effort scholars should devote to analysing how they do something and the nature of what they do as distinct from actually doing it.

Around the middle of the 1950s, some ten years after the end of World War II and when the Cold War was fully established, a group of scholars arose who, impressed by the apparent success of their colleagues in such disciplines as economics, but depressed by the lack of success of scholars in international relations, began to apply the techniques of the social sciences to its study. The reasons this should happen at that time I shall discuss briefly later, but undoubtedly it happened. The pioneer of this approach is generally held to be Lewis Fry Richardson, a Fellow of the Royal Society on account of his work in meteorology (Richardson, 1960a, b and 1993; Ashford, 1985). He started work at the end of World War I, shocked, as were numerous of his contemporaries, by his experiences at the Front as a member of the Friends' Ambulance Unit and determined that such an event would not be repeated. Many young men of the day who decided that the War's horrors should be known fully wrote poetry and novels; Richardson collected statistics and invented a social science. The activities are not mutually incompatible and may be commoner than is supposed.[7] Unfortunately, as we know too well, neither science nor art were successful in their pacific intentions. Richardson not only collected statistics but also developed some theoretical models of various international processes – noticeably his theory of arms races, worked out in the deductive form familiar to natural scientists and economists. His work was largely ignored until the surge of interest in social scientific approaches some time after World War II. Work in this explicitly social scientific mode has gone on ever since in international relations. There have been major developments in data collection particularly of the period since 1815, and developments in theory where the theory is explicitly conceived of as being testable by precisely the statistical data which the data collectors were amassing (see 'Some social scientific contributions to international relations' later in this chapter, and also in Chapter 7). The groups frequently overlapped.

Nevertheless, the detachment of classical scholars working in this tradition from what else was going on in the study of social behaviour was surprising and extreme, particularly in Britain. Thus, a major 'early modern' scholar of international relations, Martin Wight, was in Oxford in the late 1930s, when the debate over logical positivism was passionately pursued. Hedley Bull, an admirer of Wight, was in post-war Oxford at a time of great excitement over the philosophy of science as well as the philosophy of the social sciences. Karl Popper held his court at the London School of Economics, which along with Oxford was in those days one of the centres of traditional scholarship in international relations. Popper was extremely influential with a number of younger economists working in Britain in the 1950s and 1960s. This makes it stranger that the epistemological debates which so absorbed the economists, psychologists and most other social scientists did not spill over into the discipline of international relations even if only for a considered rejection. They surely cannot have been regarded as too trivial to merit consideration, though this seemed to be a theme of Hedley Bull's single, though famous, contribution to the subject (Bull, 1969). It was not the same in the United States, where scholars were more warmly disposed towards behaviouralism, though in the early stages paying scant attention to the epistemological bases. Outside the United States, an interest in empirical theory was confined to a handful of scholars. In general, international relations scholars as a group have always been sceptical of the possibility of a theory of behaviour which would explain war. The sceptics, who are barely visible in economics, are a powerful school among international relations scholars, perhaps because of the discipline's origins in history with its atheoretical mode of approach.

Other social sciences were booming in the early post-war years. Economics seemed to be becoming a genuine and effective policy science. For the quarter-century after World War II, it seemed that predominantly capitalist economies such as those of Western Europe and the United States could provide a respectable rate of growth with full employment and low inflation by using an economic technology based on a Keynesian theory of the economy. This seemed to exemplify the development of theory and its use in technology in a parallel way to that in which it had evolved in the natural sciences. In social psychology, the analysis of small-group behaviour provided some reasonably well-attested generalizations and scientific principles from which group performance can be improved[8] in specified ways. Along with this success went the development of the computer, which offered immense possibilities in the understanding of complex systems by simulation and in the handling of data in quantities hitherto undreamt of. The application of mathematical methods to the social sciences was going apace in all disciplines and seemed to be producing a body of deductively based knowledge. The development of theory in mathematical form has been central in the development of economics and still is. A genuine accumulation of knowledge appeared to be taking place, accompanied by a lot of self-conscious thought about the nature of the social sciences at that time (and ever since, for that matter). By the 1950s, there was a steady adoption of a rather extreme positivist approach, and many social scientists could be called, and many called themselves, logical positivists. A classical expression of this view was given in Milton Friedman's famous essay 'The methodology of positive economics' (1966),which was very influential among economists and well received outside the discipline also. He argued that predictive ability was the sole criterion of a scientific approach and that even if a theory or model was based on empirically false premises, if it predicted correctly that was all that was required. Even those who disagreed with him, such as Archibald (1966), did so within the same broad framework. Whatever the variations, the general notion of a social science based on testable (or refutable) generalizations had a firm grip on many of the practising social scientists at that time.

It was in this context that the rise in behavioural international relations took place. The puzzle is not so much why it should have come then, given the state of the rest of the social sciences, but why it should have taken so long. Richardson's work was seized upon as a basis for a behavioural international relations, while, from a rather different perspective, the theory of games was seen as a significant tool for the analysis of international behaviour. The new international relations scholars espoused the general behavioural principles taken as a matter of course by most of the other social scientists. The classical scholars remained above the fray, however, for reasons which to me are still puzzling and obscure.

Only Peter Winch, whose work I shall discuss later, was a voice crying in the wilderness against the behavioural trend, though, as far as most social scientists were concerned, he might as well have saved himself the trouble. His ideas, published in 1958, were discussed vigorously by philosophers but paid scant attention to at the time by social scientists, who felt themselves to be in the full flood of discovery. His views would have provided no consolation to the classical realists had they taken note of them.[9] The classical realists were and are as open to his criticisms as the behaviouralists.

The future path of the social sciences has not proved as glittering as it seemed rational to hope in the 1950s and 1960s. Economics has been a disappointment. Unfortunately the growth and stability of the post-war Western economies did not persist and the Keynesian theory, at least in its pure form, became increasingly inadequate both as an explanatory tool and a guide to policy. Many governments replaced it as a guide to policy with a monetarist theory which quickly looked equally inadequate. At the moment, there is no widespread agreement on the theory of how a predominantly capitalist economy works at the aggregative level, and how, if at all, it can be adjusted, so that it works at something more or less corresponding to full employment. However, economists as a profession appear to be methodologically optimistic, as Blaug exemplifies. They are reluctant to consider the possibility that it might be impossible to formulate such theories as an issue of principle because of the totally different nature of social behaviour on the one hand and the behaviour of inanimate things on the other. Some specialists in other disciplines such as political science and, of course, international relations are less coy about entertaining the prospect.

The apparent successes of the social sciences were not surprising to its adherents at the time. The natural sciences were held in general high repute, as they had been since the nineteenth century, and the glittering successes of technology based on science, from medicine to space exploration, were self-evident. It seemed natural that social scientists should try to emulate the natural scientists' successes. The high repute of the sciences seemed to decline after about the 1960s, though for reasons unconnected with the philosophy of science. It is argued that science has brought us the nuclear bomb (which it already had in the 1950s), environmental degradation with probably worse to come, and a tendency to arrogance in highly technological professions such as medicine. This is, of course, true, but it does not contradict the fact that the scientific method has enabled us to gain an extraordinary understanding of the natural world, confirmed by the toughest of tests, the ability to manipulate it in predictable ways. To argue that human beings have made regrettable use of the powers of technology is different from arguing that the knowledge basis from which it is derived is flawed, and, indeed, has nothing to do with it. To blame science in some abstract sense for the nuclear bomb (or the military aeroplane for that matter) is to miss the point. However, for whatever reason, science as an activity is less highly regarded by many people in the 1990s than it was in the 1950s (for example, Appleyard, 1992). It seemed obvious to many in the general intellectual ethos of the 1950s that to be scientific was a 'Good Thing' and that international relations could only be improved by becoming more scientific and hence by emulating the emulation of the natural sciences by the other social sciences. If this should turn out not to be possible (and many could scarcely conceive that this should be so), then it would be grounds for the most profound regret. This view, though still widely held (I include myself), is less general than it once was. There always were some who distrusted science and the scientific approach (a group which seemed well represented among classical scholars of international relations – Martin Wight stands out as a prominent example). However, the general ethos was more positive towards science and the general view that reason and rationality were the guiding principles for a satisfactory society. The Enlightenment was taken for granted as a positive step for the human race, and the idea that it was in some sense a mistake, as some of the French post-modernists appear to be arguing, would have been regarded with incredulity.

Four common misunderstandings
There are a number of points which it will be simpler to clear up an at early stage. The view I advocate is sometimes called 'positivism', particularly by its critics. This is the first misunderstanding. While this is not outrageously misleading it is nevertheless inaccurate and carries with it some connotations I am anxious to disown. I prefer to call my position empiricist, though even this means broadening

the concept of empiricism, particularly when it comes to discussing mental events such as perceptions. In political science and international relations it is also called 'behaviouralism' on the grounds that it deals only with manifest behaviour. Positivism is often used to mean logical positivism, a view which, in its extreme form, even its earlier protagonists such as A. J. Ayer subsequently disowned. In this view, all proper problems can be solved by the methods of the natural sciences. The only meaningful statements are either *analytic* (that is, logical or mathematical) or *synthetic* (that is, empirical or decidable as true or false by observation of the external world, either directly or indirectly). Other statements are meaningless. That is, they cannot be true or false, they just are without any meaning – the term is used in a literal sense. As other statements include ethical statements, metaphysical statements and aesthetic statements, this view eliminates many traditional philosophical concerns. However, for my purposes it would be an unnecessary debate to get into even if these days it were not rather old-fashioned. I wish to establish the possibility of a social science of international relations (and thus the social sciences in general). Strictly I do not need to concern myself with debates about the nature of ethics. I can be content with a demarcation criterion as proposed by Popper, where we can demarcate scientific statements, being empirical or logical, from non-scientific statements without having to commit ourselves to any view about the non-scientific statements.[10]

However, the view that moral debate in international relations is precluded if we adopt a social scientific approach is the second misunderstanding. There is no need to carry over from logical positivism a pile of conceptual baggage which is irrelevant to the primary argument of this book. Many behavioural scholars hold strong moral views about the behaviour of the international system and became involved in the discipline for moral reasons: they wish to make the system work better according to their principles but they think this is possible only by first subjecting the system to a rigorous scientific analysis. Richardson explicitly held this view. Thus the arguments in this book are unconnected with debates about normative international relations, a field which is currently very active (for example, Brown, 1992; Nardin and Mapel, 1992). It is perfectly possible to do both.

The third misunderstanding is that social scientific work necessarily involves quantification. Admittedly, a lot of work in the social scientific tradition is quantitative, and the stress on the centrality of generalization makes it natural that various forms of measurement quickly become involved. Further, the emphasis on deductive theory naturally draws it towards mathematical methods with their close (though not always absolutely necessary) links with quantification. However, the two are not identical. A lot of case study work is completely consistent with the social scientific mode but need not involve quantification as such. Further, work for which the ultimate tests will be quantitative might have a long pre-quantitative period before the final stage of quantitative testability is reached. Likewise, theory development does not have to be mathematical. While not all behavioural work is quantitative, the reverse is not the case. It is hard to see how quantitative work, in the sense of actually measuring things, statistically or otherwise, can be other than behavioural as it involves generalization. However, there can be and is normative work which is mathematical: a classic is Arrow's *Social Choice and Individual Values* (1963), and from long ago there is a work whose title emphasizes the point, *The Theory of Games as a Tool for the Moral Philosopher* by R. B. Braithwaite (1955).

The final misunderstanding is the confusion between behaviouralism and the realist theory of international relations (itself not to be confused with realism as it is used in philosophy). Briefly, the realists argue that international relations is explicable in terms of three principles: that states are overwhelmingly the primary actors; that states are primarily motivated by the search for power; and that the behaviour of states is largely explicable in terms of their relationship with other states (that is, that internal and external politics are largely separate). Clearly, there are differences between different theorists but these principles characterize them all.

Curiously, some have argued that realism and behaviouralism are the same, the second being little more than a sophisticated version of the first. However, others have seen behaviouralism as being a challenge to realism. The first view stems from an accidental characteristic of data, whereas the second stems from an accidental characteristic of the history of thought. To some extent realism lends itself to behavioural analysis at the level of testing. Many statistics are collected by states and thus a lot of data are available for an investigator at that level. At other levels it is often much harder. Further, while inter-state war is by no means the only sort of war, a great many wars are between states and it seems appropriate to try to explain them in terms of state behaviour. This might bias people into putting a disproportionate effort into examining realist hypotheses simply because of the availability of data. This is not always such a good thing from the point of view of a realist as these hypotheses do not do well under test (Vasquez, 1983). Vasquez, indeed, delivers a severe blow to the credibility of realism by using behavioural methods. However, the availability of vast quantities of data from state sources as opposed to any other does seem to bias behaviouralism, if not in favour of realism, then towards a consideration of the state-centric aspect of the realist picture of the world.

The superficially opposing view of behaviouralism as a challenge to realism comes from the accident that the classical theorists such as Morgenthau were dominant in the discipline during the 1950s when behaviouralism was beginning to emerge as a serious school of thought. Morgenthau and later Bull were very opposed to behaviouralism, as has been made clear already. However, their opposition was methodological, not substantive. Indeed, some of the earlier behaviouralists were realists. In fact, the two schools of thought concern different things. Behaviouralism is a methodology while realism is a theory of how the world behaves. It is perfectly possible to be a realist-behaviouralist, an anti-realist anti-behaviouralist or an anti-realist behaviouralist, though in the first and third of these one should, in the last analysis, be willing to give up one's position in the light of evidence. The one position which is incoherent is the one which many hold: it is not really possible to be an anti-behaviouralist realist. A realist, who, after all, depends for the coherence of the view on generalizations, should also be a behaviouralist, however inadvertently.

Why the problems are important

As the questions asked in international relations are of such importance, it would seem to be appropriate to get on with trying to answer them rather than self-indulgently reflecting on the nature of knowledge. After all, the natural scientists, whom some of us so much admire, spend little of their time pondering the nature of explanation and rather more of their time actually explaining things, often to the profit of the human race. Unfortunately we face some serious problems which, though they are abstract, have practical implications. Scholars are fundamentally divided on how they would answer these questions. Many argue that they are not answerable or, if they are, they are answerable only as questions of subjective opinion. Others argue that there are ways of answering such questions which are in some sense objective. This is a much more basic disagreement than is found in general in the natural sciences. It is a disagreement about the nature of knowledge. That is, there are differences first about how to start investigating these subjects; whether it is worth starting in the first place as there is nothing much one can find out. If one rejects that, then there are disagreements secondly about the sort of things it is possible to do having found something out.

Consider the case of the Cold War. The standard view held in the West is that the Soviet Union did not venture further after 1948 (with the overthrow of the Czech government) because it was deterred by Western powers and in particular the United States. This justified the nuclear deterrent. This view is widely understood. An alternative view held by many on the political left and a number on the nationalist right is that the Soviet Union did not particularly want to come further West. The goal of Russia for many centuries had been to build a solid block of buffer states to guard against the historically expansionary West. Having done this, the Soviet Union, as the successor of Greater Russia, did not want to move further. Thus, the Soviet government was not being deterred: it had no desire to do what it was accused of wanting to do. A further alternative is that the Soviet Union was deterred, not by the armed forces of NATO, but by the complexities of trying to hold down yet more reluctant allies which would have been more trouble than it was worth. On this view, the recurrent uprisings in Eastern Europe were the West's best guarantee. All this presupposes a potentially malevolent USSR and a basically benevolent USA. Another view is that we had two superpowers which, as superpowers will, wished to expand. The *status quo* was preserved by mutual deterrence until one collapsed through internal weakness. This view stresses power. Another view stresses the ideological cleavage. It was a battle of ideologies which again led to mutual deterrence. However, the motivation here is very different.

I have suggested five alternative hypotheses but even these are not exhaustive. Some of these views are mutually inconsistent. Members of governments, whether those of superpowers or other states affected by the Cold War, would take different decisions according to which theory they held. The range of effective decision itself is an issue of contention. There is therefore an important set of questions involved in how one distinguishes between the various interpretations and the various theories which lead to these interpretations. Is it possible to do so in any sort of objective sense? In general the social scientist is arguing that it is possible to do so in principle even though the practice may turn out to be difficult. Others argue that, in the last analysis, which view is adopted is a matter of taste (Frankel, 1988). It is not possible, on this view, to distinguish between the hypotheses even in principle.

This last view, if really taken seriously, has horrendous implications. The policies we adopt depend, of course, partly on our values, which in their turn determine what we wish to be the case. They also depend on what theory we have about the world. Our theories tell us what to expect from different courses of action but different theories will lead us to expect different things. If theories are issues of taste then we have no rational basis for selecting one rather than another and we can have no rational set of expectations[11] about the future. But policy can be carried out only on the basis of some rational anticipations of the likely future consequences of our choices and the likely future consequences of alternative choices. Thus we need to look carefully at the source of these rational expectations and see whether we can have some basis for formulating them. It is unlikely that Frankel really meant what he said in an extreme form. However, there is a legitimate question as to how far we can have theories which enable us to anticipate the consequences of our actions and how much these can be grounded in a solid understanding of human behaviour as distinct from our prejudices. This requires the sort of conceptual analysis carried out in this book.

In the case of the Cold War we are then faced with a number of crucial questions. If it is possible to distinguish between the various hypotheses in principle, how in practice does one do so? What is the evidence which is required? What, indeed, constitutes evidence? These are all points of serious contention. For most of the time in the natural sciences, the equivalent problems are not acute. People know how to distinguish between hypotheses, and know what evidence is relevant and what it consists of. Thus there is little need for the practising scientist to worry too much about it. This is not the case in the social sciences. Consequently we should worry about it as an issue which quickly relates to what we do.

Some social scientific contributions to international relations

I am advocating a particular approach to international relations. As work in this tradition has been going on for some decades, I should indicate what has been happening in this tradition and give a brief outline of some of the major clusters of work in behavioural international relations. I believe these are genuine advances in our knowledge about the behaviour of the international system. It is this style of work I seek to justify so it is desirable to indicate what it is. As a survey it is in no way comprehensive. It is a brief sketch, a cartoon sketch perhaps, in which I try to indicate a complex and detailed picture with a few lines. Like a cartoon, it will also have its strongly idiosyncratic flavour though perhaps more for its omissions than its inclusions.

Testing is central to empiricist studies and much of this is bound to be statistical. Hence the provision of data is a requirement. This was seen as crucially important by Richardson, whose data, published posthumously as *Statistics of Deadly Quarrels* (Richardson, 1960b), were a model of statistical care. Other workers such as Quincy Wright (1942) had produced data of great importance though with less awareness of the problems of reliability and meaning than Richardson. The data are still worth consulting in their own right, and Wilkinson (1980) has given a considered judgement on the work.

The need for data spurred on a number of scholars in the earlier days of behavioural international relations. They sought data which would both give a picture of the past and be brought up to the present time as far as possible. The Correlates of War (COW) project, operating out of the University of Michigan, is a particularly significant one. The data are largely from 1815 onwards. The end of the Napoleonic Wars was a big jump in European history at least. There is diffidence in going before that date because of the issues of reliability – always a problem in social statistics and in particular historical statistics. Richardson was likewise uneasy about going too far back, though Quincy Wright was less cautious. The data are not collected abstractly, without any problem in view: the organizers of the data such as Singer and Small who have carried out many studies using the data (as reported in Singer, 1993), and many more scholars both associated with the study and outside it have used the data for carrying out a number of important studies of international systems. Though perhaps the most commonly referred to, the COW project is not the only one. Cioffi-Revilla (1990) gives a good overview. The Dimensionality of Nations (DON) project is particularly concerned with interstate interaction and has resulted in a mammoth study by Rummel (1972). These all perhaps go to indicate that data exist in international relations and in large (though never sufficient) quantities. The collectors and users of the data are fully aware of the data's limitations.

Apart from the actual data themselves, the statistical approach has led on to many other studies and a general 'statistical attitude' with its consciousness of the need for testing. It provides the raw material for the testing of generalizations. Without statistical data there are narrow boundaries to the testing of generalizations, but untested or at least untestable generalizations are of doubtful value in the construction of knowledge about the social world. Thus, the statistical attitude leads on to such work as that of Vasquez (1983), whose acute critique of realism, referred to above, consists of a statistical analysis of realist hypotheses.

International crises have been a central topic of interest among international relations scholars of all schools, though behavioural studies have been particularly useful. This interest is due to the fact that wars are normally (though not invariably) preceded by crises, while they are methodologically easier to study than most things in international relations. They take place over a short time period, normally between small social groups such as governments, and thus the number of variables involved is limited. The interest of social scientists started early on with the studies at Stanford University by Robert North (North *et al.*, 1963) using content analysis of the 1914 crisis. The International Crisis Behavior (ICB) project from the University of Maryland is a statistical study which analyses all crises between 1929 and 1979. Psychologists understandably have been interested in crisis behaviour and one of the classics in the field is Irving Janis's concept of 'groupthink', a concept originally devised in organizational psychology but later applied to decision-making in international relations. Another classic is Graham Allison's analysis of the Cuban missile crisis in terms of different decision-making theories. These studies, which are predominantly in the social scientific tradition, represent genuine advances in knowledge.

Scholars such as Herman (1972) have used gaming and simulation techniques to study crises though both techniques have been used for a much wider set of problems. Guetzkow was one of the pioneers of their use in international relations (Guetzkow and Valadez, 1981). Subsequently, world modelling approaches to environmental and resource problems, using elaborate computer models, have illuminated those issues, albeit controversially. General world modelling (for want of a better term) as represented by the Globus model (Bremer, 1987) has likewise proved insightful in emphasizing the complex interacting nature of the economic and political system while showing the possibility of some limited policy predictions.

A lot of classical realist theory is based on the assumption that decision-taking is done by rational actors who aim to pursue the goals of the state as effectively as possible. Some important contributions from so-called 'rational choice theory' and 'theory of games' show the difficulties involved in such assumptions in conflict situations, notably those illustrated by games such as 'chicken' and 'prisoners' dilemma' (see 'Games, theory of' in glossary). Though testable theory is derived from such models, an important aspect of this work is to show the conceptual difficulties involved in such concepts. The conceptual aspects of co-operation and conflict become clearer when stated in formal terms and enable computer simulation work such as that of Axelrod (1984) to lead to interesting and relevant results. Formal modelling of the sort used in game theory and its derivatives is a very powerful method. Again Richardson was one of the leaders, with a model of the arms race, though this was not of the game theory genus. Though the application of the Richardson model has so far been rather disappointing, it has been methodologically highly innovative.

A whole range of other topics could be referred to. Negotiation, mediation and similar processes have been looked at through a variety of social science disciplines such as social psychology and game theory (Raiffa, 1982). These are selective examples, though important ones. I shall refrain from the cliche of saying the list is endless, which it clearly is not, and that it is uniformly successful, which likewise it clearly is not. Some work in the field has been disappointing and some trivial. However, the cumulation in the various fields has been anything but trivial, at least if it is as meaningful as its adherents such as myself claim. There is the possibility that the generalizations on which most of the work depends will prove spurious though it is central to my argument to say that they are not.

The basic argument of the book

The main argument concerns how far the study of social behaviour, and in particular that in the domain of international relations, can be modelled on the study of natural behaviour. In other words, can the pattern of a social science be presented as being of the same general form as the pattern of a natural science? In the earlier stages of behavioural international relations, during the 1950s, it was thought that the structure of a natural science was basically unproblematic. Some details needed sorting out but the general nature of a science and the character of scientific explanation were believed to be understood. From writers such as Bertrand Russell through to the Vienna Circle's logical positivism, further developed by Karl Popper, a reasonably satisfactory picture of a natural science seemed to have been constructed. It was then thought that this model of science, which the economists in particular were following with apparent success, could be adapted to all the social sciences without fundamental modification. Both of these views have been challenged. First, problems have been raised about this view of the natural sciences in a moderate form by scholars such as Kuhn (1962) and in an extreme form by Feyerabend (1975). The earlier near-total dominance of the original model has wilted, though, with some modifications, it is still the leader of the field. Secondly, it is argued that, in any case, the parallelism between the social and the natural sciences is false. Whatever the nature of the natural sciences and whether the empiricists had it broadly right or not, social behaviour, it is argued, is fundamentally different from natural behaviour and must be analysed in a totally different way. Thus it is possible to be an empiricist as far as the natural sciences are concerned and still refuse to accept that this is an appropriate approach for the social sciences though it is hard to see how the reverse could be the case.

However, I shall argue that the damage done to the earlier view of the social sciences by these critiques is not fundamental. The objections to a social scientific study of international relations are surmountable and alternatives are flawed. Though there are significant qualifications to be made to the earlier empiricist model as it was accepted in the 1950s when the behavioural movement began to get seriously under way, the positions widely held in the 1950s as regards the natural sciences were broadly right. The qualifications are not trivial but what remains is still recognizable as the same structure. I do not wish to disparage the opposing view. I shall address the serious objections to the empiricist view.

The argument fundamentally concerns what is rational belief about social behaviour. It is easiest to start with a few beliefs which I do not challenge. Given these, we want to see what follows from them; in other words, what beliefs are interrelated such that one set of beliefs entails, in a logical sense, another set of beliefs. Thus, I take for granted the external world which exists more or less as we perceive it or, when our perceptions appear to mislead us such as on such issues as the apparent flatness of the Earth, as given by more coherent accounts which also depend on experience. This is not to argue that experience does not need to be organized but that brute experience at some point constrains our rational belief about the external world.

This has some particular implications. I take as unchallengeable the belief that the Earth is more or less spherical and goes round the Sun rather than vice versa and that this is a matter of fact and not a matter of taste or social convention. Its repudiation would require disbelieving in a lot of the facts of common experience and, with the knowledge and experience of the present day, would involve living in a fantasy world. It is unlikely that anyone reading this book would want to challenge it, though a few moments' thought as to why may not come amiss. This is where I start as far as the natural world is concerned.

As far as the social world is concerned, I view the proposition that there is a much higher level of unemployment in the UK today than in 1950 as a matter of fact and I hold that definitions which yielded different results would be perverse. That unemployment would be incomprehensible to a medieval peasant is irrelevant if the purpose of our analysis is to reduce or eliminate unemployment today. The 'fact' and its cure are in the present-day environment where they are perfectly comprehensible. However, this is a question which is more open to rational disagreement than is the case of the heliocentric theory of the solar system. A debate today challenging the heliocentric view of the solar system is either an exercise in argument or silly. A very convoluted argument, using eccentric definitions, can be made out to counter the other position I assert about unemployment. I would regard such an argument as probably a waste of time and involving us in being able to say practically nothing about the social world. However, it involves a lower level of silliness than does the first. I shall show that, if one accepts these two views, one can say a great deal about the nature of the social world in quasi-scientific terms.

An outline of the book

Given the nature of the argument, the first step must be to describe this basic approach to scientific explanation. This is done in the second chapter. It contains a relatively uncontroversial account of a particular approach to scientific explanation, the covering law mode of explanation, though, of course, whether that approach is appropriate or not is controversial. However, I also raise some objections to the supposed symmetry between prediction and explanation which some of the more severe supporters of the covering law model of explanation firmly espouse. I suggest that a rather weaker mode of explanation may be more relevant to the social sciences. Chapter 3 approaches more directly the special issues involved when we try to explain social behaviour in the same way. In particular, I look at one of the central issues in the philosophy of the social sciences, namely what is involved in the distinction between explaining social behaviour and understanding social behaviour. This is primarily an expository chapter. Shifting more to controversy, Chapters 4 and 5 discuss problems which beset both the social and the natural sciences. Refutation, the supposed corner-stone of science, particularly in the Popperian picture, is a much more awkward concept than appears at first sight. In Chapter 4 I consider the issues of paradigms and scientific research programmes as they relate to the development of international relations. Chapter 5 deals with the issues of tautologies, their uses and abuses. I discuss whether scientific theories can ever be refuted when looked at as a whole. In Chapter 6 I return to the issues of social behaviour in a less expository and more argumentative style. I consider the understanding mode of analysing social behaviour, in particular the views of Peter

Winch, and show how it is possible to reconcile the undeniable issues which Winch raises with a scientific and explanatory mode of analysis. Chapter 7 moves on to the problems of quantification in international relations. This is an important issue if we are concerned with testing hypotheses in the area. It also raises more concerns which relate to the issues of tautology and other issues raised in Chapter 5. By redefining terms and measures and manipulating functional forms it appears we can either confirm or refute practically anything, particularly when we have the sort of degree of flexibility we have in international relations. As the economist R. W. Coase once remarked, 'If you torture the data sufficiently, nature will always confess'. If we do not have rules which prohibit some conceptually possible states of the world, then everything is possible. What we say becomes vacuous as there is no way of showing it to be false. I shall argue that there are limits to the scepticism suggested by Chapters 5 and 7, but the range of possible rational belief is broader than we might have liked. In Chapter 8 I discuss the issues of rational choice theory, a branch of theory of great interest and importance in itself but also one where the understanding and the explanatory mode seem to meet. I conclude with a discussion of values and their relevance to science and the scientific endeavour international relations. The discussion of ethics and morality in international relations is of great importance. We end on a classically empiricist note by affirming that the analysis of what is the case is separate from the analysis of what ought to be the case.

Notes

1 Unfortunately 'behaviouralism' is often confused with 'behaviourism', a once-popular approach in psychology. Behaviourists endeavoured to explain behaviour as a set of input–output mechanisms which did not need the concept of the mind to produce an explanatory schema. Behaviouralism is not the same as behaviourism though confusion is understandable. Both explicitly espouse the scientific method. However, as I shall argue later, most of the work done by behaviouralists would be meaningless without concepts of interpretation and hence the mind.

2 I adopt this term as it is used by Hedley Bull in his well-known article 'International theory: a case for the classical approach' (1969) I cite this article frequently (like many others) and normally critically (unlike many others) in this book. It is one of the rare discussions by classical theorists of epistemological issues. It has the further merit of being clear, which makes it particularly appropriate as an object of criticism.

3 Quincy Wright, widely regarded as one of the founders of the behavioural tradition with his monumental *A Study of War* (1942), was an international

lawyer. His was an unusual intellectual development, particularly at the time. He was a remarkable scholar.

4 A major exception is Charles Reynolds (1973, 1981, 1989, 1992), though in my view his epistemology is very different from that of the classical school of Bull, Morgenthau, Wight and so on.

5 On a Roman Catholic view of the Christian Church, the Church is also to be seen as an organic body in the same way as the state is seen by Hegel. A difference between Protestants (in particular Low-Church Protestants) and Catholics is in the view of the former that the Church is an organizational structure of individuals to pursue their common goals, rather like a rather large-scale club, or a business firm, whereas the Catholic view is organic as described.

6 'State' and 'nation' are to be distinguished. In most definitions, a state is a legal entity in which a government controls a given area of land and the people living there. A nation is harder to define but definitions normally involve some concept of a common culture, the identification as a nation, and the self-definition of its members as members of the nation. In organic theories of the state it is more likely that state and nation might be held to coincide or that they ought to coincide as in the nation-state (Deutsch, 1963).

7 Kenneth Boulding is a well-known poet–social scientist who was a prominent early worker in the field of behavioural international relations and peace research. The discipline in which he was trained was economics.

8 I use the word 'improve' with diffidence as it requires various normative criteria. For a fuller discussion of the issues involved, see Chapter 9.

9 Charles Manning, Professor of International Relations at the London School of Economics, did take note of Winch. He was a prominent idealist and a long way from scholars such as Morgenthau. However, he did not really construct his international relations on the sort of basis that would have matched up with Winch's position.

10 Though Popper did have strong views about metaphysics and was very opposed to the logical positivists for their distrustful attitude.

11 'Rational expectations' has a technical meaning in economics. The meaning here is less specific and would include the economists' concept of rational expectations as a rather special case.

2
The classical picture of science: theory explanation and predicition

Theories

In this chapter I shall give a brief outline of some of the basic concepts of scientific theory, scientific explanation and related notions as they are employed in the natural sciences. These views are widely held, and disputes (which are many) concern the range of their application rather than their applicability to comparatively restricted processes. It is this model of scientific explanation which many social scientists, including scholars of international relations, seek to emulate, some, indeed, claiming to have succeeded rather well. Thus, we need to be clear about the nature of these issues as a background to the discussion, which is, essentially, about whether this mode of analysis and explanation can be applied to social behaviour. Further, some of the concepts we shall develop in this chapter – for example, the relationship of experience to science – will be used in the later analysis of social behaviour.

The central concepts are those of 'theory' and 'explanation'. A theory is a set of generalizations about the behaviour of the world. These generalizations are interrelated as described below. An explanation (dealt with in more detail below under the heading 'Explanation') relates specific events to a more general class of events and it is most satisfactory if it is related to a theory. Thus, if asked to explain why a house fell over the cliff into the sea, we offer an answer in terms of how cliffs in general weaken under the impact of the sea, why particular forms of rock are stronger than others and a host of other generalizations. We relate these to the specific characteristics surrounding the house. It is a relationship of the general to the particular, where the general are the relevant theories which 'cover' that particular event.

Central to the notion of a scientific theory is the concept of generalization. In its simplest form it is simply a matter of saying that whenever certain conditions are fulfilled, some specified consequence can be expected. Thus, if a stone is released, it falls to the ground; further, it always falls to the ground. It is a statement about the consistency of behaviour so that, from some set of initial conditions, a set of consequences can be deduced. Generalizations of this sort must have been intuitively recognized from an early stage in human life.

However, science involves more than merely observing the world and noting the generalizations, though systematic observation of generalizations is a crucial part of it. A scientific theory relates the various generalizations in a deductive framework so the truth of one is not independent of the truth of some others. Thus, in the case of classical mechanics, the theory sets off with a set of postulates from which we can deduce a number of consequences. If the initial postulates are true, then the consequences are necessarily true. Hence, from Newton's laws of motion★ we can deduce the laws which apply to the behaviour of a pendulum. Then we can check these laws relating to the pendulum by direct observation, but we have grounds for believing in them even before we have carried out the systematic observation of the behaviour of the pendulum. The deduction is a strict one. If Newton's laws of motion are the case, then the equations covering the behaviour of the pendulum are necessarily true. This is a general process. We start off with a set of postulates which we assume to be true. These postulates are generalizations about the behaviour of whatever system we are interested in. They may or may not be directly testable. From these postulates we deduce that further generalizations are true and call these 'laws'. This is known, cumbersomely, as the 'hypothetico-deductive method'. The chain, from laws of wide generality to laws of lower generality (that is, describing much more restricted processes), can be a lengthy one and in sciences such as physics often is. In economics, the chains, though short by the standards of physics, are nevertheless substantial. In international relations our logical chains are relatively short, with the Richardson model★ being probably the longest at least of the well-known theories. In general, these laws are testable in the sense that they can be confronted with facts and found to be consistent or inconsistent with them. If they are found to be inconsistent so that the law is falsified, then at least one of the propositions from which they were deduced must also be false. The logical system 'carries' truth (or falsity) along with it. If the initial propositions are true, then what it deduced from them is also and necessarily true. The point is that the structure as a whole is involved. If a proposition at the end of the line is shown to be false then the truth of anything from which the proposition is deduced is thrown into doubt. The problem might be corrected by a relatively modest restatement of some of the earlier propositions, including the postulates. However, at least one of the postulates will be involved, and any of the laws of the systems whi..h are deduced, either directly or indirectly, from that postulate will have to be restated even if only slightly. Thus, a scientific theory is not merely a collection of isolated generalizations but a set of interconnected generalizations whose truth is interdependent. One of the powerful aspects of science is this interrelatedness and the ability to build up by deduction from a set of postulates a large edifice of propositions which it would have been difficult to perceive without the logical structure.

We must look more carefully at the nature of the statements which are involved in a scientific argument. They are 'empirical generalizations', but what are these? The central argument is that science concerns the structure of the external world which is ultimately determined by experience. However, if one set of experiences persuades us to make a particular empirical generalization (such as seeing a lot of white swans) then another set of conceptually possible experiences would make us reject that generalization (such as seeing a red one).

A statement can be true but vacuous such as 'In London it is always either raining or not raining'. It is vacuous in that whatever is the case it is necessarily true so it tells us nothing about the state of the weather. However, if we say 'it never rains in August in London', then we have made a statement which could be false, and in this particular case can quickly be shown to be false. Because of its potential falsity this tells us something about the actual world if it is true. That is, a scientific statement has delimited what is true from plausible alternatives which nevertheless are not the case. Any factual statement about the world, such as 'All swans are white', excludes the conceptual possibility that there exists a red swan. The sighting of a red swan would refute the proposition. Clearly, this involves not *defining* a swan as white. If we do so, then observing white swans merely establishes that swans exist. If we come across something which is both apparently a swan and apparently red, we have to deny either that it is a swan or that it is red. Not to do so violates the definitional criteria for being a swan. As scientists we are concerned with observing what is not necessarily true but is in fact true but could be false. For a scientific proposition to be genuinely empirical it has to be conceptually possible for it to be false. If we cannot specify what would refute it or something which is logically deduced from it, the proposition is not an empirical proposition at all.

Explanation

There are two modes of explanation. The first is as described above where an event is interpreted in terms of a scientific theory. It is generally referred to as 'causal explanation'. The second responds to a question 'Why did Joe go to New York?' with an answer of the form 'in order to get married'. That is, rather than relate the specific event to a set of generalizations, it is related to a goal which someone wishes to achieve. Such explanations are known as teleological. They are used more by way of analogy in the natural sciences but in the social sciences they are of great importance. I shall consider them in Chapter 8 and for the moment concentrate on causal explanation and the form of explanation known as the 'covering law model of explanation'. I shall initially explain it in its purest form and modify it later.

Suppose we wish to explain some set of events. These are described by a set of statements, known as the *explanandum*, and which we shall denote by E(1), E(2), ... , E(k). Thus, in the above example, these will be statements about the collapse of the house into the sea after it has occurred. They are statements about specific conditions at some specified time and place and are not generalizations. The *explanandum* is explained in terms of other statements known as the *explanans*. These consist of two separate sorts of statements. First, there are expressions of the relevant laws which we shall denote by L(1), L(2), ... , L(n). These are generalizations which apply whenever the appropriate conditions apply and are not peculiar to this instance. Secondly, there are the specific initial conditions, which we shall denote by C(1), C(2), ... , C(m). Like the E statements these are statements which describe specific events in time and space and are not generalizations. Clearly these initial conditions must take place either earlier than, or simultaneously with, the events they explain. They must not occur later. In the example above, they are propositions about the nature of the rock or soil at the time, the rainfall, the positions of rivers and so on which are the specific variables to fit into the theory.

This, then, is the background and, as related, will not cause too much surprise. However, in the strict version of the covering law approach, for an explanation to be a true and full one the E statements have to be *logically deduced* from the conjunction of the C statements and the L statements. Thus if we know the first two sets of statements to be true, and the laws to be true, we can deduce the last lot without doubt from them. This is more obviously so if the statements in question are mathematical statements, which is often the case. The schema can be laid out as follows:

$$C(1), \quad C(2), ... , \quad C(m)$$
$$L(1), \quad L(2), ... , \quad L(n)$$
$$\overline{}$$
$$E(1), \quad E(2), ... , \quad E(k)$$

However, according to this view in its strong form, if we do not have a sufficient structure fully to deduce the Es from the earlier statements then we are deluding ourselves that we have a full explanation. Thus, if we find that the explanation was incomplete without inventing another law it is not appropriate, on the basis of this one case, to assume that the missing law is in fact true. It might incite interest in looking for such a law, though in the case of the land-slip this is not too likely as the relevant laws are well known. However, we do not have a full explanation unless we confirm the likely truth of the missing law independently of the particular case we are trying to explain. More probably, in the case of the landslip, we will find ourselves with a missing initial condition. Thus, we might realize that we would have had a full explanation if we hypothesized the existence of a hitherto unknown stream. If we look for it and find it then we have achieved a full explanation. However, for the full explanation the existence of the stream must be determined by means (such as looking at it) which are independent of its role in the explanation. Once independently confirmed, the stream can play a proper role in the explanation and make it a complete one.

The covering law model leads directly on to a model of prediction. In the case of explanation it was presumed that both the initial events (described by the C statements) and those to be explained (described by the E statements) had already happened. Suppose we take the case where the events described by the C statements precede those described by the E statements in time. As the E statements are logically deduced from the rest, it can readily be seen that, from a formal point of view, it is not very important whether the events have or have not occurred. If they have occurred it is explanation whereas if they have not it is prediction.

It is often argued that prediction is the sternest test of science and, indeed, that if a supposed theory cannot predict, then its full scientific credentials are in doubt. This reasoning derives directly from the covering law model. If explanations are full and proper explanations, such that the explanandum really is deduced from the explanans, then prediction is possible. If prediction is not possible, so it can be argued, then we do not have proper explanations. The two activities are intimately tied together, divided only by their placing in time. In this sense, prediction and explanation are symmetrical concepts.[1]

This reasoning is impeccable from a formal point of view[2] but it is too strict. Many systems which we would undeniably call scientific are not very predictable except in a general sense. It is true that eclipses of the moons of Jupiter can be predicted with remarkable accuracy: predictions of the weather, earthquakes and tidal surges fare less well.

In many cases the difficulty comes in knowing what the initial conditions are. Thus, we have difficulty in predicting earthquakes because the timing and extent of the earthquake depend on the precise location of the tectonic plates, which cannot be determined with sufficient precision. The geological laws involved in an earth-quake are perfectly well understood and there is an obvious sense in which we can explain a particular earthquake. Strictly it does not meet with the requirements of the covering law model but this is for practical reasons. This suggests that making prediction the criterion of science is too strict, though still conceptually appro-priate as a standard to aim for. In principle the initial conditions could be specified and observed but in practice it is impossible. This leaves open the possibility that further developments in observational technology will surmount the problems. However, there are some further objections in principle deriving from considerations of chaos theory. In some cases it may be impossible *in principle* to specify the initial conditions with sufficient precision to make prediction possible. This is a much more fundamental objection as it means that no developments in technology will make prediction possible.

Because of the significance which is sometimes given to the issue of prediction as a criterion of scientific success, and because this criterion no longer seems to be appropriate, I shall devote the next two sections to the issue, the first to the practical problems, the second to the conceptual.

The practical problems of prediction: the zebra principle
Hempel, Lakatos and Popper all assert, in one form or another, that the real test of a scientific theory is its ability to predict and that prediction is the true criterion of whether a particular theory is correct or not (Hempel, 1965a; Lakatos, 1970; Popper, 1959). I shall argue both that this criterion is too stringent in many cases and that it is in principle over-demanding in others. Both arguments are important but the second shows the criterion to be even conceptually inappropriate, though this view could have become recognized only with the recent developments in chaos theory, of which more below. This is not to say that, when the full panoply of the covering law applies with full knowledge and completely deterministic laws, it is inappropriate even if it is rarely practicable. However, it can no longer be maintained that it is a necessary condition for a satisfactory explanation, as earlier philosophers of science thought.

Predictability can be achieved when a small error in the initial conditions leads to only a small error in the prediction. However, if a small error in the initial conditions leads to a big difference in the prediction then our predictions are likely to be poor unless our measuring instruments for the initial conditions are sufficiently precise and we are able to carry out the appropriate measurements. This is the problem with earthquakes. A small difference in the initial conditions leads to very big consequences – that is, an earthquake or not.

I shall discuss the difficulty of obtaining a comprehensive list of the antecedents necessary to explain something in terms of the explanation of the evolution of the zebra and for this reason call it the 'zebra principle' (Nicholson, 1983). The zebra evolved, probably incrementally, from proto-zebras and earlier animals which were more remotely zebra-like and so on. The zebra, having arrived, proved suitable for its environment and flourished. However, the precise combination of genes and chromosomes which produced the zebra was just one set of a vast number of possible sets (not strictly infinite but extremely large). Most of these sets would never occur, for reasons which may not be strictly random but which are essentially impossible to trace through. Of the possible sets, only a small number would have produced animals which were viable and, of the possibly viable animals, only a small number will actually appear. However, the development of the zebra can be explained in terms of antecedent conditions which would be hard to fault as a proper explanation in covering law mode. Likewise, its survival when it existed can be explained. However, if we had an account of evolution up to the zebra we could not have predicted the arrival of the zebra on the basis of any evidence we could in practice acquire or are likely to be able to acquire. Thus there is no practical symmetry between prediction and explanation in this case.

We can still, of course, make a conditional prediction and argue that, just prior to the arrival of the zebra, if a zebra-like animal were to develop it would be viable in a certain environment; we could argue that a zebra was possible in the sense of viable, even if we could not predict it would happen. Thus sparrows did not evolve in North America but were brought from Britain. They were clearly viable and had they evolved there they would have been part of the indigenous bird population of North America. If we went to a desert island we would not be able to predict in advance what flora and fauna there would be. We would be able to predict possible patterns, given the climate, soil conditions and so on. Some of the patterns would be conditional on other aspects of the prediction.

For example, climatically a bird nesting on the ground might be possible. However, its existence would also depend on whether or not a rat-like rodent (which would eat the eggs) also lived there. Thus we could not predict that a particular type of animal or plant would be found, but only that particular, mutually consistent groups of animals and plants would be found. This is clearly a very long way from unambiguous projections of the unknown, though, equally clearly, it is a long way from complete ignorance. It is a prediction of what is possible, not what is necessary, and is probably not unique. A unique prediction would require an enormous amount of data covering the initial conditions where, if the data were a little bit wrong, it could have big effects on the predicted consequences. These incomplete predictions are nevertheless quite consistent with the covering law approach to explanation. We know, *ex post*, exactly what fits in to every part of the explanation. However, we are unable to find the initial conditions prior to an observation of what is to be explained.

In terms of social behaviour, this aspect of prediction is important. Certainly, in the existing state of knowledge there is no possibility of unambiguous projection into the future. Further, looking at the experience of the natural sciences, there seem good reasons to suppose that this may be in principle impossible, though this is not yet certain. It would be ironic if the social sciences proved better than the natural sciences in this regard. However, this form of reasoning leads us to the 'X is possible' mode of prediction. Just as we could not in advance have predicted the kangaroo in Australia, nor can we predict a revolution, except perhaps very close to the event. We could say, however, that under certain conditions a revolution is possible and in others impossible. We are still not too good even at this, but, if we could, it would put us on a par with the earthquake predictors.

In the limits of an 'in principle' argument, the practical difficulties of maintaining the symmetry between explanation and prediction would not matter. We could dismiss the practical problems with a philosophical disdain and argue that the underlying principle would still hold. The above points were familiar to the philosophers of science cited, though they did not stress them. However, the problems raised in the next section are problems of principle which demolish the criterion of predictability as a universal rule.

The conceptual problems of prediction: chaos theory
In a completely closed system,[3] without random elements, one would expect there to be total predictability at least in principle. Oddly, the development of 'chaos theory' has shown this not to be

true. This has come about in the past few years, though qualms were appearing in the early 1960s (Lighthill, 1986). Essentially it can be shown that it is impossible to predict beyond a certain time horizon in some closed systems governed by totally deterministic laws. Notice I say 'some' closed systems, not all.

Chaos theory is now talked about widely and has many popular books and even television programmes made about it. Extravagant claims have been made so that it has become difficult to say just what its significance is. However, it certainly has some conceptual significance in the present context as it contradicts the notion that explanation and prediction are symmetrical even in principle.

As the characteristics of a chaotic system are counter-intuitive, some explanation of the issues involved will be useful. I shall begin by describing a non-chaotic system which has a *bifurcation* in it to illustrate one of the basic concepts. This system behaves in a limited number of different ways (say two) where there is a boundary between the two. Initially, suppose we have a bowl of water and slowly reduce the temperature. At 0°C it alters its form very significantly from liquid to solid as it reaches this particular boundary. Prior to this point, as the temperature decreased, there were small changes as it altered its density but nothing so marked as a change in its form. For continuous changes in the temperature variable there is a point where there is a discontinuous change in the nature of the water as it changes from liquid to solid. This raises some problems in weather forecasting. It might be predicted with confidence that there will be high precipitation in a particular area. However, if the temperature at the appropriate height in the atmosphere is somewhere around zero it will be very difficult to predict whether this will take the form of a heavy rainstorm or a heavy snowstorm. A small error in the temperature variable will give a large error in the nature of the storm. If the temperature were safely at around 10°C, there would be no problem. There would be a rainstorm.

Thus there are certain points in such a system where predictability is difficult, though, of course, we know where they are. As long as the system is safely in the area where it might go to one or the other, it is stable and predictable in the sense described in the last paragraph. However, if it is near the boundary then a small change in the initial conditions might alter its behaviour, from one to the other. As even in the most exact physical systems there are limits to observational accuracy, it follows that predictability in the area of the boundary is uncertain. As observational techniques are often poor, particularly in the social sciences, this boundary of uncertainty can be large. Such boundaries are known as 'bifurcations'. The phenomenon is well known and its relationship to prediction is generally appreciated.

Consider the following example which, by virtue of its ecological setting, is closer to the interests of scholars of international relations. Suppose we have a population which reproduces itself period by period at some particular rate. The stocks of some particular fish such as cod would be a case in point. Suppose the rate of increase of the stocks were estimated at 5 per cent per year, then the overall fish stocks will be believed to be increasing steadily. If, as is the case with fish stocks in the wild, it is difficult to estimate with any precision, then the true rate of increase might be 4 per cent. However, this is not too serious as the qualitative behaviour of the system is still the same. Conversely, if the fish stock is decreasing by 5 per cent a year it will be decreasing steadily and at some point will be in danger of extinction. In the same way, if the true rate of decrease were 4 per cent, the qualitative path of the system would be the same only slower. Fears about the future viability of the stocks would still be in order. It is around the 0 per cent change that the difficulties lie. This is the border between increasing and decreasing. If it is truly 0 per cent, the fish stock just reproduces itself and is a stable state. However, if it is really a 1 per cent increase, this is rather different from a stable state. Similarly, and more worryingly, it is the case if the population is decreasing at a rate of 1 per cent. Small changes in the area around the bifurcation point lead to major changes in the system's behaviour. If we cannot measure the system to an appropriate degree of accuracy, then, when it is in the neighbourhood of this bifurcation point, we are unable to say which of the radically different patterns it will adopt. Thus prediction is poor in this area of the system, though not of course in the safe areas away from the bifurcation point.

We can elaborate this argument. Denote the population in period t by $P(t)$. Let a represent the rate of growth, so that $a = 1$ implies a constant population or a zero rate of growth, $a = 1.05$ denotes a 5 per cent increase and so on. Then

$$P(t) = aP(t-1) \qquad (2.1)$$

If we assume that a is constant over time, so there is a constant rate of growth or change, and we start at period 0, then

$$P(t) = a^t P(0) \qquad (2.2)$$

Thus, if $a = 1.1$ and $t = 10$, then $P(10) = (1.1)^{10} = 2.6P(0)$. Its graph will look as in Figure 2.1. That is, the population will increase by a little over two and a half times. Now it is clear that if $a > 1$ we have a system which is growing, whereas if we have a system where $a < 1$, the population is declining. The boundary case is where $a = 1$ and the system reproduces itself at a constant level. This is illustrated in Figure 2.1.

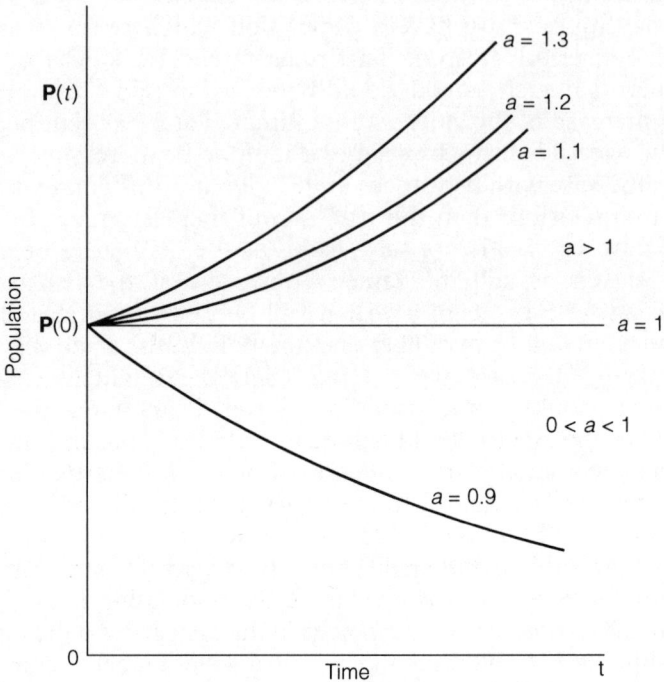

Figure 2.1   A population growth system

Note that there is a sense in which all cases where the population is growing can be regarded as qualitatively the same. Suppose we compare two growth rates where $a = 1.5$ and $a = 1.7$. The second is faster than the first but nevertheless the general qualitative pattern is the same. The long-run path of the system is more or less the same. If measurement error means we confuse the two it is not too serious as the later errors will be proportional to the initial errors. However, suppose we compare $a = 1.1$ and $a = 0.9$. Here we have two very different patterns. The long-run path of the system is very different, growing in the first case as above, and shrinking and almost disappearing in the second. $P(10)$ will equal $0.35P(O)$ and ultimately it will shrink to close to zero. There is a qualitative change in the system at $a = 1$. Suppose our estimates of the value of a are only approximate, as is the case in the estimation of such things as fish stocks. If the range of error is 0.2 and we make estimates around 1.5 then we would not normally be very concerned. For all estimates within the range, the population will be growing. If we make estimates around 0.5 we may be concerned, if we do not want the population to disappear, but at least we can be confident of the general path of the system. If our estimates are close to 1, however, we do not know whether the population is increasing or decreasing and the nature of the qualitative path of the system is unclear. Thus, small errors in the estimation of the parameters of the system can lead to large errors in our prediction about the system's behaviour. Alternatively, a small shift in the system's behaviour can have large consequences. This occurs around the point[4] $a = 1$. In general the system is robust in that minor shifts have minor consequences.

Systems with bifurcations are common in the social sciences. Of particular relevance in the field of international relations is the Richardson arms race model. In the unstable case of the Richardson model, there is a line around which a point might go off into one of two very different sorts of trajectories. However, this occurs in just a small region of the model and for the most part the behaviour of the model is stable. This sort of situation is very common and conceptually unsurprising.

The curious thing about chaotic systems is that bifurcations are found universally and not just in limited regions as was the case with the example above. Thus the system becomes less and less predictable as time goes on. That is, its trajectories from two almost infinitesimally close points diverge widely and this is true *for all points in the system* and not just for a small region as in the more familiar models with bifurcations. It is this last characteristic which is surprising and counter-intuitive.

We can illustrate this, though in no sense prove it; the argument here is by assertion. In a fascinating paper, Lighthill (1986) describes some work of Miles (1984) where those with a sufficient knowledge of differential equations can verify the results. First, consider an ordinary pendulum where the ball has a given weight and the length of the pendulum is also given. If the pendulum is pulled back to a specific point and then released, it is possible to say where the pendulum will be at some specified point of time, say two minutes, in the future. A practical experiment requires fairly careful measurement but the theory is clear. We normally think of the swinging of a pendulum as being a very well-behaved sort of activity. Suppose we now look at a more complicated pendulum system in which the pendulum swings from a point which itself is oscillating. Though the system is more complicated, it is usually possible again to compute where the pendulum ball would be at some specified time in the future. However, Lighthill shows (or rather Lighthill asserts on the basis of Miles's showing) that, for certain values of the oscillations, and for certain lengths of the pendulum in relation to its weight, the position of the ball is unpredictable beyond a certain point. This is true for all starting-points.

This is an apparently bizarre result coming in the midst of the epitome of orderly behaviour, classical mechanics. It is not true for all pendulum systems but it is for some and is very disconcerting. However, it is now generally accepted that this unpredictability characterizes many natural systems which have been generally assumed to be deterministic. It is this sort of phenomenon which is described as chaotic and the general theory behind it is known as 'chaos theory'. We should be careful about what it says in the case of the pendulum system. It is not saying that the pendulum will suddenly stop unexpectedly or go into some wild form of oscillation. It merely states that the precise nature of the fairly orderly oscillations is not predictable. Further, the sooner after the first release of the pendulum one considers the system the more closely one is able to predict the position of the ball. The un-predictability increases with time and the system is predictable over short periods. Thus, we are dealing with unpredictability within some constraints.

There are many systems with bifurcations for some points in the system. Systems for which differential equations are an appropriate model often have them and, indeed, it fits in with common sense. That it happens for all points is rather more surprising but, on reflection, it can be seen to be an extension, though admittedly a radical one, of a well-understood form of behaviour. Mathematically it is less surprising. The phenomenon arises because the relevant differential equations do not have a steady equilibrium solution to which the system tends.

An example of a natural system which is chaotic is the meteoro-logical system. This is not a completely closed system by any means. As the whole environmental debate makes clear, it is only too significantly affected by human agency. Nevertheless, most of the human input is relatively constant, or constantly changing over periods such as a year, and it is its cumulative effects which are disturbing. Thus they are predictable, broadly speaking, over such periods and should not be a major impediment to meteorological prediction. In meteorology the basic laws of the movement of gases, precipitation and so on are well known and the failure of long-term forecasts has often been attributed to the great complexity of the system. Thus, it was supposed, as we found out more, computers improved and as, perhaps, we learnt yet more about complex systems, long-term meteorological prediction would improve. It was generally assumed that two very similar configurations of weather at point t in time would lead to two very similar configurations of weather at time $(t + 1)$ no matter how far ahead $(t + 1)$ was from t. In particular, this means that errors or inadequacies in the observations at t will lead to errors in prediction at $(t + 1)$ of more or less the same magnitude. However, it now seems possible, even likely, that the systems are in fact chaotic, so the above conditions do not apply. This means that long-term weather forecasting is impossible even in principle, and not just as a matter of practice, where the problems are such that, at some stage in the future, they might be expected to yield to analysis. Thus very similar configurations of the system at one time can, and perhaps in general do, diverge very markedly at some later time. This leads to the so-called 'butterfly effect'. If a butterfly flies from one buttercup to another in June in England instead of staying put, the minute difference in the climate 'causes' a hurricane in the Caribbean the following year. While this example might be fanciful in that all butterflies have a similar effect, the general point behind it is not.

The lack of predictability does not weaken our explanations of the weather system. However, these examples show that the supposed symmetry between explanation and prediction falters, even at the conceptual level, quite apart from the practical problems. To make prediction the criterion of a proper explanation would be so restrictive as to be essentially impossible.

Chaos theory is of great importance to natural scientists and in all probability to social scientists. Economics is the area of social science where chaos theory models have been most widely applied (George, 1990). To date it has had little impact in international relations. That it has not is not very surprising. With the major exception of Richardson's analyses and related work there has been comparatively little work on dynamic systems in any formal sense (Schrodt, 1981; Zinnes and Muncaster, 1984). It is in such systems that chaotic phenomena are to be found. Whether the underlying phenomena will at some stage turn out to be appropriately described by chaotic models is hard to say, though it is, of course, quite possible. Certainly the developments in economics suggest it might be. However, the point of this argument was conceptual, and it is valid whatever future developments of chaos theory in international relations there may or may not be. We can no longer hold to the view, even in principle, that explanation and prediction are symmetrical concepts.

Definitions: the connections between theory, reality and language

The theory so far has been described as a set of statements which in some sense describe the world. So far we have been vague as to how. However, if language is to be used to describe and analyse experience, then it must be tied into experience in some comprehensible way.

There are certain objects which are a direct part of our experience and which we wish to communicate about. Initially we learn the use of words and hence communication by simply having them pointed out to us. We learn the use of the word 'cow' by being shown one and having our mentor say 'cow'. Similarly with cars, aeroplanes and houses. Such direct definitions of words where in effect we are involved in a process of saying 'This is a dog' are known as 'ostensive definitions'. They directly relate the experience of seeing a dog with the word 'dog' and are the direct link between the language and the reality it describes. However, many, perhaps most, of the definitions of terms concerning the world (and I am not concerned here with the usage of language for other purposes, such as moral discourse) are not direct in this way. We define words in terms of other words. Such definitions are known as 'nominal definitions'. A dictionary is a collection of nominal definitions. Ostensive definitions are not confined to nouns as the above examples might suggest. Colours are likewise communicated by ostensive definitions, and verbs such as 'running', 'climbing', 'singing' and so on are learnt by experiencing or witnessing the activities. From a basic vocabulary which has been learnt ostensively and by direct contact with experience we can build up the rest of the scientific language by means of the nominal definitions. However, though the scientific vocabulary can always ultimately be traced back to an ostensive definition, the route is normally a long and tortuous one. The link between our experience and the statements we make about the inside of a star is remote. This remoteness raises some difficult points as we shall discuss later, but the link, nevertheless, exists (Quine, 1961; see also Gochet, 1986).

The statements made in an explanatory framework, whether particular or generalizations, are linked to experience, though perhaps remotely. However, these statements, being verbal or mathematical, can be manipulated logically so that we can say what implies what, and, if one set of propositions is true, which others are true because of it. However, logic applies to language and mathematics. Logical manipulation is essentially an arrangement and rearrangement of symbols. It carries over from the real world if these symbols are interpreted or defined in terms of entities or activities in the real world, but there must be some explicit act of linking the language to the world.

Let us illustrate this with the case of a pendulum, though this time swinging in a simple system and not according to the chaotic principles of the previous section. An instance of a pendulum is a small spherical ball which swings on the end of a string of length L. The pendulum swings with a period of oscillation T given by

$$T = 2\pi \sqrt{L/g}$$

π is the constant pi and g is likewise a physical constant, namely the acceleration due to gravity. The reader should notice that the bare description of the pendulum is given in terms which are probably part of everyone's common experience. The assertion of the rule or law by which the pendulum swings depends on a rather wider knowledge of the procedures of science. Given this, we can deduce the period of oscillation of a pendulum which has a string of length 30 cm. However, we can do this if we interpret the particular variables in terms of entities or behaviour in the real world, which in its turn means observations. The relationship between the formal terms and what they represent is straightforward in this case. Length is something one can observe and measure easily. Time, though it depends on a more complex measuring instrument than a standardized measure (namely a watch or clock), is closely related to common experience. The understanding of the mathematical formula takes a little learning but is essentially a form of learning a language. The point I am making is that the real world is modelled in terms of the language (here a mathematical one); we can manipulate it logically as logic is the preserve of the language. This can be carried over to the external world inasmuch as the language corresponds closely to the entities in the external world. In the case of the pendulum the mathematical model and the 'reality' correspond closely and there is no real problem. In lots of other cases, such as we meet often enough in the social sciences, this is not the case.

The case of the pendulum is the most direct form of test where the refutation can be directly carried out. However, what is relevant is that it is not the single proposition in isolation which has to be refutable but the proposition within the whole context of the theory. Thus it has to be the theory as a whole which is refutable. This extension has some important implications. There are some concepts which are inherently unobservable but which nevertheless play an important role in scientific theories. Consider the case of the concept of 'centre of gravity'. Clearly this plays an important part in classical mechanics. If we want to find out how far a bus can lean over without falling over, we carry out a calculation using the concept of the centre of gravity in a very precise manner. We could not very well make the calculation without it. Nevertheless, however hard we try, there is no way in which we can make a direct observation of the centre of gravity. This is not because of the inadequacy of our measuring instruments. It is in principle unobservable and cannot be identified independently of the deductive structure in which it is embedded. Thus its existence is dependent on what it does. It is thus conceptually different from the earlier case (p. 34) when we explained a landslip by hypothesizing a hidden stream which, we argued, would need independent observation if it were to play a proper role in the explanation of the cliff fall. In that case we required a specific observation. In the case of the centre of gravity we have an abstract term involved in the set of generalizations which leads by a process of logical deduction to other generalizations which can be independently determined empirically. However, it would be unreasonable to exclude such terms from scientific discourse because they are not directly observable, nor, indeed, do they exist in any independent sense. We have to modify the earlier statement of refutability to emphasize that it is the theory which is testable, not the individual propositions. The location of the centre of gravity can be confirmed only by the predictions which are made using it and the other propositions which play a role in classical mechanics. Such terms play an important role in science. Gravitational fields, electromagnetic fields, electrons and so on are of this nature. They are known as 'theoretical terms' (Braithwaite, 1953). This particular argument plays a significant role later in the analysis of theories in the social sciences, in particular in Chapter 8.

Observation and communication

The activity of science deriving a coherent picture of the external world can be illustrated in Figures 2.2 and 2.3. Observer A and observer B are observing O, which is some aspect of the external world. For the moment we assume this is something relatively simple concerning day-to-day experiences. The observations of A and B we assume to be the same and together they formulate language in which they can communicate. This is based initially on common experience. They can communicate with each other about their common experience. However, language enables them to go further, for they can broaden the language by defining terms nominally. They move from the simple language L(1) to the broader language L(2) with words defined nominally.

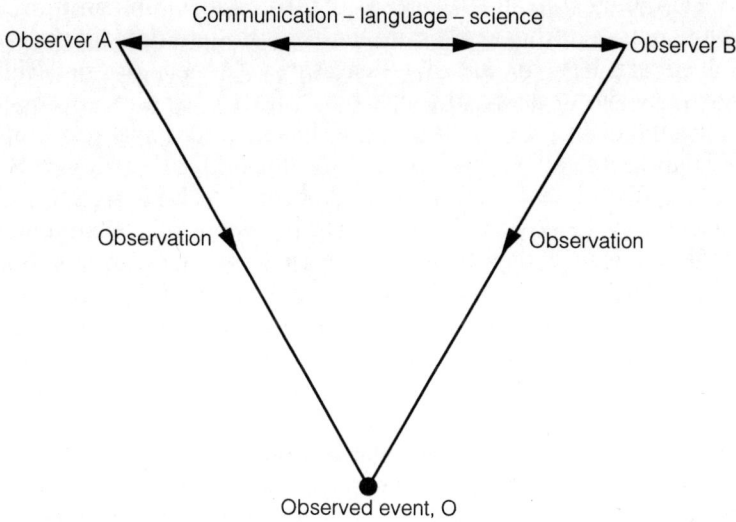

Figure 2.2 Direct observation

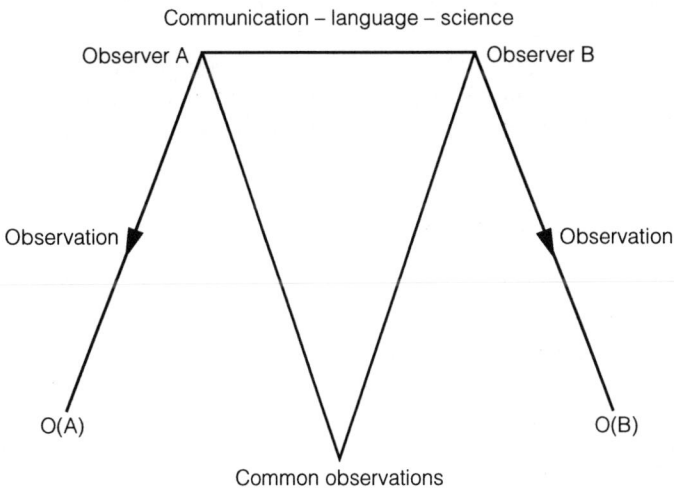

Figure 2.3 Observation and communication

Having worked out their language they are now able to partici-
pate in step 2, illustrated in Figure 2.3. Observer A carries out observations concerning O(A) which observer B has not carried out.
Likewise B carries out O(B) which A has not carried out. By virtue

of the language they have worked out, observer A can communicate to B the nature of these observations even though many of the terms involved are not (or are not necessarily) a part of the original ostensively defined vocabulary. This means that the impressions and mental events which observer A has acquired as a result of the observation of O(A) can be communicated to observer B. In observer B's mind, the same mental events can be generated, or at least the same beliefs can be generated by means of the language, as if a direct observation had been carried out. Communication is good, and a language efficient, if the messages which A intended to give to B are in fact understood by B. In the case of simple statements such as 'the cat is sitting on the mat' there is little reason to doubt that communication is good. However, it does depend at some stage on the shared, common experience of both A and B. It is argued by some that even the simplest common experience is mediated by some prior (presumably earlier learnt) context and there are no such things as 'brute facts' which we all agree on as giving an identical common experience. Thus, in a society where a cat is regarded as a god there is a lot more to asserting that it is sitting on a mat than if it is merely a domestic pet. Observer B might understand the physical fact but fail to understand a lot of the implications. This is a point I shall return to. However, initially I shall simply assert (a) that, whether god or not, there is a certain amount of physical 'fact' which is communicated for which there is near-universal common experience, and which we can reasonably call objective; and (b) that a lot of observations can be made which do not run into this problem – in few cultures are many animals regarded as gods. Hence we have widespread if not universal agreement about common experience.

In the case of natural sciences as a whole, it can be presumed that communication is good. However, there are further issues involved. The observations which are of importance are not crude observations of particulars but some are of generalizations and even generalizations in the context of a theory. Hence if observers A and B are now regarded as scientists they have done more than just build up a language: they have built up an understanding which they share of the scientific process. The question then is whether this scientific process is objective or whether there is some degree of choice in accepting it. I shall argue the former but it is not uncontroversial.

'Why necessarily?' and 'how possibly?'
The strict application of the covering law model shows how something which is to be explained necessarily follows from a set of

laws and initial conditions. Thus, the request for an explanation of something is expected to be in the form of 'Why was it necessarily the case?' We have suggested that, even in the natural sciences, this standard is often too stringent to be practically useful. In the social sciences it is almost always too stringent. A weaker form of explanation is to ask not why something was necessary but how something was possible.

Consider World War I and its causes. True covering law theorists would ask for a set of initial conditions and laws of social behaviour which, when taken together, would mean that World War I would necessarily take place. They would admit that such an explanation was beyond our powers at the moment. In view of the vast amount of detailed knowledge available about the period, this would probably be attributed to a paucity of reliable social laws. All we are able to do is provide 'explanation sketches', as Carl Hempel, the most vociferous advocate of the covering law model as applied to history, called them in his original paper in 1948 (Hempel, 1965a). However, the true 'why necessarily' conditions are to be aimed for and an explanation without them is inadequate. For practically all circumstances this is not what historians do, nor does it seem an achievable goal in the near future or possibly at all. What we can ask is why it was that World War I was a possible event in 1914. Was it also possible in 1894? More significantly, was war possible in 1908 when, in the Bosnian crisis of that year (with its grim reminders of a more recent age) the conditions were remarkably similar to those of the 1914 crisis? Let us consider more carefully what asking whether something was possible or not means. Clearly war was possible in 1914 because it happened. Thus some necessary conditions were in place. At some point they were supplemented by a sufficient condition. To ask whether war was possible in 1908 is to ask whether the necessary conditions were in place then also. Clearly a sufficient condition, such as the assassination of a sufficiently symbolic person, was lacking (from the definition of sufficient condition), but some necessary conditions may have been missing also. The study of the causes of war is still not sufficiently advanced for us to be too sure about necessary conditions but it seems more likely we shall get some better ideas about these well before we are able to predict the occurrence of war. This sort of analysis fits most conveniently into a view of the world in which the basic necessary conditions are the underlying causes which can be triggered off by some relatively minor specific conditions. Analogously, a boulder might be delicately poised to fall into a valley. The necessary conditions are in place. A flock of birds alighting on the boulder might be the proximate cause of its falling down. A strong wind would have done as well. In asking whether war was possible in 1908 we are asking whether the European system was likewise poised such that a normally minor set of circumstances could have switched it into war. This sort of question seems to be much more accessible to research than asking whether peace was inevitable then but war inevitable in 1914.[5]

We can ask the same sort of question about all sorts of social events. What made the French Revolution possible in 1789? What made Napoleon possible? What made the move to the European Union possible in the post-war years? These are all weaker questions than asking why something was necessary in what, by implication, is a determinist world.

Clearly, 'how possibly' is a weaker mode of explanation than the strict covering law. It is worth examining the notion in greater detail. It is advocated in historical explanation by Dray (1957) in response to Gardiner (1952), who followed Hempel as an advocate of the covering law as a model of explanation in history. He argued that the 'how possibly' approach was much closer to what historians do and makes sense of the sorts of historical explanations which are in fact proffered. Both versions, however, can be regarded as explanations in the empiricist sense, though probably Dray would not be happy with this interpretation. In both forms, people are trying to make a set of events coherent by reference to our general knowledge of behaviour. The 'how possibly' form of explanation is a clearer description of what historians do when they claim to explain. It is also what social scientists do in their explanations of events. A strict covering law explanation is a rarity.

The 'how possibly' form of explanation fits in neatly with the *ex post* results of a probabilistic situation. Thus, before a horse race it is a probabilistic matter as to whether Red Rover will win or not. If he does win, then we can explain how this was a possible event but hardly that it was a necessary event – or, if we could, we could be rich. Most events in international relations are probabilistic. We argue before the event that something is possible but not necessary. Before the Iran–Iraq war we could have argued that this event was possible. We could also have argued that it was possible that Iraq would win rather quickly. In fact, many observers gave a high probability to the possibility of an early Iraqi victory but it would have been rash to say it would necessarily be the case. We could, moreover, have given reasons why several options were possible and perhaps been willing to give probabilities in the sense of degrees of belief to the different possibilities. Thus, an event whose outcome we view probabilistically can be explained 'how possibly' after the event but definitionally not 'why necessarily'. This does not refute the covering law model, which does not require determinism – the attempt would be made to explain probability distributions. However, it does more clearly explain single events which occur in uncertain or risky situations.

The 'how possibly' form of explanation likewise relates closely to the zebra principle. We cannot say why the kangaroo was a necessary development in Australia as the practical information requirements are beyond all hope of acquiring. However, we can say why it was a possible development given the climate, other flaura and fauna and so on. In other words, we can explain its viability but not its inevitability. This requires us to retreat from the strict covering law approach.

'How possibly' and 'how necessarily' are obviously related. 'How possibly' involves giving an account of some process and admitting that within the domain of one's current knowledge alternative processes might have happened. But one is going to exclude some accounts. I can say in general why a flood in February in coastal areas of Britain may happen in 'why possibly' terms by referring to high tides, bad weather, low-lying coastline and so on. These are necessary but not sufficient conditions, and many other possibilities could occur which I could comment on similarly. The knowable initial conditions are too general to give a 'why necessarily' account. However, two hours before an actual flood the initial conditions are sufficiently closely specified to give a 'why necessarily' account. As we get closer to the actual event we find that many possible states of affairs did not in fact happen. We eliminate the alternatives in the 'how possibly' account until we are down to a 'why necessarily' account in a limiting case. It might be a great rarity for us honestly to be able to say this, but, logically, 'why necessarily' is a limiting case of 'how possibly' where all the possibilities but one have been excluded.

In the case of World War I, one might use some informal laws to say that in 1913 a war between Britain and France on one side against Germany on the other was possible. However, a war with Britain and Germany against France was very unlikely. The same could not be said about the period of twenty years earlier. However, by excluding options – that is, by narrowing the range of what is deemed possible – one gets to one possibility which is then a necessity. The closer one gets to an event the more one can eliminate possibilities. War in August 1914 was one of a great many possibilities in August 1913. By August 1914, the range of options was very narrow and, though not perhaps necessary, war was very close to being necessary. The nearer to a situation one gets, the closer to a necessity. The same happens with a flood. Some options, possible at one stage, are eliminated as time moves on.

Whether we are looking for a 'how possibly' account or something narrower also depends on the question we are asking. Consider the American War of Independence. If we ask why it happened in 1775, we could give only a 'why possibly' explanation. The way in which independence happened could be argued to be dependent on relatively minor events and could have happened in many different ways, not necessarily involving war. We could presumably exclude some of these ways but not all. However, if we want to explain the overall event of the United States becoming independent from the British government sometime in the late eighteenth century we could endeavour to provide a 'how necessarily' explanation as it is hard to imagine it would not have happened in some form or another.

We should not let the more relaxed nature of 'how possibly' dull our ambition. Obviously a 'why necessarily' explanation is to be preferred if achievable. If a 'how possibly' can be reduced to a 'why necessarily' this is clearly something to be pleased about and to be tried if possible. The issue is that the weaker forms are not just poor relations. They have merit in themselves.

The questions get more difficult when we consider something such as the rise of Nazism in Germany in the inter-war years. Is a 'why necessarily' explanation possible? Clearly, if we reduced the question to 'what was the cause of the rise to power and subsequent policies of the man, Hitler?', the answer is no. He could have died in childhood. All we can analyse are the conditions which made Hitler's rise possible. However, if we ask the broader question, 'What was the cause of the rise of an expansionary, authoritarian and anti-Semitic regime in Germany?', the answer is less clear. If we go sufficiently far back in time, say to 1815, the answer has to be in 'how possibly' terms. However, by 1919 a 'how necessarily' explanation looks more plausible.

I have deliberately avoided bringing probability into this account though it is clearly lurking in the wings. Strictly, something is either possible or not possible; there are no gradations. However, some things are clearly possible but very improbable such as that conclusive proof will be offered that King George V of Britain was the illegitimate son of Gladstone (the reverse would be impossible, of course). Above, I have referred to things as being 'unlikely' meaning that they were possible but less probable than other possibilities. Thus probability has sneaked in through the back door. It is hard to keep it out totally, otherwise the analysis would be trivial in that, if we allowed even the remotely probable into it, the range of possibilities would become ridiculously large. However, it is probability only in a very weak sense which would permit a few gradations such as very probable, fairly probable, improbable and so on, and where 'not possible' can mean both 'impossible' in the strict sense and 'of very low probability' in a numerically undefined sense. Numerical definition at this point would certainly not be useful and may not be meaningful.

Notes

1 One can, of course, have a prediction in the sense of a pure projection without an explanation. Thus, after a little observation, it is easy to forecast tides at a specific point on the coast without having any idea as to an explanation of the phenomena either formally or informally.

2 Indeed, it can be extended and elaborated. In particular, we should note 'retrodiction' where, from a particular set of initial conditions, we can predict that something hitherto unobserved must have happened in the past and then test it by looking. In general we can say that if some statements $(s_1, s_2, \ldots, s_n)$ in conjunction with laws represented by $(L_1, L_2, \ldots, L_m)$ imply statements $(r_1, r_2, \ldots, r_k)$ then we have an instance of the covering law irrespective of the timing of the events described by the sentences.

3 A 'closed system' is one where the variables interact only among themselves and are not influenced by outside factors. Any outside factors are at least constant over the period of analysis. Thus, in laboratory experiments, the experimenter endeavours to create a closed system where only the factors which are being examined vary. An 'open system' is one where outside factors impinge on the system and cause it to alter in its behaviour. In real life, as opposed to the laboratory, systems are usually open.

4 Interpreted as a population of fish increasing ($a > 1$) or decreasing ($a < 1$), there is just one point where the system changes its style of behaviour as a cannot be negative. For interpretations where a can be negative, there are two other points where the system changes its qualitative style of behaviour. For $0 < a < 1$ we saw that it goes smoothly down towards zero. However, if $-1 < a < 0$, each alternate term will take on the opposite sign so we will get an oscillating series in which every term is smaller and closer to 0. An instance would be $-\frac{1}{2}, +\frac{1}{4}, -\frac{1}{8}, +\frac{1}{16}, \ldots$ and so on, converging to zero. Thus, if a is around 0, the possibility of a different mode of behaviour for slight alterations in a becomes possible. If $a < -1$, the series oscillates in sign but the terms become bigger, diverging further from zero. Thus, around $a + -1$, there is another possibility of a switch in the systems behaviour.

5 In Bueno de Mesquita's analysis of war causation (Bueno de Mesquita, 1981), he hypothesizes that a positive expected utility of going to war is a necessary condition for a war to start. It is not, however, a sufficient condition, which, by implication, might be a comparatively minor factor. This analysis is consistent with the discussion above.

3
The characteristics of social sciences

The distinctive nature of the social sciences
At the most general level a social science is the study of human beings in a social context. As argued before, international relations is just one of those contexts and we would expect the same problems and possibilities to be involved in it as with any other social science. Given the basic level of our questions, there does not seem to be any reason for thinking that international relations has any peculiarities not shared by other social sciences.

Social scientists in general discuss voting, economic growth, and the responses to catastrophes such as earthquakes. If their speciality is international relations, then such questions as the causes of war and the other phenomena mentioned at the beginning of the book are the areas of interest. The central question is, to what extent can these phenomena be described by the same sort of procedures as natural phenomena, such a planets or genes, and are the differences, which clearly exist, of such a nature as to preclude their analysis by the same sorts of methods?

First, we have to look very carefully at what these phenomena consist of. They are not purely physical events. They are events which are interpreted by the actors involved. The physical actions involved in voting would seem to an observer from Mars to be trivial and barely worthy of note. They become significant only in the context of their interpretation by the people who are voting. Thus we are looking not just at physical events but at their interpretation by those involved in those events. At least to some degree, we are considering the mental events which go on in the minds of the actors concerned.

In the case of the natural sciences we noted that scientists communicated about objects external to themselves in language which had its origins in sentences about observables. The objects, however, were things separate from themselves and which had no perceptions of their own. Observers, whether scientists or not, make remarks about stones, but the stones themselves have no view whatever on the matter in hand.[1]

The major difference for our purposes between stones and human beings is that human beings do have a view about the matter in hand. Many crucial debates in the philosophy of the social sciences wage around the significance which should be given to the actors' own perceptions of the situation.

Let us consider the matter in terms of an example, that of a battle, which is particularly appropriate given our central interest in international relations. Figure 2.1 in the previous chapter dealt with purely physical events. It related the observers of an inanimate physical event to that event by perceptions and themselves to each other by communication expressed in a language. This language may well be a mathematical one.

In the battle illustrated in Figure 3.1, the event is carried out by the actors, and indeed the event is an interaction between them. Thus we have not only the observers observing the battle from the outside but the actors, who are a part of the phenomenon under observation, observing themselves. They are part of the action and part of the observation at the same time.

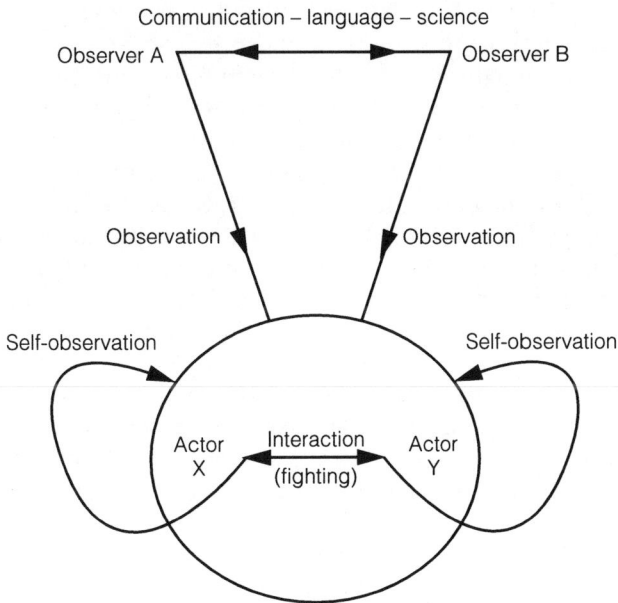

Figure 3.1 Perception and communication about a social process

In the case of the battle, it is likely that all the observers, whether internal or external, will agree on their interpretation of the event at some basic level. They will agree that it is a battle on some minimum definition of a battle of two groups of people trying to dominate the other using force, including, and indeed centrally involving, the killing of opponents. They may not agree about much else. The participants may well disagree profoundly on the interpretation of the causes of the battle, one holding that it is a reconquest of their ancestral lands, the other that it is a ruthless attempt to exterminate their society. (It is not uncommon, of course, for both to hold that their ancestral lands are being taken from them.) However, the possible differences among the participants are something which I shall return to at a later point. In some cases, like the battle, the differences between participants might or might not be a significant issue; in others, such as a social or religious ritual, it might not be very important. For the moment I shall simplify things and assume that there are two categories of people: the observers, who interact like any other scientists, and the observed, who can play some sort of double role. The differences in interpretation between the internal actors and the outside observers are sometimes very important. This factor is not a minor qualification but is the central issue around which the social sciences, and the disputes in the philosophy of the social sciences, revolve. The crucial issue is that social behaviour is interpreted by the actors and not just by the observers as is the case with natural events. Thus, any theories involving battles as relevant events within them are dealing with two types of concepts. First there are the physical events: people kill each other. Secondly, there are some mental events. The participants and other people involved in the activity interpret what they are doing in a way in which we doubt that colonies of ants do when they go through the superficially similar acts of fighting other ants. Not only those directly involved, but the whole society in which the activity takes place, interpret it.

Let us consider the case of the battle more closely. As far as people killing each other is concerned there is only a minimum degree of interpretation involved. The presuppositions involved in describing it as an event are very close to an observation in the natural world. There is unlikely to be much disagreement. If we come to analyse the cause of the battle, as opposed to the war of which it is a part, there is greater scope for interpretation. It may be seen as part of a strategic plan by one or both parties or as a semi-accidental meeting of the armies. If the former, there may be disagreements about how carefully the strategy was formed and in what detail (a common way of looking at battles by strategists or historians of war). Even if the battle was seen as part of a grand plan, such as Napoleon's invasion of Russia, it nevertheless might have involved a lot of accidental factors to the point of being determined by them (as Tolstoy argued). Though there may be disputes, the nature of the disputes is generally understood by the disputants. However, we are bringing into the argument more than just the physical events involved. The views of the actors are playing some role. Perhaps even more centrally, in order to talk about strategy we necessarily need to know how the actors regard the events and the concepts they use in analysing them. We may not agree with the actors' analyses but we have to understand them.

The issue of interpretation becomes even more central if we consider the war as a whole of which the battle is part. From the point of view of the observer looking for purely physical events alone, the war would appear to be an intermittent collection of battles between more or less the same groups of people, or at least by groups who would appear to have some contact with each other (such as the people who form an army and those who form a navy). However, the behavioural definition of a war might be rather difficult, relying, not always very convincingly, on statistical groupings of acts of violence. At times, apparently similar events (such as the two world wars) involve considerable differences when looked at from on the one hand a physical and on the other a behavioural point of view. (I use the word 'behavioural' to mean a form of physical behaviour which can be identified without interpretation or, at least, with a minimum of interpretation.) In the case of World War I, the casualty rate per month jumped at the beginning of the war and remained at a fairly high level throughout. If one did not know the dates of World War I but were shown the casualty figures alone, one would be able to date it by behavioural data to within a few days of the official dates. In the case of World War II this did not happen. Battle deaths in Europe varied and went up and down from 1936 (the Spanish Civil War) until the invasion of the Soviet Union by Germany, when they shot upwards. Looked at purely behaviourally it would be very difficult to identify a beginning (though easier to identify an end), and 4 September 1939, which is the date Western Europeans identify as the beginning of the war, or any date near to it, would not stand out as being of any particular significance. The definition of 'a war' in this sense involves the actors and their perceptions and is not just a matter of behavioural data alone.

Now let us consider a more extreme case, that of 'ownership', where very few physical events occur and where the issues largely consist of people's attitudes. If I say I own a house, then anyone in a wide range of societies has a clear understanding of what I mean. However, by observing my behaviour in connection with the house we cannot tell whether I own it or not. It could be established that I live in it but I can live in a house without owning it and own a house

I do not live in (even the phrase 'live in' involves some degree of interpretation). Nor is this just a remote conceptual possibility; many people do both. The evidence of ownership is contained in some written document which establishes legal ownership. We could argue that this was one representation of an attitude of mind, shared by me and others in the society of which I am a member. The crucial thing is the events and understanding which go on in my mind. The events, without this understanding, are more or less meaningless. What I am considering in this case are mental events. The issue is comprehensible only if I am in a culture where the concepts involved in these mental events are understood by me.

While few, with the possible exception of some extreme behaviourists, would dispute that human beings' consciousness significantly modifies the analysis and has some consequences which do not arise in the case of the natural sciences, there are serious differences as to what this difference is. These range from regarding a causal analysis as totally invalid to regarding the issue of understanding and empathy as a minor detail. I shall distinguish between seven different approaches or positions, though the borderlines between some of them are unclear while others are mutually contradictory.

Position 1: It is argued that social understanding is all we can do and that causal analysis is impossible. This is the view of Peter Winch, whose position I examine in greater detail later (Winch, 1958).

Position 2: Understanding and causal analysis can be merged. We can still use causal analysis, but this analysis deals in events in which a necessary condition is that they are understood by the actors. I shall defend this position in this book.

Position 3: Evidence by means of understanding is unreliable and should be eliminated (as with strict behaviourism in psychology) or kept to a minimum as in behaviouralism in international relations (and political science and, more generally, economics).

Position 4: Understanding and explanation are possible and legitimate though different. Thus, an empathetic understanding of situations is quite legitimate and possible but should be kept separate from causal explanations, which nevertheless fall broadly under the rubric of the third position.

Position 5: Understanding and explanation are possible, legitimate and different. However, explanation must also incorporate understanding. This is the fourth position modified by the second.

Position 6: Causal analysis is impossible and understanding is often unreliable, so there is not a great deal we can say. This is held by some post-modernists. It is a plausible interpretation of R. G. Collingwood's view of history (Collingwood, 1946).

Position 7: There are often multiple understandings of a situation; indeed, this is usual in any complex social situation such as a war. This issue is central, meaning that even the 'understanding' mode of analysis is not straightforward. This is also an issue which has been raised by the post-modernists.

A closer analysis of 'understanding'

The core issue is that of understanding. We must look at this position with more care. At least at some level it is a central difference between the social and the natural sciences. I shall discuss in particular the views of Peter Winch, which derive quite directly and explicitly from Ludwig Wittgenstein in his *Philosophical Investigations* (1953). At least as far as international relations is concerned, few would deny that the views of the actors were relevant to the issues. In analyses of arms races, for example, analysts more or less take it for granted that the actors involved would agree that an arms race was going on and, at least in broad terms, agree with the concepts involved. However, behaviouralists would argue that this did not preclude them from dealing with them as events and relate them to other events in a perfectly standard scientific manner (i.e. position 2 and possibly 4; if the latter, then necessarily 5 also). There are many studies which do precisely this. However, Winch (1990, p. 133) stresses the interpretation of the actors as central, and argues that understanding events in the terms of the actors is the only valid way of examining social behaviour and that the formulation of generalizations, central to the behavioural approach, is invalid. There is thus an asymmetry between the opposing camps. Behaviouralists (and I cannot think of a serious counter-example) accept the legitimacy of the understanding mode of looking at social events. They do not doubt the propriety and interest at looking at events through the eyes of the actors. They merely argue that this is not all one can do and, further, differ on the significance and degree to which it is legitimate. However, Winch is not so tolerant. He argues that his way is the only way and that the other methods are illegitimate. I shall argue later (Chapter 6) that, while the methods advocated by Winch are perfectly proper in themselves, the added twists he puts into them to justify their exclusivity are not valid.

Let us consider Winch's arguments in terms of a game of tennis. There are rules for the scoring of points and for adding the points up which determine which of the players in a match is the winner.

The crucial issue is that there are rules. The whole procedure becomes meaningless without these rules, and observers can be said to understand the game only if they understand these rules at least in general terms. This involves understanding what it means to keep a rule and hence to break it. All forms of human social conduct are of this sort. Language is very clearly so. It involves an extremely complex set of rules of both vocabulary and grammar which must be understood (though not necessarily explicitly) in order to communicate in the language. Lecturing, driving a bus, religious ceremonies all require a knowledge of rules and their significance in a broader set of concepts in order to give them any sort of meaning. This meaning, at least initially, must be that of the actors involved. The argument clearly applies within the domain of international relations. Diplomacy, for example, is clearly guided by explicitly understood rules. Further, we know when they are broken as in the case of the siege of the US Embassy in Iran. We can go further than this and understand the nature of the rules which the apparent breakers of the diplomatic rules were adopting. That is, their conduct was not random but involved following a different set of rules. In order to say that we have understood the event as a whole we have to understand that set of rules also. A response to something like the siege of the US Embassy in Iran is to ask about the Iranians 'What made them do it?' This can be construed in two ways. First, it can be seen as a request for the rules applied by the Iranians and the set of concepts in which these rules are embedded. Such an answer should be expressed in a way which can be understood by someone more familiar with the traditional rules. The implication is that the Iranians had developed a new set of rules. Secondly, it can be seen as a request for an explanation as to why the Iranians broke the traditional diplomatic rules in the full knowledge they were doing so. They may have thought they could get more out of everyone else's shock that a well-established set of rules had been broken. Both versions, however, require a clear concept of rules and of what it means to keep and to break them. The possible Iranian counter-request of 'Why were the Americans so surprised that we did it?' is likewise a request for why the Americans thought that this set of rules was so important – in some sense, a request for a rule about rules.

Diplomacy is a highly structured form of activity in the international system. Less structured is the behaviour of states in crises. If we consider a classic study such as Graham Allison's study of the Cuban missile crisis (Allison, 1971) from the point of view of the decision-making of the United States government, we can interpret it as a discussion of the rules which were followed by the actors. Allison analyses three different possible modes of decision-making by the United States government in the course of the crisis, which he calls the Rational Actor Model, the Bureaucratic Politics Model and the Organizational Processes Model. He asks which provides the best description of the decisions which were in fact made. This could be interpreted as asking which sort of social game the actors were playing and according to which rules. The argument can be followed only by people (admittedly a very large number) who understand the general way of thought of the actors involved.

The argument of the above paragraph would be accepted in broad terms by most people, including most behaviouralists. While the precise language of 'rules' and, even more, 'games' might not be to everyone's taste, the general position is difficult to object to. While physical events are involved in social behaviour, the conceptual schemes – that is, some ideas – are also involved. Therefore we are to some degree talking about ideas and their interrelationship. However, at this point views differ sharply. Winch (1990, p. 133) discusses the process whereby historians and other social scientists use data to 'produce scientific generalizations and theories establishing connections between one kind of social situation and another'. He continues

> I have tried to show . . . how this involves minimizing the importance of ideas in human history, since ideas and theories are constantly developing and changing, and since each system of ideas, its component elements being interrelated internally, has to be understood in and for itself; the combined result of which is to make systems of ideas a very unsuitable subject for broad generalisations. I have also tried to show that social relations really exist only in and through the ideas which are current in society, or alternatively, that social relations fall into the same logical category as do relations between ideas. It follows that social relations must be an equally unsuitable subject for generalisations and theories of the scientific sort to be formulated about them.

This claim is central to Winch's argument. Later its rebuttal is central to mine (Chapter 6, 'Ideas and social behaviour', p. 113). Notice it is not just a claim that ideas have to be understood in and for themselves but also that ideas are constantly changing. The problem of changing rules is a potentially damaging argument for the case I am arguing and needs close attention.

We shall just emphasize what the argument is. To do this it is useful to make a distinction between 'ideologies', which are whole structures of ideas such as religious or political doctrines, and 'social events', which are events such as international crises that can be understood in a wide variety of ideologies. The Winchian point is that, though crises are not dependent on a narrow form of ideology, they still require interpreting in the context of some ideas. They are not just uninterpreted physical events. This is just another way of stressing the need to understand them in the way the actors understand them. Thus, if ideas are required and if social events such as crises are meaningful only in the context of some ideas held by the actors, and them alone, then it follows that they too cannot be analysed in a scientific manner (using the phrase 'scientific manner' in a narrow sense). However, if it is possible to talk causally about ideas in the form of ideologies, it follows without much difficulty that the broader context of interpretation can be made. These are central points of disagreement over which the debate will be engaged later in Chapter 6.

In this chapter I shall deal with two further issues. The first concerns some problems of generalization in the social sciences which are not dealt with by Winch as they would be redundant given his more basic dismissal of such a possibility. The second concerns the issue of multiple perceptions in a form which is also not considered by Winch.

The legitimacy of generalizations in the social sciences

The core methodological problem in international relations and other aspects of the social sciences is whether we can legitimately generalize or not. Central to the social scientific approach to international relations and social behaviour in general is the notion that we can identify certain sorts of situations as 'the same', or at least 'the same' in some crucial and relevant respects. Thus we need to be able to identify a class of crises, of revolutions, of situations of the balance of power or whatever, and argue that they are sufficiently the same for us to be able to make generalizations. There are two major difficulties. The first I shall call the information problem. Actors in apparently similar situations know different things. In particular, people know what happened in similar situations in the past and can modify their conduct in the light of this information. Hence, the knowledge of actors is different in what are otherwise similar situations. Thus, unless this knowledge is kept secret or for some other reason is not known to later actors, there is never a true replication of an event. The second I shall call the complexity problem. Many social events are very complex so nothing is quite like a predecessor and for this reason also it is hard for there to be a true replication of an event. Thus two revolutions, such as the first

French Revolution of 1790 and the Russian Revolution of 1917, had some similarities but also very many dissimilarities even apart from the knowledge the Russians had of the French Revolution. The first of these distinctions is more fundamental than the second.

First we shall consider the information problem. Viewing events through the eyes of the actors brings us up against a severe problem in considering events which take place at different times in history, such that the experiences and interpretations of the actors are different. Thus, actors in the events on the international scene which took place after the 1914–18 war were deeply affected by the war and may have acted differently because of it. But this means that such events are different in some possibly crucial respect from those which preceded them and it might make a difference as to how we classify things. Similarly, some social events seem to achieve symbolic importance and affect what happens afterwards. Munich is a classic case which affected all subsequent attempts at international negotiation for years to come and made 'appeasement', which had been earlier a perfectly respectable notion, something which had to be avoided at all costs. The question is whether this is a surmountable problem or one which funda-mentally prohibits the use of generalization in international relations or, by extension, in any of the other social sciences.

The most convinced of empiricist philosophers acknowledge that there are differences between the natural and the social sciences. When a human act is repeated it is common for the actors to know what happened on previous occasions and modify their conduct in the light of this. Thus, the repetition is not a true repetition but takes place under conditions of modified information. At its simplest, this can be an observation by the actor of what went before, followed by some simple modification of behaviour (which need not necessarily achieve its objective). At its most sophisticated it can involve the formation of a theory of the relevant processes which offer grounds for a successful adjustment. There is no necessary presupposition that the theory induces behaviour to con-form more closely to the theory (thus making it self-fulfilling), or makes behaviour diverge (making it self-refuting). It does different things in different circumstances. However, that an observation of some behaviour can alter future instances of that behaviour is clearly possible. Similarly, in a more structured form, a knowledge of a theory of behaviour can alter that behaviour and make the theory false. There is no parallel to this in the natural sciences. It does not mean that all behaviour takes place in different circum-stances as a result of the information generated. If an action is repeated often, after a while the learning which takes place is trivial or non-existent, and a lot of human behaviour is of this sort. However, modification of behaviour as a result of learning can and does happen and is a feature of social behaviour.

I shall illustrate the point by taking the case of crises, an issue of continuing interest to the international relations specialist. Crises succeed each other in time. A particular crisis appears at a certain point in time and the actors in that crisis have some knowledge of the preceding crises. Because of this they might, and sometimes do, alter their behaviour. The actors in the next crisis have knowledge of what happened in previous crises and, even though it might be similar in many other respects, the actors have different relevant knowledge. This is more than a hypothetical point. We know, classically in the case of the Cuban missile crisis, that a knowledge of what had happened in 1914 influenced the United States decision-makers, in particular Kennedy, in the way they considered the crisis. The galling experience of the Bay of Pigs in the earlier part of the Kennedy presidency reinforced their views and explicitly affected the behaviour of the actors in that particular case. The two cases of the Bay of Pigs crisis and the Cuban missile crisis are most unusual in that many of the same individuals were involved in both. Thus, they were learning from their own experience. However, people learn from other people's experiences also, though perhaps less vividly. Suppose there are a sequence of crises $C(1)$, $C(2)$, ... , $C(n)$. We cannot assume that behaviour in any one of them is independent of its position in the sequence – indeed the contrary. If $C(2)$ had occurred before $C(1)$ then it might have followed a different path owing to the lack of information about $C(1)$ which, in the event, was available. However, if we drop different-coloured cannon-balls from the top of the Tower of Pisa then it does not matter whether we drop the blue before the green before the red or the red before the blue before the green. The sequence is irrelevant as the cannon-balls do not learn from the experience of their predecessors.

Consider another type of social situation which is simpler than a crisis. Suppose that three people are testing a new type of parachute and the observers have persuaded three volunteers to jump whose parachutes, like the cannon-balls, are coloured red, blue and green. Assuming the testers are allowed to watch their predecessors (as presumably they would be), it does matter whether the green goes first or last. The green will presumably learn from the others and modify his or her conduct in the light of the earlier experience. Thus, if we build a theory of learning into the process we can overcome the problem of changing, for, though each member of the sequence differs from the predecessor in terms of the knowledge available, this can be built into the system. The question then arises, where is the theory of learning coming from and is it subject to the same problems at a higher level?

In the case of simple social processes which are often repeated there is no great problem. We can conduct series of trials of parachute jumpers and see how jumpers later in a sequence alter their behaviour in response to the experiences of their predecessors. With sufficient trials we can construct a theory of such change. If people make several jumps, they will learn from their own experience also. We use such a theory to short-circuit the process and tell novice parachute jumpers of the experience of predecessors to save them the trouble (and dangers) of learning. We use the theory of learning to alter the process of learning to make it as effective as possible. For more complex human activities, such as learning a new language, the same principles apply as we learn about learning. However, no infinite regress is involved in this argument, as learning about learning is the same sort of activity as learning about any other form of psychological or behavioural process.

Not only do we require a theory of learning in the sense of how learning works and modifies behaviour but also when learning is likely to work. In novel situations people are likely to look around for situations which look similar to give them some guidance. In routine situations they are more likely to follow established procedure unless such procedures begin to become clearly unsatisfactory. Some individuals are more prone to seek for precedents, as are some groups, and we can have a theory of this too.

While instances of parachute jumping might be regarded as the same, it is not so obvious that instances of such complex events as crises are. Revolutions are even more complex. Clearly there are some similarities between the French Revolution and the Russian Revolution but are there enough to regard them as an instance of 'the same' type of event? Likewise, can arms races (Richardson, 1960a), alliance formation (Singer and Small, 1968), instances of deterrence (Huth, 1988) all be regarded within their classes as sufficiently similar to warrant the possibilities of generalization? Where, if at all, does the issue of complexity become crucial and eliminate the possibility of classification? If revolutions are *sui generis* but parachute jumps are not, where is the borderline between them?

The procedure which can be adopted is to break down the complex social events into a set of simple ones. For this to work one has to hold that, in the processes of analysis and synthesis between simple and complex, there are some basic consistencies which hold. One of the most important contributions to our knowledge of crises has been Irving Janis's interpretation of many forms of behaviour as 'groupthink' (Janis, 1982). The concept of groupthink did not originate in international relations but in social psychology, particularly as related to industrial and commercial decision-making. This aspect of crisis decision-making can be separated out – and we have a sufficiently large number of similar, though not identical, events to have a coherent and reasonably testable theory of groupthink which is applicable to international crises, just as it is to other forms of small-group decision-making. The possibility of analysing complex situations in bits and putting them together again makes them analysable. The degree to which this is possible is again disputable.

The learning processes from one complex event to another can similarly be related. President Kennedy very explicitly learnt at the time of the Cuban missiles crisis from the examples of 1914 and his personal experience of the Bay of Pigs (Janis, 1982). However, this was not a novel form of learning, divorced from any other sort of human learning, and we can incorporate the change due to learning in any analysis.

Thus we have two different concepts of social behaviour. The first asserts that generalization is possible. If so, we can move on to formulating deductive theories of social behaviour in the standard scientific way and devise a social science of behaviour in this mode. This is what many social scientists assert they do anyway. The second concept asserts that generalizations about social behaviour are usually impossible. Its adherents may accept some limited exceptions but argue that fruitful generalization applies only to some narrowly restricted classes of events which are very simple, in that not many steps are involved, such as parachute jumping. Other sorts of learning which, though complex, are nevertheless frequently repeated and apparently highly structured such as learning a language might be the subject of generalization also. In both these instances, the learning processes between one instance and the next are very similar, so the actions can be regarded as effectively the same. However, social events of any size and complexity, which means more or less anything studied in the social sciences, do not fall under this rubric. On this view they are effectively excluded from analysis by scientific methods as normally understood. The research strategies implied by the different concepts are totally different. If we follow Winch, the whole corpus of work in the behavioural tradition involving data-gathering and formal modelling is meaningless. Richardson (1960a, b), Deutsch (for example 1953), Rapoport (for example 1974), Singer (for example 1968, 1993), Boulding (1962), Guetzkow and Valadez (1981) and all the other toilers in the vineyard have wasted their time. All we can do is look at the events in the world and, in the case of the international relations specialist, the international scene in isolation and as instances of themselves and themselves alone. Classes of events, inasmuch as they exist at all, are so fluid as to be essentially worthless for the purposes of analysis.

Multiple interpretations

We can suppose that most people within a society have much the same sort of idea about voting and that there is not a great deal of difference between them as far as their conceptions of voting are concerned. However, there are many cases where people's ideas do differ. People in different societies may show a significant difference in their interpretations of something. In the case of a complex phenomenon, even within the same society there may be people who have very different understandings of the same institution.

Once again, let us consider the case of a battle. Viewed from the point of view of the private soldier, possibly conscripted, or in the army because the alternatives were even worse, a battle is both dirty and dangerous. A lot of the orders seem to be incomprehensible and he[2] simply does what he is told by his immediate superior. There may be some underlying feeling that what he is doing is defending his country, or Christian civilization, but this is unlikely to be very clear. His loyalties are to the immediate group of which he is a member such as his immediate colleagues in a platoon or to the wider group of the regiment. He may feel a pride in acting like a brave soldier, or he may just want to survive. He will be unfamiliar with the whole nature of the battle, and know only about his own little bit, and perhaps not much about that. If he is fighting in one of the classic battles of history such as the Somme or Agincourt, he is likely to have known of this only after the event if, of course, he survived.

Viewed from the point of view of the general, it is a stage in a war, a professional exercise which may have very different consequences depending on whether the battle is won or lost. The general will normally see this both in terms of the overall goal of the states on whose behalf he is fighting and also in career terms. In modern battles, most generals are well away from the front and unlikely to be in any personal danger. This was not true until the twentieth century (and less true then in naval engagements). Earlier, generals had run high risks. Even in the twentieth century, while there are some counter-examples, generals have usually started at a more junior level and are aware of what it feels like to be in a battle and have some empathy with those in the midst of it.[3]

Viewed from the point of view of the peasant over whose land the battle rages, it is an outrageous nuisance similar to, though perhaps rather nastier than, an exceptional storm or flood or an earthquake. It may be that the peasants are grateful to one set of participants because they are protecting their lands but this is historically unusual. Stores of food, fodder and fuel are lost to the army (on rare occasions paid for), the land is destroyed, often long after the battle is over, and the women run the risk of rape. There is very little good to be said for it. Only rarely are peasants likely to see it in the broader political or strategic context.

Others, closer to the battle, might see more opportunities for gain. Inflated prices for small comforts can provide a useful profit. For Brecht's Mother Courage, war was a useful institution. However, as with the peasant, it will seem an Act of God and any political and strategic significance will be lost.

We could extend this indefinitely. Every actor in the battle will see it from a different perspective. As social scientists we are dealing with events as interpreted by human beings. There is normally some sort of physical event, but what makes it of interest to us is how people, either the actors or others, see it. But if everyone sees it differently, does this mean that there are several events coexisting for the same set of physical events and, if so, how do we treat these things?

This does not seem such a damaging critique as some postmodernists claim. There are some physical events going on, many of which would be interpreted in the same way by everyone; for example, someone being killed or a bomb falling. Probably such events as a group of soldiers advancing would also be agreed upon – only the very basics of what a battle was about would be required for this common interpretation.

There are two reasons why this is not a particularly damaging critique of a social scientific position. First, people can comprehend the multiple perceptions of the problem, including, with effort, the actors in the system. We can easily see that the battle can be perceived both as a strategic move and as an Act of God. The answer to the question 'What really is the battle?' if people think of it so differently is that it is the physical actions plus the perceptions of the physical actions by the various people involved (note I say involved – I am keeping the observer as a separate actor). That these perceptions and interpretations are inconsistent does not matter. They are facts about the people, not about the physical events, and are part of the object of study.

The second reason is that, while sometimes we are interested in the collection of perceptions, often we are interested in just a range.

If we are interested in the response of communities to catastrophes, then we will look at a battle from the point of view of the peasant and the local entrepreneur, not the general. In itself it may seem to be something which comes more or less at random, like a flood or a pestilence.We are not very interested in why the battle happened but in the particular details of the battle in terms of the destruction it caused. In much the same way, if we are involved in earthquake relief we are interested in its causes only inasmuch as there may be an after-shock. We are interested primarily in the damage it caused and people's response to it. However, if we have a historical interest in the growth of a particular state, the details of the battle are of no concern. Its consequences are what count and people's view of it at the time are of no interest.

The post-modernist point that there are multiple perceptions which on the whole the empiricists have either ignored or down-played is an important one and one which needs to be incorporated into our structure. However, it is not damaging to the general corpus of empiricist interpretation and can be absorbed without difficulty.

Notes

1 Some animals may have some view about what is going on which might raise problems for some biologists. However, I do not address this problem.
2 Despite recent developments, wars have been fought overwhelmingly by males. Hence, in this context, the male pronoun seems appropriate.
3 This was the case with several senior officers in World War II who had had experience of World War I. The British general Montgomery was very influenced by his own experiences as a junior officer and his cele-brated caution is attributed in part to this. Likewise, Churchill, in general a bellicose enough man, was deeply worried about the possible casualties involved in the invasion of France in 1944, again partly because of his personal experience of warfare and probably his disastrous involvement with the Dardenelles campaign in World War I, which had involved a large number of casualties (Taylor, 1965).

4
The difficulties of refutation: the development of knowledge

Imre Lakatos and the process of theory refutation
The earlier description of a scientific theory was rather cold and clinical and revealed very little of the process of scientific development. The work of Kuhn (1962) and Lakatos (1970) broadens this account and in so doing raises some basic issues concerning not only the development of science but its nature. Their arguments were made almost entirely in terms of the natural sciences. In the first two sections, where I describe this work, I shall similarly concentrate on the natural sciences, though less exclusively. However, social scientists of all sorts have been very influenced by this work. In the later sections of the chapter I shall discuss some of the controversies the issues have raised in the social sciences.

If one were to take a very strict line, then an observation which refuted a theory would lead to the rejection of that theory and the search for some replacement. This is a distortion of what people do. Scholars do not like their theories being rejected, and put up a fight to protect them. The first step is to check whether the observation was a mistake in the simple sense and try again. If the error persists, then the theory behind the observation might be checked – for example, does the instrument operate within the requisite ranges of error? In the case of the social sciences the measurement procedures are extremely malleable and can be easily deemed to be at fault (see Chapter 7). If this fails, some modification of the theory might be entertained which still leaves its essential structure intact. Thus, the functional form of a relationship might be altered, such as a linear relationship being replaced by a gently sloping quadratic equation. There are many stratagems which the researcher can use before coming to the reluctant conclusion that the theory is wrong, and all will be pursued by a devoted researcher. A quick reading of Popper (1959) might lead one to suppose that he advocated that scientists accept with joy, or at the very least resignation, the refutation of their theories in that it meant yet another step had been taken away from error. This is psychologically implausible as well as being of dubious rationality. A more charitable reading of Popper and an extension of his views by Lakatos makes him, in

Lakatos's grand if linguistically contorted phrase, a 'sophisticated methodological falsificationist' (Lakatos, 1970).

The numerous ways in which it is possible to fend off the objections to a theory suggest that it might be always possible to fall back on some stratagem to save a theory, and there is no end to the road of theory preservation. In this case either the Popperian criterion which demarcates science from non-science is inadequate or perhaps indeed there is no such demarcation principle. Perhaps science is subjective after all.

First let us clarify what is being refuted, as confusions can arise. Involved, or possibly involved, are singular statements, empirical generalizations, theories and research programmes. *Singular statements* assert that something happened somewhere at some time ('at some point in the space–time continuum', as some would say). Such an event is observable either directly or by its implications. To neglect probabilistic statements for the moment, it is determined as either true or false by observation; that is, some form of experience. A *generalization* relates two or more variables, as mentioned before. Provided the prior conditions are met, this is not restricted to a particular point in time and space. The conditions may not hold forever. Propositions about swans and their whiteness hold only when and where swans exist and, rather obviously, if swans become extinct, there will be no instances of white swans to check up on. However, whenever they do exist, any general propositions about them hold. If the statement is deterministic, then one counter-instance, expressed in terms of a singular statement, is sufficient to destroy the truth of the statement in principle, though not in practice. However, repeated attempts to confirm it will run out of excuses. After sufficient counter-instances, the empirical proposition will be regarded as false. I would therefore argue that an empirical statement can be falsified beyond reasonable doubt. Further, and contra Popper and the Popperians, provided it survives genuine narrowly defined tests sufficiently often we can regard it as confirmed, the more so the more frequently it passes the tests.

The refutation of *theories* is more complex. I have argued that a theory consists of a set of logically interrelated propositions such that if one falls, the others fall also. Further, empirical propositions are placed in the theory such that if one of them is found to be false, then the theory as a whole is regarded as false. This at least is the extreme case, the naive falsificationist case. However, this is not really how theories are regarded. A theory can be modified into something which is clearly of the same family as the original theory and with the new theory the offending proposition may come out correctly. How resilient theories are to such changes, and, indeed, whether they can be totally resilient, is an important question which has been approached in different ways. It will recur in this book but for the moment I want to concentrate on one of these, Imre Lakatos's concept of the methodology of scientific research programmes.

A *scientific research programme* is a more dynamic version of the process of scientific development than that portrayed in the original account of a theory in Chapter 2. According to Lakatos, a theory is not refuted in the abstract merely because of a few counter-instances. A particular proposition might be discarded but not the theory as a whole. In part this is because the significance of a counter-instance is hard to detect. It might involve some minor tampering with the theory, or the counter-instances might be due to some misspecification of the initial conditions. Thus the erratic behaviour of the planet Mercury, which is the planet nearest to the Sun, was not explained by Newtonian physics. However, Newtonian physics did not collapse because of it. It was assumed there would be something to account for it, such as yet another planet which could be incorporated without difficulty in the general Newtonian picture. This was a perfectly proper and rational attitude to take. It was subsequently shown, however, to be entirely explicable in terms of Einstein's theory, and thus what had been an insignificant counter-example to the one theory proved a much more significant corroboration of its replacement. A theory is refuted only in terms of another which explains all the other did and more besides. Lakatos wants to say that it 'predicts' novel findings which had not been expected, but this seems to be an optional, if useful, extra and leads Lakatos into some convoluted definitions of prediction.[1] I think my criterion is sufficient. While this leaves a number of problems unsolved, as we shall see in Chapter 5 on tautologies, it clarifies the concept of refutation. A theory is modified and replaced by something better; it is rarely abandoned.

Theory development is a dynamic process. A theory which is shown to be inadequate is replaced by one which is rather better but typically by one which is of the same family ('family' is my word, not Lakatos's). We have a sequence of theories, $T(1)$, $T(2)$, $T(3)$ and so on, each of which explains more than its predecessor and thus supersedes it. This sequence of theories is known as a scientific research programme. The family relationship is carried on by the 'negative heuristic' or 'hard core' of propositions which will not be doubted, at least during the course of the research programme. In general it is not to be supposed that all observations will fit neatly into this framework and objections will be raised. The response is not to abandon the hard-core assumptions but to defend them by means of *ad hoc* or 'auxiliary' hypotheses which will protect the core against recalcitrant facts. These auxiliary hypotheses are expendable and will be abandoned or modified if new observations require it. However, they will always be modified in such a way as to defend the hard core of the research programme.

In international relations, an obvious candidate for a research programme is that of realism. Realism views the international system as dominated by states whose behaviour is the central focus of what is to be explained. Further, the states' central goal is to maximize power. Power is the ability to coerce other actors, where for the realist the actors are other states, and power is normally conceived of as military power. This can be regarded as the hard core of the realist research programme. The straightforward realism of Morgenthau (1948) during the earlier post-war years was developed into 'neo-realism', notably by Waltz (1979). Neo-realism still maintained the same hard core as classical realism though added to it the possibility of other actors. More significantly, it was viewed, at least by Waltz, as basically systemic or holistic such that the system of states is the dominant entity. This is opposed to the reductionist view in which the system is simply the sum of the individual actors and where the system's behaviour can be deduced from the actions of the individual actors alone. There are controversies over the extent to which the Waltzian version of realism is holistic or reductionist. This is central to the theory but not to its use in our analysis. Neo-realism is clearly a successor to classical realism, in the sense that first, it is clearly of the same family and making the same core assumptions, and secondly, it subsumes the first in that it explains the same things at least as well (or badly) and incorporates rather more besides. The expansion of explanatory power is what Lakatos regards as central to a developing or progressive research programme.

It is normal for the scientific community in any particular area to be following more than one research programme at the same time. Scientists are competing with each other in trying to find alternative explanations for the same broadly defined group of phenomena. They are characterized by different hard cores and thus, in general, they will be inconsistent with each other though it is possible that the inconsistencies will be ironed out at some subsequent stage. The question is how to choose between them. This is a central question and it is here that Lakatos differs from Kuhn in a way which can be seen as central to the development of science as a rational activity. We must not be in too much of a hurry. A research programme should continue, provided it is still 'progressive'. That is, it must be able still to continue to incorporate new facts under its umbrella without becoming grossly overburdened with *ad hoc* hypotheses and where the modifications of the auxiliary hypotheses continue to add to the explanatory domain of the theory. However, a research programme is 'degenerate' when the auxiliary hypotheses which are incorporated manage to explain only those particular facts they were called in to explain and otherwise add nothing to the theory beyond this. The research programme sinks, so to speak, under the weight of its *ad hoc* hypotheses. In the competition between research programmes which, according to Lakatos is the usual state of affairs, a degenerate programme slowly gives way to a progressive programme. It does not give way to an absence of theory. Even a bad programme is better than nothing in Lakatos's view, which is probably psychologically true, though I can see no fundamental epistemological reason why it should be true.

Lakatos argues that his concept of research programmes provides what he calls a rational reconstruction of what goes on in a developing science. It certainly provides a criterion for selection between research programmes. However, the criterion is not a clear-cut one; perhaps it would be naive to suggest there could be such a criterion. How long it is before a research programme is regarded as degenerate may be a matter of taste. Even in a research programme in good standing it would seem likely that some *ad hoc* hypotheses, dragged in to explain some awkward fact, do just that and nothing more. It is when too many auxiliary hypotheses do only that, that we get worried. But how do we define 'too many'? A research programme may go through a passive stage when nothing much seems to be happening and alternative research programmes seem to be running away with all the prizes. In economics, the Keynesian research programme in the 1950s and early 1960s dominated the monetarist one, which seemed for a while to have become degenerate. By the later 1960s this was reversed, though now the situation is unclear.

At some point, however, there should be a clarification as to which research programme dominates the other, though this may well take a long time. However, it is hard to imagine the flat earth theory getting a new lease of life or, for that matter, the phlogiston theory, but a theory has to become thoroughly degenerate before it can be written off as hopeless (Thagard, 1992). Even a definition of total degeneracy is hard to formulate explicitly even though we might feel we know it when we see it.

Thomas Kuhn and paradigms

Lakatos's methodology of scientific research programmes was developed in response to Kuhn's theory of scientific revolutions, which historically should come first. However, this is not a historical survey.

Kuhn took a rather different starting-point. He was interested in the nature of fundamental jumps in scientific belief. In particular, he examined the replacement of the view of the Earth as the centre of the solar system by that in which the Sun was the centre of the solar system. This was the central case in terms of which he developed his theory (Kuhn, 1962), though it is also illustrated in a number of other instances. Kuhn's position is that there are two different modes of scientific change: the period of 'normal science' and the period of 'scientific revolution'. 'Normal science' is what it says it is, science as it is normally practised. Scientists try to solve puzzles within a generally agreed set of principles. They agree about such things as what counts as evidence which confirms a theory or hypothesis, what are appropriate hypotheses to test and so on. There is broad agreement on the basics of the discipline and what are interesting questions within it. Most chemists, for most of the time, know what they mean by chemistry; they have a common recognition of good chemistry, and would expect to agree with their colleagues on this. When a discipline is in such a stage of normal science the practitioners of the discipline are said by Kuhn, in his now very famous term, to be working in a common 'paradigm'. The paradigm is what appears in textbooks. In the days and disciplines when the difference between original works and textbooks was not always clear, the paradigm was contained in the seminal works of the discipline such as Newton's *Principia*. This phase of working could be interpreted in standard covering-law terms without difficulty.

However, occasionally there are 'scientific revolutions' when the whole basis of the discipline is fundamentally cast into doubt. In terms of Kuhn's concepts, there is a 'paradigm change' where one paradigm is replaced by another. In Kuhn's view, this type of change is qualitatively different from the change which goes on in normal science. It is not just a bigger and better version of the same thing. The paradigm defines the concepts, and the change in paradigms means that the concepts themselves change. Thus astronomers adopting the heliocentric view and those adopting the geocentric view were not just offering alternative theories of how the blobs of light which were the planets could be explained. They all agreed the planets existed in some form – they were not doubting their common experiences. However, they were involved in a discussion about the whole nature of the concept of 'planet'. The whole structure of the solar system was open to a radical reinterpretation and not just some discrepant observations within it.

This total reinterpretation of a scientific system is different from normal science. There are no longer rules for determining whether one hypothesis should be preferred to another between the systems. Thus they are 'incommensurable' and there is no overall criterion of choice. Unfortunately they are also incompatible. One cannot hold both views as to the structure of the solar system nor is there any way of reconciling them. One has to choose but there appears to be no principle of choice. Thus, it would seem that ultimately the choice between paradigms does not have any rational basis. This is the point at which the fundamental difference between Lakatos and Kuhn appears. Lakatos holds there is a principle of rational choice between radically different pictures of the world, as I have described earlier. However, Kuhn appears to accept that in these, admittedly rare, circumstances of radical change no such principle of rational choice is possible. I shall return to this point below.

Historically, of course, paradigms do give way to other paradigms. Slowly more and more people switched from the view that the Earth was the centre of the planetary system to the view that it was the Sun. It is worth looking at the process more closely. First, holders of both paradigms agreed that the central observational problem was the movements of the planets. The Copernicans (see 'Solar system: theories of' in the Glossary) believed they went in a circular orbit round the Sun while the classicists held that they went round the Earth, not directly but in a set of epicycles. The Copernicans had not taken the circle as just the most plausible path but because they viewed the circle as a very privileged shape indeed; it was the perfect shape. Hence it was a much more central aspect of the theory than it might seem to modern thinkers. In terms of its explanation of planetary movements, neither had a commanding superiority. There were serious discrepancies between the predicted observations and the actual observations in the case of both theories. Thus, at this stage, on the basis of the evidence alone, there was no overwhelming reason to discard the Earth-centred view of the solar system. The Earth-centred theorists also claimed another advantage: their view was more in accord with the scriptures. While this is not a source of authority the empiricist would accept, it weighed heavily at the time. There are reflections of the debate in the disputes over evolution even today. The critical point came when Kepler proposed that the planets went round the Sun in an elliptical orbit, which, seen in the light of the remarks above, was a more significant adjustment in the context of the time than an equivalent modification of a functional form in a theory would appear today. The incorporation of the elliptical motion, along with the theory of the speed with which the planets travelled in the various parts of the trajectory, gave very precise predictions of the planetary motions (it should be remembered there was a wealth of observational data over long periods about the movements of the more readily visible planets). Thus, with Kepler's modifications, the empirical evidence for the heliocentric theory of the planetary system was commanding and it totally dominated its rival. However, it still took a century or so before the Earth-centred theory completely faded away in scientific circles. It was still possible to add on new hypotheses to save the older theory, though the defences grew more and more tortuous and unconvincing. In the earlier days, even after Kepler, there were many who resisted it, and the new paradigm replaced the old more through the death of its adherents than by their conversion. We should note, however, that in no sense did the 'facts speak for themselves'. They spoke only when there was an appropriate theoretical framework for them to speak in.

Another prominent example in the history of sciences is the theory of evolution. Darwin's account of the origin and development of species introduced a new paradigm which was in contradiction to the biblical account. However, it was more than just a different account of the same facts; it was an entire reinterpretation of the meaning of, for example, the fossil evidence. This is not the same as two different theories within the overall theory of evolution. The conventional Darwinian theory was that all sorts of genetic change took place through random processes. As far as survival was concerned they could be good, bad or indifferent. However, those changes which made an organism survive better tended to be perpetuated, because the organisms were able to breed more than their genetically less favoured colleagues, and hence in the long run to supplant them. While the change in itself did not discriminate between useful and useless or harmless characteristics, the process of selection did. Thus, long-necked proto-giraffes survived better than short-necked ones and thus bred more. This, in very brief summary, is the generally accepted view (Dawkins, 1989). However, an alternative and initially not inherently implausible view was proposed, which was that useful characteristics acquired in the course of life by an organism were passed on to the offspring. Thus, the proto-giraffes of one generation stretched their necks and slightly lengthened them, a characteristic which they passed on to their offspring. Understanding of genetics has decisively refuted this point of view, but I would define it and Darwin's explanation as alternative theories within a common paradigm and not separate paradigms. They were dealing with the same set of phenomena which did not involve a disagreement about the nature of the facts under review. Fossils, for both, were fossils. This means that the disagreements were of a totally different nature from the disagreements between biblical accounts and evolutionary accounts, where, as said, there was a totally different interpretation of the nature of the facts under review.

This, as the case of the planets, makes sense of the notion of facts being 'theory laden'. It is argued that there are no such things as 'brute facts' but only facts as determined in a theoretical framework. That is consistent with this account, though what are facts is determined at the level of the paradigm rather than the level of theory. The discussions of such problems – for example, the particularly elegant analysis of Russell Hanson (1962) – notably take place in what is here referred to as a paradigm, though Hanson published in the same year as Kuhn and hence before the more recent meaning of the word had acquired its currency.

To return to the dispute between Kuhn and Lakatos. Kuhn's view was that the conversion from geocentric to the heliocentric view of the planetary system cannot even be interpreted as a rational process: Lakatos argues that it can. Despite a superficial similarity between the concept of a scientific research programme and a paradigm, they are fundamentally different, at least in the uses to which they are put. The methodology of scientific research programmes is a way of incorporating the dynamics of change into the classical picture of science as essentially a rational and cumulative advance of knowledge. It merely stresses that there are blind alleys which scholars inevitably go down from time to time. The argument involving paradigms is that paradigms are inherently incommensurable: they cannot be compared. As they cannot be compared, there is no rational way of choosing between them. Thus, in the last analysis, science is not a rational process. If there is no rational way of choosing between incommensurable paradigms at any point in their development, then the development of science cannot be regarded as the rational activity that philosophers such as Russell, Popper, Lakatos and, indeed, the whole tradition of the Enlightenment claim it to be.

How do we evaluate this argument? First, this is not a psychological argument. Whether one looks at the process through Lakatosian or Kuhnian spectacles, the actual process of conversion is not necessarily one where all the converts were people who had evaluated the evidence and made a careful choice. In the Copernican case, I have suggested there was a period when there genuinely was no rational dominance of the one paradigm over the other. People no doubt switched for emotional reasons, for career reasons, through peer pressure as everyone else in their group did (or did not), or because some deeply admired colleague did. The argument is not about people's motives but about whether a rational choice was available. Lakatos holds that this rational choice became available as the Earth-centred 'research programme' (or 'paradigm') became degenerate and the solar-centred remained progressive to a point where it was difficult to deny the superiority of the new. Thus while there may have been stages where the incommensurability posed a problem and where there was no rational choice, there became a period where a rational choice did become possible. Lakatos would presumably have argued that such a period would always become the case. Lakatos also argued that 'normal science' is itself a myth as there are usually competing research programmes in any science. Indeed, it might be worrying if there were not.

The clinching argument in favour of Lakatos, in my view, is the debate about the solar system today. It is virtually inconceivable that anyone with a modicum of scientific knowledge could support a flat-Earth, Earth-centred theory of the solar system (and by extension, the universe as a whole). There are huge and fundamental controversies in cosmology but this is not one. The heliocentric theory of the solar system is totally dominant and it is inconceivable that the geocentric theory will make any sort of come-back. Thus, now there are rational reasons for believing in the heliocentric theory. However, if the two paradigms had been totally and genuinely incommensurable, this could not have happened. It should still be possible to hold on to the Earth-centred theory as, in the end, a choice on the basis of the evidence would not have been possible. This is not to say that there was not a considerable period where they were incommensurable, but at some stage there did become appropriate criteria and few would argue that one could rationally maintain an Earth-centred theory. This is not just because of the social consensus that this is the case but because the evidence of experience makes it impossible to accept the older view.

The statistics, of course, suggest that a large number of people do in fact believe in the older view of the solar system. It appears that one-third of the British people still believe that the Sun revolves round the Earth (*Guardian*, 27 March 1995). This is a shaming comment on the educational system rather than on their rationality. The belief appears to be a passive one and attempts to justify it are rare even among the bizarre groups who believe in astrology and other hangovers from medieval times. One suspects that people have simply not thought about the problem but if they did, and were reassured that it did not conflict with any religious principle, they would accept the orthodox position. This is not the case with evolution. The scientific community regards the arguments for some sort of evolutionary theory as overwhelming. Most accept an essentially Darwinian account, somewhat updated, and even the heretics are heretics within some form of evolutionary fold. However, 'creationism' is a more active belief than that in the Earth-centred solar system. 'Creationists' of both Christian and Muslim varieties prefer the biblical or Koranic account and argue that where there is a scientific theory which conflicts with the religious account the religious account is necessarily right. This is a totally different principle for determining truth and in this case makes the competing theories genuinely incommensurable. Religious accounts of this extreme form put their holders in very awkward positions. Effectively they are picking and choosing not merely among scientific theories but among criteria for belief. At times they want to accept experience but the job of relating this experience to belief is very difficult.

That Kuhn hit upon some significant feature of the development of science seems incontrovertible. Whether his interpretation of this feature is appropriate is open to dispute. The notion of a paradigm is useful if it is restricted to the few very basic shifts in scientific theories such as the Copernican revolution or the Darwinian revolution. The definition of a paradigm is extremely difficult and not helped by Kuhn's promiscuous profusion of definitions (Masterman, 1970). If we concentrate on the most fundamental version of paradigm (which is what is at issue here), I suggest the following. The 'facts' which are being discussed are defined in terms of the paradigm. There can be conflicting accounts of these facts which involve different theories. When the proponents of the different theories agree on what they mean by the facts, and can agree what sorts of observations would show one theory to be true as against others, then the theories are conflicting theories within the same paradigm. When there is disagreement about the whole interpretation of the concepts within the theory, we move to a different paradigm. I have argued that, whatever the degree of incommensurability there is in the short run, in the long run such incommensurabilities are rare.

The 'inter-paradigm debate' in international relations

'Paradigm', purportedly carrying the Kuhnian meaning, has become very fashionable in many circles. International relations scholars have not been immune to this, and the 'inter-paradigm debate', in which the different approaches to international relations are held to be different paradigms in the Kuhnian sense, is an avid topic of discussion. The conflicting paradigms, are viewed, supposedly, as incommensurable accounts of the field, though at times this view is ambiguous. Michael Banks (1985) argues that there are currently three paradigms which in different ways attempt to characterize the study of international relations: the *realist paradigm*, the *pluralist paradigm* and the *structuralist paradigm*, though there is some hedging on the issue of incommensurability. Banks has closely followed Vasquez (1983), who discusses the concept of a paradigm in some detail in the discussion of realism, but even with Vasquez the issue of incommensurability is left rather vague. However, Reynolds (1982) in a rather different sort of analysis of imperialism is quite clear that the conceptual frameworks he uses, which are not identical with those of Banks, are mutually incommensurable and inconsistent, though he steers away from talking of paradigms as such (to the relief of some of his readers, who get a little tired of hearing of paradigms at the slightest sign of an intellectual disagreement).

Only in small degree is this a pedantic quarrel about the dictionary definition of a word. There are some basic issues involved around the whole concept of incommensurability in international relations and social science. This is intimately linked to concepts of the testability of theory (sometimes referred to as its 'operationalization') and to the ways in which change and development occur in international relations as a field of study in the social sciences. Thus, can propositions be tested only within the context of their paradigm and is there any way of establishing one paradigm's superiority over another? In its turn, this leads on to the issues involved in the selection of the most appropriate research strategies in international relations. How significant is the question of incommensurability in the social sciences and, by extension, international relations? Hollis and Smith (1991), for example, accept the Banksian argument though they do not develop its implications. These implications, if taken seriously, have horrendous consequences which I am excused from examining, as I shall argue that incommensurability is less of an issue for the social sciences than the above scholars imply. I have argued already that, in the natural sciences, incommensurability is largely a temporary phenomenon (albeit sometimes quite a long-period form of 'temporary') and that there comes a time when the rejection of one paradigm in favour of another is not dependent on the social conventions of a scientific community but cannot rationally be resisted. It does not follow that this is the case in the social sciences. It may be that incommensurability is much more widespread, though I shall argue not.

My basic criticisms of the proponents of the inter-paradigm debate and of the pervasiveness of incommensurability in international relations are three. First, if we take the issue of incommensurability seriously, the debate aborts a set of interesting arguments well before it is appropriate. If two schools of thought are different paradigms then discussion between their proponents is futile and in particular any notion of synthesis is a waste of time. A 'debate', at least a debate consisting of rational argument, cannot take place if the two paradigms are incommensurable. Secondly, the terms in which the debate is phrased restrict it to international relations and, as so often in the past, isolate the discipline further from the rest of the social sciences in a manner which is harmful to its development. Thirdly, by raising the issues to those of a fundamental paradigm in the Kuhnian sense we impose a totally false picture of debate and hence the nature of change in the social sciences. Controversies can be important and serious but still fall short of the cosmic significance ascribed to them. These objections do not apply equally to different authors, as will become clear, but they are all involved in the general controversy.

I elaborate by first summarizing the argument about the inter-paradigm debate as presented by Michael Banks (1985). The division into realism, pluralism and structuralism is accepted in substance by many scholars and, indeed, it seems a fruitful categorization. I try to state these 'paradigms' in ways which would be acceptable to their adherents, though there are considerable differences within the paradigms as well as between them (which, whether or not they were true paradigms, would not be surprising). If the argument were to be phrased as 'conceptual approaches' or 'theoretical frame-works' or something of the sort, the characterization of the different schools would be quite acceptable. This is not the burden of the argument. While my argument is that these different schools are not paradigms, at least in any Kuhnian sense, I shall retain the term for the moment to maintain consistency with other expositions.

Proponents of the realist paradigm argue that international relations is essentially about states and their interactions. States pursue power as their dominant motivation, and internal and external politics are largely separate forms of activities. It follows not only that the behaviour of one state can be understood only in terms of its relationship with other states but also that internal factors are of no substantial importance except as determinants of the power base. Further, interactions between social groups which cross state boundaries, other than those which are surrogates for the state's behaviour, are of minor importance. As an example, it is argued that religious links are at best secondary to state interactions and at most provide a bit of 'friction' in the inter-state relationship, which is what is predominant.

Proponents of the pluralist paradigm argue that other actors besides the state are also of great significance. Multinational corporations, religious groups, and other organizations which cross state boundaries are not peripheral actors, as the realist would claim, but dominant in any discussion of international relations. States are one type of actor in the system though pluralists would disagree as to their significance. Some argue that they are of little significance. Pluralists also argue that a state is not a homogeneous entity but a complex coalition in which it is unclear that the state is maximizing anything, much less an ambiguous and ill-defined concept such as power.

Structuralists argue more generally still that international behaviour can be understood only in terms of social, political and economic structures and that the greatest of these is economic. Many contributors to this genre are Marxists or, like Johan Galtung, very influenced by Marxist thought (for example, Galtung, 1971, 1976–80). The central feature of a structuralist explanation of phenomena is that the role of decision as compared to structure is small.

Conceptually, Charles Reynolds's approach to the analysis of imperialism (1981) is remarkably similar to Banks's interpretation of the three paradigms, though his general approach to international relations is otherwise very different. The discussion is set in the context of a very self-conscious approach to the problems of explanation. He discusses four analytical approaches to the issues of imperialism. The first interpretation or mode of imperialism places it within the power politics mode of explanation (roughly corresponding to Banks's realist school). This is illustrated with material from the post-1918 world. The second is economic imperialism (roughly corresponding to the structuralist account) and involving considerable discussion of the multinationals. The third mode is ideological, illustrated with the example of Hitler and the Third Reich. The final one is the sociobiological form of explanation, which is illustrated at the political level with the example of Japan in the 1930s. The last two categories do not correspond with any of Banks's categories.

While, unlike Banks and Vasquez, Reynolds does not refer to the concept of a paradigm as such, he is much more explicit than Banks on the issue of incommensurability. Thus, referring to the various approaches he says 'Clearly they are incommensurable as theories or world views. In choosing one as a valid characterisation of world politics and apportioning it explanatory power, we are compelled to reject the others' (Reynolds, 1981: 20). He goes on to say 'I said earlier that these models of imperialism are incommensurable. They are mutually exclusive, making universalist claims that deny any authority to rival schemes' (238). A lot of his argument is a justification of these points.

That this is an account of different schools of thought in international relations would be widely accepted, though others might offer different sets of groupings. However, are they 'paradigms' in Kuhn's sense? It is not clear what Banks's view on this is. Initially he is apparently dogmatic: 'Today, the field contains not one but three such general explanations: realism, pluralism and structuralism. Strictly, they should be called "paradigms", but they are also more casually termed perspectives, approaches, world views, frameworks or general theories' (Banks, 1985: 9). To affirm that 'paradigm' is not used casually he later remarks, 'Awareness of just how deep were the new divisions came hesitantly at first, beginning with discussion of the importance of Kuhn's "paradigm" philosophy for the field, and then accelerating' (11). Vasquez, whose influence Banks readily acknowledges, devotes a whole chapter to the issue of paradigms in the Kuhnian sense and is unambiguous in his identification of realism as a paradigm in the strict sense of the word. However, he later talks of the relationship between paradigms as 'a discussion about choice of analytical frameworks' rather than 'a militant confrontation between mutually incompatible world views', and asserts that the paradigms are tackling different problems. Thus the form of incommensurability involved could better be called 'local incommensurability', discussed below, namely a temporary incommensurability which will at some stage be overcome such that comparisons are possible. Unfortunately, this is an important qualification, as I discuss below. If 'paradigm' is used rather carelessly to mean simply a school of thought then, after all, we are involved in an unimportant semantic problem about the definition of a word. However, if this is not so, and strong incommensurability is implied, then this involves a basic dispute about the status of various forms of international relations scholarship and the nature of the development of thought within the discipline. This is an issue which should neither be neglected nor left ambiguous.

I shall now consider the alleged cases of incommensurability discussed above, starting with the realist, pluralist and structuralist trichotomy. Realism and pluralism were described above. They are both versions of a decision-making research programme but with different actors and different variables entering into their utility functions. One can decide on their relative explanatory power on the basis of general scientific principles, which would include parsimony. Suppose one wants to explain war, defined not necessarily as inter-state war but as any case of organized, large-scale violence. We can consider the various possible actors and goals they might be assumed to be pursuing and see which of the theories comes up with the most parsimonious explanation. The realist and pluralist research programmes are in competition with each other for producing the most broad-ranging and parsimonious explanation of the issues involved. There is no particular reason to assume that they are incommensurable. Similarly, we can take the case of an economic (or structural) explanation of imperialism and compare it with a realist one. Non-state actors are not a twentieth-century invention and clearly such enterprises as the East India Company were major actors in the eighteenth and early nineteenth centuries. However, were these genuine actors or merely surrogates for the state? The answer to this is not merely a matter of taste. We can examine this in terms of all three programmes and perhaps find that one is progressive and dominant, leaving the others to fade away. Alternatively, we might well find that some synthesis emerges with bits of each fitted together systematically and not in some *ad hoc* way. In the long run we can expect theoretical developments to take place which would make such questions decidable. They are not, as the theorists I am criticizing appear to maintain, inherently undecidable. The case of Reynolds's discussion of the biological bases for behaviour is slightly different. The argument here is that there are basic aggressive drives which underlie behaviour and which effectively determine them. Again, of course, this can be represented tautologically. However, this sort of theory is at a different level of analysis from the other theories and is potentially consistent with any of them. Only if the sociobiological theories totally determined behaviour would they be potentially inconsistent (or, of course, consistent). To claim this, however, would be equivalent to claiming that underlying motives determined by biological factors meant that an analysis of the overt motives was either unnecessary or incommensurable. They are incommensurable only in the trivial sense that they are asking different questions, not in the sense of answering the same questions in different but non-comparable ways.

The various frameworks in international relations can be regarded as competing research programmes much more satisfactorily than as paradigms. There is no particular need for an early reconciliation. In a field which manifestly has failed to find satisfactory explanations for so much of the behaviour which is central to its concerns, theoretical diversity is to be welcomed. This is provided in the notion of competing research programmes. However, we should notice that the very concept of competition implies comparison. At least at some points, the proponents of the various programmes are trying to do some of the same things better than the other. The result may be that one programme 'wins'; that the programmes have amalgamated at some higher level; or all have been defeated by a so far undiscovered programme. However, the result must be acknowledged according to some generally accepted common sets of criteria. Kuhn's paradigms, at least on the strict interpretation, are incommensurable. They cannot be compared and therefore they cannot compete.

This is not to argue that there may not be 'local incommensurability' in the sense that in any stage of the development of theories it may not be obvious how two theories which appear to cover similar ground are to be compared. As each school follows its own programme, there is probably not too much point in being obsessed with issues of comparison, just as there is not too much point in being over-fastidious, at least in the earlier stages, about the finer points of testability. However, at some stage it is useful to spend effort on seeing how different programmes can be compared and not to be too readily discouraged in structuring the theories to make them commensurable. The very act of comparison is likely itself to be illuminating, but is likely to be aborted by speedy assertions of incommensurability. Otherwise we rapidly get to the point of choosing our theories according to taste and prejudice and dismissing the notion of social science which can be attested to by observation. This is the implication of being prepared to fall back on concepts of paradigms too readily.

As a simple research strategy there is a lot to be said for the methodology of scientific research programmes. It is a proper and rational research strategy to try to milk a programme for all that it is worth and be undeterred by some failures. Thus, it is perfectly sensible to try to see just how much behaviour can be explained in terms of states' behaviour. The auxiliary hypotheses used to bolster up some apparent anomalies in the programme might well turn out to be very revealing. It would be foolish for a realist not to try, and for proponents of other programmes not to follow the attempts with interest, to see how such strategies might support their own programme. However, efforts at comparison and synthesis are also important and, on the view I am urging, possible. If the claims for incommensurability are to be taken seriously social science is going to be a badly disjointed affair with hardly anyone being able to talk to anyone else except to retreat into a corner with a plaintive cry that 'My paradigm's better than your paradigm.'

Change and paradigms

The loose use of 'paradigm' to mean little more than a school of thought (as in 'realist paradigm', 'Keynesian paradigm', 'monetarist paradigm' and so on) is widespread. The word has caught the

imagination and is used in a variety of inconsistent and often incoherent ways. Doubtless it is here to stay and defenders of the purity
of language must sadly hang up their dictionaries and tend their
gardens. Language changes: I should not abuse my professional
colleagues unduly for participating in such change. It is common
for humble concepts to be raised to the status of fundamentals while
their purveyors, in their own eyes at least, move from the social
scientific equivalents of mere meddlers with microscopes to
Darwinian giants.

There is, however, one reason for regretting this particular
derogation of the language. Kuhn considered cases of major change
in the development of science. Whether Kuhn correctly interpreted
such changes or not is open to dispute but it seems that he did identify
an important characteristic of scientific development. However,
the sorts of changes which are going on in the social sciences are
simply not of this magnitude. Social scientists are continually
looking for their Newton or their Galileo and are returning disappointed. This may be because there has been no paradigm change
in the social sciences of the same sort of magnitude as the generally
accepted changes in the natural sciences. Indeed, why should there
be? One would not expect them frequently. It may be that the one
paradigm change there has ever been was that inaugurated by the
development of systematic social science during the late eighteenth
and early nineteenth centuries by people like Adam Smith. This
was more of an evolution rather than a revolution but was no less
important because of it. However, the notion that social science is
constantly in the grip of changes of the magnitude of the Darwinian
revolution parodies the concept.

Note

1 This is in any case rather different from 'prediction' as used in Chapter 2.
There we were concerned with taking a set of particular events and
predicting other particular events. In the context of scientific research
programmes, it must be interpreted as the prediction of hitherto
undiscovered laws which in their turn will be tested by their prediction of
particular events.

5
The difficulties of refutation: tautologies, their use and limitation

The strategy of refutation

The methodology as well as the epistemology advocated by the Popperians is to propose hypotheses and theories in refutable form and then try to refute them. On this view, a good theory is a vulnerable theory; that is, one for which one readily can conceptualize what would refute it and proceed to search for it. Bearing in mind our qualms about the alleged distinction between verifiability and refutability, this nevertheless seems an impeccable way of going about things and as likely as any other strategy to produce empirical theory.

The characteristic of an empirical statement is that it can in some way or another be tested. Thus we need to know what are confirming observations and what are disconfirming observations. Ayer, strongly influenced by logical positivism and the Vienna Circle, proposed the 'verifiability criterion' as the standard by which one judged whether a statement was empirical or not (Ayer, 1970, originally published in 1936). For a statement, other than those of logic and mathematics, to be a part of science, it had to be possible for it to be verified, either directly or by a verification of its logical implications. Popper argued that this was too weak and a statement needed to be refutable (Popper, 1959). That is, one has to be able to specify the observations which would falsify the statement and then see if the conditions which would falsify it hold or not. Verification and refutation are in some sense asymmetrical processes. If we attempt to verify a proposition we can look at numerous instances but we cannot, by looking at a finite set of observations, justify asserting the truth of a potentially infinite set of observations such as 'all swans are white.' The more white swans we have come across in the past, the more confidence we may feel that all the swans we will come across in the future will indeed be white, but we do not establish it. This is the classical problem of induction. However, a single counter-instance of a swan which is not white refutes the proposition. Also, the stronger condition is needed because some forms of verification can be trivial. Thus, one can 'verify' a tautology such as that a billiard ball is either red or not-red. Having defined what to do in various ambiguous cases when the colour verges on orange or purple, we can carry out as many verifications as we want and always confirm the truth of the statement. This is the source of the Popperian emphasis on refutation, though it is implicit in all but a rather trivial notion of verification. We can perfectly properly look for confirming instances of a theory, but we have to take care to look for cases which at least conceptually could be false. To verify properly, a verification must be able to fail.

There are, of course, both logical and psychological aspects to the whole debate between verifiability and refutability if it is to be a genuine one. The logical problem is the one stated above. The psychological point is what one does when faced with a scientific proposition. Obviously, one tests it – but what does this mean? It can only mean carrying out observations which can either confirm or disconfirm it. However, if it is a genuinely empirical hypothesis in the sense that the counter-instances can be formulated, then the process of testing is logically the same whether one is a verificationist or a refutationist. Scientists (whether natural or social) who have just proposed a theory naturally look initially for some confirming instances in the sense of looking for cases where it is most likely to hold. This is a perfectly rational procedure. If it does not hold in the potentially favourable cases it is not likely to do so in the less favourable. Furthermore, it is only human to hope that one's theory is true. As confidence is gained with easier cases, then one might turn to harder cases and be ready with some reasons why it might fail in these instances. After all, a failure might well require a modification of a theory, not its total rejection. However, one's psychological motivation might quite reasonably be to prove a theory rather than disprove it. The same may well not be true of one's professional rivals and colleagues. They may be quite happy to see the theory refuted which has made you famous (or, perhaps more modestly, meant that you got tenure). Further, they will do their very best to refute it for you. The essence of the science is that it is carried out by a social group with a strong competitive element. The refutations come from this rather than the noble feelings of scientists anxious to refute their cherished theories.

However, there are three sets of qualifications to the general disapproval of tautologies. Two are methodological and one is epistemological. As far as methodology is concerned, it is not so clear that a constant awareness of refutation is a particularly useful way of proceeding. Lakatos, himself a devoted Popperian, developed what he called the 'methodology of scientific research programmes', referred to in Chapter 4. In this, he proposed a clarification and modification of the actual process of devising refutable theories which made it a more credible process. In Lakatos's schema, refutability is still the cornerstone but more as a final court than as an everyday event. I think we need to go further than Lakatos and admit that, in a developing branch of an empirical discipline, vulnerability is not such an overwhelming virtue and even tautologies have their place. The second problem concerns the definition of terms. Concepts such as 'power' in international relations are so loosely defined in their general usage that a whole range of precise definitions are consistent with them. If one definition fails to give a required result another can be brought in and may well succeed. With ingenuity, one can select a set of definitions which will confirm a wide variety of hypotheses. The problem has particular importance with respect to quantification, which is of great significance in international relations (see Chapter 7). In the social sciences, the degree of flexibility we have in definitions is at times disconcerting.

These are practical problems (which is why I call them 'methodological'). However, there are more difficulties than at first sight appear about the whole concept of refutability. It is accepted generally that there are no final truths in science and any theory can be overturned in the light of future discoveries, either factual or theoretical. This is common ground in all epistemologies of science. However, Quine (1961) argues that, because of the holistic nature of knowledge, all theories are redeemable, or refutable, in principle if viewed in the whole system of science and not just in isolation. We discuss his view at the end of the chapter. First, however, we shall clarify the concepts of tautology and refutation and consider the uses of a more permissive attitude to tautology than the Popperians think proper in scientific analysis.

Tautology
A tautology is a statement which is by definition true. Similarly, a set of statements can be tautologous in that, taken together, they cannot be false. All possible states of the world can be consistent with them. Take the case of 'false consciousness' as an instance. In standard earlier versions of Marxist theory it was argued that people identified with their class. In particular, it was believed that the working class in a developed capitalist economy would regard their class as the group with which they would primarily identify, rather than such other potential sources of identification such as nation (or state) or religion. In 1914 most Marxists (and some non-Marxists) thought that war would be impossible because the working classes of the different countries would refuse to fight each other. Clearly the war did happen and the working classes of the

different countries did fight each other all too vigorously. This appeared to contradict and refute a basic Marxist hypothesis. It could be saved, however, by saying that the working classes, drugged by propaganda, misperceived their true interests and, in the language of later Marxists, were the victims of 'false consciousness'. The false consciousness of the working class, and indeed of other groups, has been used to explain subsequent discrepancies between the behaviour of the working classes and what would have been predicted by Marxist theory, at least according to Marx.

Brief reflection makes it clear that this is tautological, at least in the form expounded. Any sort of behaviour can be explained as the consequence of the working class either perceiving its true interests or being the victim of false consciousness. Hence it tells us nothing about the world and is on a par with asserting that billiard balls are either all red or all not-red.

Tautology is a difficult problem for the social scientist, partly because it is not always easy to see. As I shall argue below, tautological stages may be perfectly respectable stages for a theory to go through and the formulation of tautologies may not always be such a barren exercise as Popper would have us believe. They should not be mistaken for genuine theories, however.

International relations is as dogged by tautology as any other branch of the social sciences. Let us consider Waltz's widely discussed 'structural realism'. Apart from his basic statement (Waltz, 1979), which is strongly recommended to the reader, there are many expositions. Consequently mine will be brief, highlighting the aspect I particularly want to use in my analysis.

Waltz adopts the realist view of the centrality of the state as the primary actor in the international system. However, unlike the classical realists he stresses the systemic aspects and regards the individual actors as severely constrained by the behaviour of the system as a whole – that is, the other actors. Thus, he has a model somewhat analogous to that of the perfect competition model in economics, an analogy which he stresses. The perfectly competitive market is a classic case of a structural system which also involves decisions. If there are a large number of actors in a market, with cost conditions given by other markets and the technical factors of production, then the price, quantity produced, and so on will be determined. However, the model is analysed in terms of decision-making processes, admittedly of a rather stylized form, in which it is assumed that businesses try to maximize profits. If they do not, they will go out of business. Thus the effective choice before the entrepreneur is between the two rather extreme alternatives: to maximize profits or to cease being an entrepreneur. This is a model, and real life is not usually quite so stark. However, the point that decision is restricted is a valid one. Notice that this is not to say that one cannot explain the behaviour of markets in terms of the individual actors, but that it is trivial to do so. One could argue that it is the imperfection of markets which makes the analysis of individual firms in fact an interesting one.

In Waltz's model, the states are the actors instead of the firm. However, like the firm either they can take an appropriate set of decisions to maintain or increase their power or they can fail in systemic terms. They have choices but they are extreme choices – do as the system dictates or go to the wall – though it can be supposed that there are some technical, lower-level choices of alternative methods of maintaining power. For example, there might be genuine alternatives about the structure of the armed forces or even of different possible alliances. Machiavelli's view of the world, both within and without the state, was rather similar (though Waltz would probably argue that, however understand-ably, Machiavelli did not fully understand the concept of a system).

How would we tell whether this system were the case or not? In the perfectly competitive system, bankruptcy is a good criterion of failure in the system and the actor can cease to exist without replacement. Quite what the equivalent of bankruptcy is in international relations is unclear. A theory such as Waltz's does not exclude the possibility of a mistake either because the actors misjudged the power situation or because they unwisely neglected the basic precepts of power politics. Thus, the British and French actions at Suez in 1956 which appear to counter the neo-realist theory do so only if we assume, very unreasonably, that people never make mistakes. Thus a very large number of events can be 'explained' either by the theory working properly, or, if this fails, by arguing that the actors have made mistakes. We can add that a system is a changing entity and that the relative rise in power of some states and the decline of others takes time, as with Britain or France. We can fend off counter-instances by arguing that not enough time has passed by yet. Further, these time lags are variable. Sometimes power changes come quickly, as with the former Soviet Union. Thus any apparent disconfirmation of the Waltzian thesis can be accommodated by means of some plausible additional hypothesis. In other words, it has become tautological in that it is consistent with any facts about the world.

What we are doing in the Waltzian case can be interpreted in one of two ways. Either we are buttressing a hard core with some auxiliary hypotheses in the manner of Lakatos, or we are exploiting the flexibility of the overall holistic system in the manner of Quine (see below, p. 101). Either, I think, is a plausible interpretation of what we are doing. However, the practical difference between international relations and the natural sciences, in particular physics, becomes clear in the light of either Lakatosian or Quinean arguments. The depth of the deductive argument is very much shallower in the case of the social sciences than in physics, where the basic propositions of physics are many deductive steps away from experience and part of an extremely complex system. In comparison, a Waltzian system or any other in international relations is simple.

The refutation of generalizations and the refutation of theories

It is prudent to insert a note of caution about the refutation and verification of generalizations and the refutation and verification of theories. A generalization is a statement about a class of events (such as 'All swans are white'). If we simply leave it at that, then it is confirmed, or refuted, by direct observations of swans. In the case of a tightly specified statement such as this, the notion of refutation is straightforward. We can consider the generalization on its own and without regard to other generalizations. However, there are problems when a statement is statistical or when there is some flexibility in the definition of the terms. I shall return to this in Chapter 7 as it has significance in our analysis of international relations.

A theory consists of a set of generalizations. They are logically interrelated such that the truth of some is dependent on the truth of others, and a generalization might be refuted because another, on which it was logically dependent, is refuted (Braithwaite, 1953, gives a good account of this). The refutation of a theory involves the refutation of a set of statements taken as a whole. A critical observation is one which refutes a generalization on whose truth the theory as a whole depends. Such critical observations (or the generalizations dependent on the observations) are rare. The Michelson–Morley experiment, which refuted the concept of the absolute ether, was one (Munn, 1973). They are non-existent in the social sciences. However, a generalization might need to be altered because of an observation which requires modification of some of the theory.

Suppose one is trying to choose between two different (though possibly neighbouring) theories; one is trying to find some set of observations which will discriminate between them, confirming the one and refuting the other. However, quite a lot of generalizations might be shared between them. If they were not, the problem of discriminating between the theories would be rather easier. Thus, when Einstein's theory of relativity superseded and refuted Newton's theory of gravitation and classical physics, it did not mean that the individual generalizations of classical physics such as the rate of acceleration of a body falling towards the earth had been refuted. It was not necessary to recompute the trajectories of shells fired from a gun, which still carried on obeying the same old Newtonian laws. These laws now had to be seen in a different and, in this case, broader context (though not for practical mechanical purposes[1]). Indeed, in the earlier days of relativity theory the problem came in finding an observation which succeeded in discriminating between the classical and the new theory; that is, a statement which was not true in both theories. Thus, when a theory is refuted, it does not mean that a whole set of generalizations in which we had hitherto believed have been necessarily refuted. It means that the set of statements as a whole, of which the 'classical' statements are a part, has been refuted and replaced with another within which many statements in the earlier theory are still held to be true.

Suppose a set of observations shows that a particular theory is clearly false as it stands, whereas a rival theory holds up. This would seem to be the end of the story, and the theory's only hope now is to appear in books on the history of science. Indeed it may be so. However, despite what Karl Popper appears to say, a refutation is unlikely to be accepted happily by the proponents of a theory. They will work hard to try to redeem it in some form or another and the next step is to see how much of the theory can be saved. There are basically two approaches. The first is to modify the theory; the second is to look both at the observations and the particular generalization which they refuted. This brings us back to the first issue raised in this section, of the refutation of specific generalizations as distinct from the theory as a whole.

First let us consider the theory as a whole. The main step is to alter the set of postulates, perhaps adding one to the list, or taking a postulate out, such that the revised set of postulates does not carry implications which were refuted. This will mean that the two theories, the successful one and the refuted one, are no longer incompatible. Further modifications may be taken such as to try to get a set of postulates which incorporate the implications of both theories and build a grander theory. This in fact is likely to be done. The point is that, if a theory contains implications which are refuted by the evidence, the theory is not jettisoned but is revised until it fits in with the facts. This, at least, is what initially happens. Revisions of a theory might initially improve it. However, repeated revisions, requiring more and more awkward stratagems to protect it in the face of a more successful rival, will lead to its abandonment, not because it has violated some rule of acceptability but because it has slowly been worn away by a succession of awkward observations. This, on a smaller scale, is what is recommended by Lakatos in his 'methodology of scientific research programmes'.

In international relations theory the procedure can often be more easily carried out, as most of the theories are rather loosely defined in any case. Strict applications of the hypothetico-deductive method are rare. Strict deductions do not exist, so a disconfirmed proposition can be largely ignored unless it is central to the argument. Thus most realists who earlier would have preferred to analyse the international system exclusively in terms of states are now willing to accept that organizations such as multinational corporations have an influence on the system which cannot readily be explained by reducing it to the behaviour of states. While it would be a parody to pretend that this was being done in terms of formalized postulates of behaviour, a rather similar procedure is effectively being carried out.

Now let us turn to the refutation of specific generalizations. The simplest form is 'All As are Bs.' It is, of course, by way of the refutation of some of the generalizations in a theory that the theory as a whole is refuted. Suppose we make an observation which is inconsistent with the generalization in question. The immediate reaction is to wonder whether there has been an observational error. If an observation is a statistical one, such as a sample survey, it may be a 'rogue survey' in which the sample was very unrepresentative of the population, as is bound to happen from time to time. Alternatively, the observation may have been of a very untypical case or at a very untypical time. Few scientists would be overly concerned at a limited number of observations which appeared to refute a generalization which in its turn refuted a theory, but if refutations of the particular generalization became too insistent to ignore, the observer would have to reject the generalization as it stood. However, it is often the case, and almost invariably in the social sciences, that the proposition can then be modified. If it is a mathematical relationship, such as an assertion that one variable will increase with another, a time-lag can be introduced. The varieties of time-lag are legion and some lag can be found to fit most sets of statistics (this is discussed in more detail in Chapter 7 on measurement). An alternative procedure is to redefine the terms. In cases such as 'all swans are white' the scope is limited, though 'white' could be adjusted to 'whitish' in the case of some ambiguous observations. However, if we are dealing with concepts such as 'power' or 'nation' there is a great deal of scope for adjusting the definitions to accommodate a wide variety of apparently recalcitrant observations. Thus, a generalization can often be saved by some appropriate redefinition of its terms.

As with the theory, this process cannot be carried on almost indefinitely. Most social scientific international relations analyses involve the researcher in using a variety of operational definitions of some concept to see how sensitive is the generalization under investigation to alternative definitions.[2] If it is insensitive then the researcher takes heart. If it is sensitive then the generalization is likely to be abandoned. For example, while 'nation' is a flexible concept which can be defined in a wide variety of different ways, it is not infinitely flexible. Some definitions would be disallowed.

The uses of tautology

Apart from the rather obvious uses of mathematical statements which are tautological, there is still a use for tautologies in the development of a science. That they occur is clear enough. Thus a common class of frameworks where this occurs in the social sciences is found when two different systems of explanation of the same phenomena are both tautological and explain everything. Thus, a power political analysis of imperialism can be made tautological. Any apparent anomaly in the system can be incorporated by some redefinition of power or by assertions about the basic subordination of non-state actors (such as multinational corporations – extending far back in time as is the case of the British, French and Dutch East India Companies). The system always has sufficient flexibility within it to cope with anything. If we now consider a structuralist picture of imperialism on the same lines as Charles Reynolds in his study of various analyses of imperialism (Reynolds, 1981), then we can do the same. Everything is explained perfectly well by means of some readjustment of the terms involved. In the new framework we appear to have explained again the phenomena completely. The incommensurability depends on the tautological nature of the 'theories' involved. We seem to be in an impasse – though an impasse with which some scholars, such as Reynolds, appear quite happy.

However, the development of tautological frameworks is only one stage in the process of trying to develop a theory of some phenomenon such as imperialism, and a preliminary stage at that. It is a useful stage nevertheless. The conceptual frameworks, tautological though they are, determine the categories which are deemed relevant to the argument. Thus, in the case of the billiard ball which is either red or not-red we are asserting that we are interested in billiard balls which we presume to exist. There is also the non-tautological implication that billiard balls can possess the quality of colour. Imperialism, after all, cannot. Further, we are claiming that colour is a relevant category for the purposes in hand. It could have been size or, within limits, shape. Thus the statement is not totally vacuous. Further, though the general statement that the billiard ball is red or not-red is a tautology, an observation is required to determine into which category a particular billiard ball falls. This may be problematic for a ball verging on the orange or the purple. Some balls may fit into either category according to the definition of red. The phrasing of the tautology has raised the issue of colour definition which will still remain in non-tautological statements. Again, the tautology has raised some non-vacuous issues.

The tautological 'theory' is only the beginning. If a theory is found to be tautologous (and it may not be obvious at first sight) then the next stage is to restate the theory in a non-tautologous form, either in its entirety or by breaking it down into sub-theories which are themselves non-tautologous even if the group itself is tautologous. One of the classic tautologies in the social sciences is the Fisher equation of the quantity theory of money. This states that the stock of money (M) multiplied by the average number of times each unit changes hands in a given period of time (V), known as the velocity of circulation, is equal to the price level (P) multiplied by the number of transactions which take place at that price level in the same period of time (T). Thus $MV = PT$. Now brief reflection shows that both sides of the equation are different ways of breaking down the total expenditure in the same period of time and therefore *necessarily* have to be the same. Thus it is not a theory in the strict sense of the word, though it provides us with some useful categories to consider. However, if we want a proper theory we can say instead that $P = f(M)$ where f stands for some function. To make it a genuinely testable theory we can specify f and then test it against some data. This has involved a vast testing industry over the last three decades which started with Milton Friedman and A. J. Schwartz (1963). However, all the different tests would have confirmed the original Fisher equation. If confirmation had not been forthcoming, then as a matter of logic it would have been due to measurement error.

I suggest that this is the appropriate way of tackling tautologous theories, and indeed is what happens. It is not to sit back and accept tautology. Nor is it to sneer at the theory's empirical uselessness and banish it from consideration in respectable society. It is to restate theories in non-tautologous form, at which point they become not merely testable but also comparable. This is where I am specifically advocating a particular sort of theoretical research programme in international relations. On the basis of the tautologies which set what appear to be interesting categories we then formulate non-tautological, testable (or 'operational') hypotheses. In the process of developing these we should not be unduly worried about moving through some tautological phase. It all comes as part of the process of theory development, though it is important to be aware that such a stage does not represent a theory in itself. Once one has broken out of tautologies there is also the possibility of combining theories which are ostensibly trying to relate the same phenomena. A partially economic and partially power theory of imperialism is perfectly acceptable once they are restated in non-tautological form; indeed, it seems odd to think that they might be mutually exclusive, something which was a consequence of the rather unfortunate and unnecessary tautological form of the theory's statement.

Marxism and psychoanalysis are the two schools of thought which originally provided the targets of Karl Popper's wrath (1968) as being tautological. His followers have continued in this tradition (oddly, they did not notice that the 'power politics' school of inter-national relations was just as tautological at the time of Popper's assaults and, in its classical form, still is). However, this does not mean that they were inherently tautological, and in both traditions there is an empiricist wing which tries to formulate hypotheses in testable form and test them (Edelson, 1984; Fisher and Greenberg, 1978, Kline, 1972).

One way of doing this is to define certain sorts of problems independently of the theory. Thus, suppose one wishes to study war. We can define war as any instance of large-scale organized violence. There is no need to specify who is doing the organizing. One could go further and follow Richardson (1960b) in defining a 'deadly quarrel'. This is any conflict where the parties try to kill the other whether at the level of the individual (where it is murder) or a group, and whether organized (such as war) or not (such as a riot). Even a brief survey of the cases of war as defined above shows that a state-centric view is inadequate. The classical realist has merely stated that this is something which is not of concern for the theory and that the relationship of states is all that is of concern. However, deadly quarrels are defined to include all such violent acts whether inter-state wars or not. A deadly quarrel is indepen-dent of the definition of the actors involved. It overlaps the realist theory of behaviour but it clearly does not coincide with it either tautologically or empirically. One of Richardson's big achievements was to jump out of the tautological trap, even if he received little thanks for it from the classicists, who had not realised they were in a trap in the first place.

My argument is that tautology is a step in a process which is perfectly legitimate and helpful in the determination of theory. To return to the issue of false consciousness. To insert it into a debate about people's sense of political identification is not absurd. On the contrary, it might be an important and relevant issue (intuitively this seems very likely). It is inadequate to leave the debate at this stage. The next step is to formulate a definition of false conscious-ness independent of the situation it is called upon to explain. It is necessary to take this next step but to pass through the stage of tautology on the way to a more satisfactory, testable theory is quite legitimate. Without doing so, we might have been unaware of the potential relevance of the variable. The same is true of the Waltzian system. To suppose that actors cannot make mistakes is absurd, but it is also easy to explain any deviant observation as the result of a mistake and thus preserve the theory against refutation. Mistakes have somehow to be independently operationalized. Like so many other precepts in the philosophy of science, 'avoid tautology' is important as an ending-point but damaging if it inhibits the process of development. The danger is in not recognizing the tautology (this failure is widespread among classical theorists of international relations), and mistaking the process for the ending-point.

The high and low vulnerability of systems
A single, precisely defined generalization is very vulnerable to refu-tation. Only one set of clearly defined set of observations satisfies it and any other observations show the statement to be false. This is particularly true when the observations concern precisely defined variables. Conversely, a tautological generalization is invulnerable to refutation, as any set of observations is consistent with it. How-ever, theories (note theories and not just isolated generalizations) can vary radically in vulnerability at any given point of time in their development. A theory can be relatively invulnerable in that it can be consistent with a wide range of observations but still not be tautological. Thus it is still potentially refutable, even though only some small set of possibilities are in fact inconsistent with it. It is important to distinguish a theory of low vulnerability from a truly tautological theory. The low-vulnerability theory is a genuine theory though its explanatory power is relatively low. In Quine's account of theories, all theories are ultimately invulnerable as it is always possible to restate some hypotheses somewhere which can rescue the phenomena (though quite how this would be managed for

the flat-earth hypothesis is not at all clear). However, even on the Quinean picture there are some theories, the vulnerable theories, which are more likely to require a restatement in the light of apparently recalcitrant facts than others.

One may be dissatisfied with the low-vulnerability theory because, though some explanations are excluded by it, most are not, and many sets of different explanations are consistent with it. If the purpose of the exercise is to explain, then this is unsatisfactory in its own terms. If the purpose is technology – that is, the theory is being used to alter things – then the situation is even more unsatisfactory as the theory gives licence to a whole range of possible alternative beliefs about consequences and hence no good basis for choice. Consider the case of threats. An actor makes demands on another actor and threatens the use of violence in order to gain compliance. The threat of violence may have two different consequences: (a) the threat makes the object of the threat comply with the wishes of the threatener; (b) the threat makes the object of the threat more intransigent. It is observationally the case that there are occasions where one or the other happens. This is a problem whenever people use threats but in the early 1990s it has been particularly conspicuous in the case of UN operations. Given a broad definition of compliance and intransigence, my two statements taken together look almost invulnerable in that either one or the other will happen. However, the normal definitions of compliance and intransigence do not define one in terms of the other so it is not truly tautological. Under most sets of definitions, there are alternative possibilities. The object of the threat may not understand the threat (a case which must often happen in threats between very different cultures) or it may ignore it. Though not tautological, the propositions about threats are not very susceptible to easy empirical test. However, we have an extremely practical problem where, nevertheless, our predictive ability is low as we do not know which of the two major possibilities will turn out to be the case. We lack an empirical theory which enables us to recognize with much confidence and in advance into which of the two categories any particular instance falls. Such theories as we have so far are relatively invulnerable in the sense of being consistent with most if not all eventualities. Clearly, this points to the next step in research: to get a theory of high vulnerability, which means a theory that can readily be refuted but which when it survives the refutation, is very useful.

Very general theories are normally of low vulnerability. The wider the range of hypotheses, and the more theoretical theory becomes (in the sense of there being more hypotheses detached from an observation base), the greater the flexibility there is. Again we come to the instances of psychoanalysis and Marxism, where we get very broad theories which can be made almost invulnerable to evidence. We face the Quinean dilemma in a severe form. However, I say almost invulnerable to evidence, in that while the central tenets of the system are almost invulnerable, some more specific hypotheses are subject to test.

Refutability and holism

For a single deterministic generalization, it is comparatively easy to see what the conditions are for it to be true or false. Normally, the result of a refutation is not to abandon it completely but to modify it as we discussed above. In principle, the same sort of process is possible in a system of deductively related generalizations. Any observation statement which is inconsistent with any of the propositions within the theory falsifies not only that proposition but also any propositions which are entailed by that proposition. However, different statements have different degrees of significance within a logical system. It is possible for a generalization to falsify the system as a whole in that every statement in the theory is entailed by it. Other generalizations, however, entail relatively little and can be discarded with only a little modification of the system. However, this is easier said than done. If we have a complex deductive system of many interrelated parts, many of which are far from the observational base, then it is possible to incorporate an apparent refutation by modifying some other statement within the system. According to Quine (1961), when we pick out a particular proposition and examine it apparently in isolation, in fact we are looking at the whole set of propositions which are to some degree interconnected. A classic case where this was particularly relevant is when Galileo first looked at the Moon through a telescope. He was interested in making propositions about the Moon but these depended on the theory of optics behind the structure of the telescope. To make the propositions about the Moon he had to take as given the propositions about the telescope, but in those days this was making a big jump. Nowadays we are fairly sure Galileo was right about the telescope but many observations, particularly in physics, depend on theories of the measuring instruments which are not always thoroughly grounded. The case of Galileo is a particularly striking case but Quine argues that this is a general issue. An observation challenges not only the direct object of the challenge but the whole set of statements in which it is embedded – and in principle the whole of our empirical knowledge.

The dependence of theory on the techniques of measurement is true in the social sciences though in a slightly different way. When using some variable such as 'crime' or 'arms level' we are taking the method of measurement of the variable for granted (an issue which is fortunately well known – the first step a politician makes on being confronted with some discomfiting bit of evidence is to attack the principles on which the data were gathered or the variable was defined). Further, a system is not only complex but it is also not absolutely rigid. A modification of one of the propositions may have little or no effect on the other propositions which are consistent with a number of variants of the propositions in question. Because of this, they can still conform with other observations which have so far verified the theory as a whole.

Let us represent Quine's approach in Figure 5.1 as a circle in which are located all the propositions of a science.[3] The circle's circumference is where these propositions 'touch' reality. That is, these are the direct observation sentences which can be directly verified or falsified. Suppose an observation statement $S(1)$ is refuted in a decisive way, so that we must rationally reject it as a part of the science. There are some statements in the immediate vicinity which were logically implied by the now refuted statement and which must be modified accordingly. However, the farther away from the refuted proposition one goes, whether farther round the circumference or farther into the circle and away from the observations at the rim, the less the statements will need modifying.[4] The same centre is consistent with a whole range of observation statements. Hence a refutation is a refutation of some of the propositions within a theory but not of the entire theory. This is Quine's version of holism. Quine holds that the inner part is almost invulnerable to observation though the degree of vulnerability is an issue for further investigation. Even the apparently refuted observation statement can be saved in that it is dependent on other statements in the theory. Thus, the attempted verification or refutation of a particular proposition is simply a highlighting of a particular statement for the purpose of the exercise. In fact it is a confrontation of the evidence with the theory as a whole. But we can choose to make other propositions vulnerable to protect the designated proposition, perhaps, as suggested above, by querying the techniques of observation. However, it is easy to fall prey to great contortions about this. Everything can be saved, but only at the cost, at times, of severe complication. If parsimony is allowed as a criterion, then some statements really will be confronted with the evidence and found wanting. However, the confrontation with evidence is easier in rigidly specified areas of the natural sciences such as physics than in the looser structures of the social sciences.

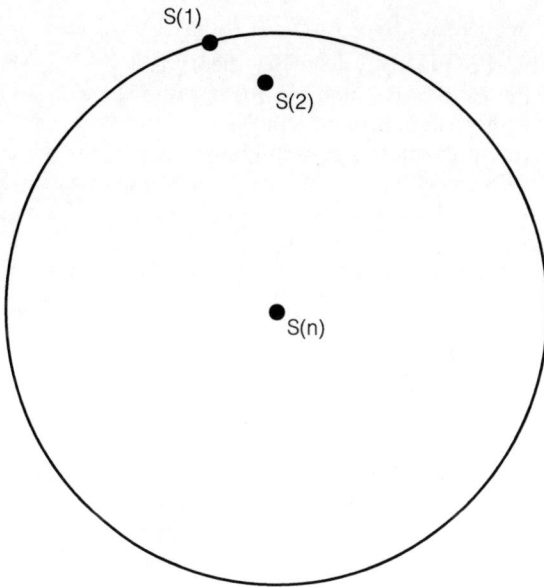

Figure 5.1   A Quinean system

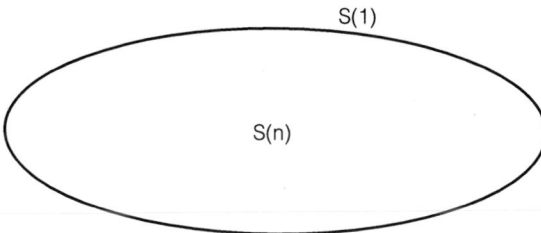

Figure 5.2   A social system

In physics, parts of the theory are a long way from the observational base. This is not as true in the social sciences, though more so in economics than elsewhere. It is more appropriate to represent, say, international relations by a rather shallow oval where none of the theoretical propositions in the middle is very far from the observation sentences, as in Figure 5.2. On the face of it this might make it appear more vulnerable to refutation. However, what the theory gains in vulnerability to observation by the fact that the propositions within it are nearer the observational base, it loses through the greater flexibility in the definitions of the propositions both within the theoretical base and on the observational circumference.

Notes

1 The correction required by relativity theory is $\sqrt{1 - v^2/c^2}$ where v is the velocity of the cannon-ball and c is the speed of light in a vacuum. For most earthly purposes it is undetectable.

2 There are many examples. A well-known one is Singer and Smalls's various conceptualizations of bipolarity and multipolarity (Singer and Small, 1968). The later objections of Moul (1988) are an aspect of the process of sciences being the process of debate.

3 I use the definite article in 'a science' as if sciences were totally separable. In principle everything relates to everything else. However, it seems that some areas of knowledge are 'almost separable' from others such that major disruptions in one field would have little effect on others. Thus, a lot could happen in nuclear physics which would leave genetics relatively intact.

4 The concept of distance used here should not be taken too seriously. However, there is some intuitive notion to it. The distance of a theoretical proposition from an observation sentence might be measured in something like the number of logical steps necessary to get to an observation sentence (but some of them might be of greater importance or 'bigger' than others). Similarly, distance along the circumference could be measured likewise in how deep one had to go into the theoretical base in order to get to a shared (theoretical) generalization.

6
Understanding social behaviour

Common understanding and conceptual communities

I argued in Chapter 2 in the section 'Observation and communication' that scientific observations about the natural world presuppose some commonality of experience that we all have and about which we do not entertain serious doubt. Thus, if I look at a blue spherical billiard ball and describe it as such, I expect to be understood because I assume other people to have had experiences sufficiently close to mine such that any differences can be ignored. This is true in everyday life just as much as it is in scientific discourse. Physical science, or so I am maintaining, depends ultimately on everyone having a body of common experience and on our assuming that the physical experiences involved are sufficiently close for us properly to regard them as the same. There is, therefore, a common understanding.

This common experience is public. It depends on our senses, such as sight, and if I make an assertion about a blue billiard ball being at a certain position at a certain time then I am assuming that this can be verified by someone else (with sight) coming along and having essentially the same experience. This is relatively uncontested. How far we can move from such common experiences to the farther reaches of nuclear physics is more controversial, though all schools of thought regard experience as being relevant at some point.

However, can these concepts be extended to the analysis of social behaviour? Is there some equivalent common experience from which a social science ultimately derives? I shall argue that, while the range is narrower, we are dealing with essentially the same sort of problem.

If we wish to analyse, say, the development of monotheistic ideas we need to have some broad concept of what monotheism means. More detailed questions about religious belief also have to be understood in terms the actors understand. This is an added problem (at least on occasion) for the social scientist from which the natural scientist is spared, but it is not as crippling as Winch (1958) appears to think. To emphasize the point, I shall introduce the notion of a conceptual community. A 'conceptual community' is a group of people who have broadly the same mutual understanding of various concepts relevant to a particular problem. Consider this in the context of voting in elections in the United Kingdom. Voting, as mentioned before, involves rather minor physical acts, so the overt physical behaviour looks trivial. However, the people who are involved regard it as having important consequences but, more to the point, would agree about what they are doing. Terms such as 'voting swing', 'constituency', 'majority' and so on are used without anyone finding them particularly problematic. Scholars carry out studies which relate voting patterns to social class (a very abstract notion, incidentally) or the relationship between disposable income and voting for the government in power, a relationship which everyone understands without any problem and, furthermore, can understand what counts as evidence for and against a specific proposition. This is because they all belong to the same conceptual community and understand the vocabulary involved in much the same way as they understand any other sort of abstraction such as 'summer'. The conceptual community extends beyond the United Kingdom to anyone who understands the concepts of multi-party elections, which is rather larger than the community which experiences the actuality of multi-party elections. The central point here is that, within the context of the conceptual community, we can relate the concepts to each other in a normal scientific manner. We can agree as to what constitute observations which establish values of the variables defined by these concepts as either being the case or not.

Voting is a comparatively easy example. However, the fact we can analyse voting behaviour in the way we do establishes the point and makes an extreme version of Winch's position hard to hold. To be a part of the conceptual community does not require being a member of a common experiential community. We can imagine social states which we do not experience. Thus it is possible to describe polygamy to someone from a monogamous society and vice versa and hope to be understood. We move on by deduction and analogy to the understanding of experiences well beyond our personal experiences. We need to do so in order to generate a social science. I am arguing that it is quite possible to do so.

However, there are other sorts of experiences which are private and which cannot be directly verified. Dreams, for example, rely on personal report. If I claim that I dreamt of a white whale last night, there is no evidence other than my report for that event. It is the same for my reports of pain or of any other sensation. However, we make the underlying assumption that people are in very broad senses the same and, while we might doubt the report of a particular dream, we do not doubt the general proposition that other people have dreams. We believe that, broadly speaking, other people have the same experiences as ourselves, including private experiences. Thus we can regard at least part of these private experiences as also part of the common understanding. This view may seem to some to be philosophically naive. How can we know that, when John says he is in love with Jill, he is experiencing the same sort of experience as anyone else who announces they are in love? We cannot know, of course, though nor can we know whether physical experiences such as that of seeing blue are the same either. However, we have to start somewhere. I assume that there are certain sorts of human behaviour which indicate to us that the people concerned are having some comprehensible sort of internal experiences, rather similar to the ones we would have in that sort of situation. Thus, if I see someone who is undernourished and looking miserable, I assume that I have some understanding of what it feels like even if it is not a totally adequate one. I can use this assumption as the basis for a theory of human behaviour.

In considering rather basic experiences such as the experience of pain and dreams we can generalize quite broadly and do not have a serious problem in thinking that almost all human beings have these experiences and can communicate to others about them. However, there are other sorts of experiences which might be more restrictive either within cultures or between different members of the same culture. Hence such concepts as 'jealousy' and 'honour' might vary between different cultures, and certainly the events which provoke the appropriate experiences are very different. Even within the same culture, mystical experiences are experienced by some people but not by everyone. Similarly, some people are unaffected by music whereas for others musical experiences are central to their lives. This obviously is a limitation on our ability to understand, though some degree of empathy is still possible even if we are limited in our ability to understand fully the experience of another person. There is, so to speak, a limited common understanding but one which allows a considerable degree of communication nevertheless. When emotional factors are centrally involved, as in questions of identity as they relate to nationalism or religion, the problem becomes more complex but none the less the same sorts of issues apply.

Sometimes we are sceptical of the validity of the other person's experience. This arises in the case of art where we cannot understand a particular painting. It is sometimes claimed that the purported perception of the artist and the claim to artistic insight are in fact dishonest. There is, of course, no final way of deciding the question.

Other cases of possible dishonesty arise when an individual claims to have been ideologically motivated for some act but one suspects that the true motivation may be a desire for power or, in the case of torture, a simple sadism which is rationalized by the appeal to high principles. Discriminating between various hypotheses becomes very difficult in such circumstances, though not impossible. Indeed, there is the possibility that someone from outside the context of the ideas might have a better understanding of a situation than the insider. This is certainly the case with some aspects of adults' understanding of children's understanding. (Though there can be colossal failures too.)

The central point is that we have members who constitute a conceptual community who can communicate about social behaviour and derive a common understanding of it ('common understanding' and 'conceptual community' are defined in terms of each other). The common understanding need not derive from a totally common experience and indeed rarely would. However, there must be some overlap of experience at some point and it is from these common experiences that people can extrapolate to gain an understanding of other people's experiences which they themselves have not had. In a trivial sense this is obvious. I can imagine the general notion of the experience of being in Cannes without actually having been there, even if I get the details wrong. I suggest this extends beyond the trivial. This involves a principle similar to that found with our understanding of natural behaviour. From some basis of common experience defined initially in ostensive terms, we can move on to definitions made in language, and understand a great deal which is a long way from any sort of experience in any commonly understood form. The differences between the experience of natural and of social events is that the latter is probably narrower and we are probably less confident about our understanding of how other people perceive things. Nevertheless, to suppose that our ignorance of other people's feelings is total is extreme.

The range of understanding
The argument about the common understanding of common experience (Chapter 3, the section entitled 'A closer analysis of "understanding"') came with the implication that the range of common understanding was sufficiently large for us to be able to say a wide range of interesting things about a wide range of people. However, the core argument of common understanding can be accepted but its range regarded as small, so small that it allows for only limited communication and hence for limited social science. A reasonably broad range of communication is a necessary condition

for social science, but not a sufficient condition. The issues dealt with in the next section, such as the alleged instability of ideas, would, if they were the case, destroy the possibility of social science even though the range of understanding was broad. I shall deal with three groups of people in this section: Winch himself; Collingwood and his philosophy of history; and the post-modernists, at least as represented by Ashley, Walker and others working in international relations (Ashley and Walker, 1990a; Walker, 1992).

Winch considers the problems of interpretation when the observer comes from a very different society as compared with the subject of study. In particular this means anthropology. As argued above (p. 105), Winch thinks we may often misinterpret the actions of another society, in particular with respect to such things as religion, and thus misunderstand the whole nature of some critical events. As understanding is the point of the exercise and, indeed, is the only legitimate thing we can do, the field of study collapses. Quite how wide the range of common understanding is for Winch is unclear, though by implication it is rather narrow. However, this is only one aspect of Winch's argument. If the range of common understanding is narrow, then social science is also narrow to the point of triviality. If common understanding is broad but the arguments in the rest of the chapter are valid, social science would still be trivial.

Winch (1958) considers the problems of understanding between very different contemporary societies. A similar argument is made by R. G. Collingwood (1946) with respect to societies in the past. Winch views Collingwood's ideas with broad though not unqualified approval. Collingwood is an idealist in the philosophical sense of idealist. He views history as being about ideas. He says of the historian that 'At bottom, he is concerned with thoughts alone; with their outward expression in events he is only concerned by the way, in so far as these reveal to him the thoughts of which he is in search' (Collingwood, 1946, p. 217). This is perhaps an extreme view and one which many historians would not accept as an account of their craft. However, it is a coherent view and one which it is easy to reconcile with Winch. This leads directly to Collingwood's methodology where he argues that 'the historian must re-enact the past in his own mind' (282) or in more detail, referring to a person who has written some documents, 'he has to discover what the person who wrote those words meant by them . . . To discover what this thought was, this historian must think it again for himself' (282–3). (Historians, we notice, appear all to be male.)

It is, of course, easy to accept that this is what some historians do

and that this is a legitimate activity. To recreate the past is an appropriate and important task. Eileen Power does this in *Medieval People*
(1946), where she makes us understand what life in medieval
England felt like. John Keegan in *The Face of Battle* (1976) does the
same, in helping us to empathize with men in battle at various times
in history (more plausibly than with historians, the people referred
to were overwhelmingly male). Collingwood argues that this is
all the historian should do. He makes the claim of exclusivity for
this approach to history. He would presumably dismiss as illegitimate an account of the industrial revolution in terms of capital
accumulation, agricultural change and the 'consequent' (a word I
assume he would disapprove of) move to urbanization in terms
which relate only tenuously to the understanding of people's
thoughts at the time. However, this sort of account of history is
central to the behavioural approach. 'Cliometrics' is the statistical
study of history, and people in the behavioural wing are inclined to
look approvingly at the work of scholars such as Singer and Small
(Singer, 1968, 1980, 1993) whose work has little or no relationship
to 're-enacting the past'. The arguments in favour of this are
directly parallel to those which relate to Winch. My argument is not
that the imaginative recreation of the past is either illegitimate or
uninteresting – quite the contrary. However, it is not the only way
of studying the past. Behavioural methodologies are appropriate
for the rather different sorts of questions which are asked and, as I
have argued and will further expound in this chapter, are legitimately
asked.

The understanding mode of analysis as applied to historical
events runs into some severe problems which are acknowledged by
the school of thought of which Collingwood is a prime representa-
tive. We can have difficulties in putting ourselves in the position of
someone in a past society either because we know too much of what
came afterwards or because the ethos of the society is so different
from our own that it is difficult to achieve the necessary level of
empathy. Thus, when we consider the position of people in
Europe, whether politicians or ordinary people, in the early years of
the century, it is hard not to reflect that they were about to be
engulfed in World War I. However, they were perhaps fortunately
ignorant of this and continued with their plans for life on the
assumption that it would continue much as it had done before.
Even those who were involved in international decision-making
were thinking of war more or less on the lines of the small Franco-
Prussian War or the more destructive but very localized Crimean
War. If people had paid more attention to the American Civil War,
they might have had some better idea of what a future European

war would have been like, but this is much easier to see now than it was at the time. We know what they did not, and it requires a formidable act of imagination for us to blank it out in our attempts to empathize with people of the time even though European society then was not so very different from that of today.

The problems are even more formidable when we try to put ourselves in the position of people in societies where belief in witches and warlocks was all but universal. That magic was all around one and might be invoked must have had a very constraining effect on people in a way which can be imagined but only with difficulty. We must also be aware that such beliefs were there. Because they were so much a part of the background structure of beliefs, it is easily overlooked. These issues are not insuperable and one can gain at least some limited understanding of what was going on. I do not think we are totally without any comprehension of life outside our own society. Collingwood regards these difficulties as very serious. Given his view of historical knowledge as being the understanding of people's thoughts, which, it appears, are not understandable, the discipline becomes a very limited enterprise.

Neither Collingwood nor Winch is concerned about the communicability of beliefs among people within the same society. Their neglect of the issue suggests they do not see it as a problem. Anthropologists and historians apparently can communicate among themselves and a broader public without worrying unduly about being misunderstood. Their concern is over the limitations, severe in their view, in how well one can understand other societies.

This is not the view of the post-modernists, who normally take a much more sceptical view of communication in general. However, post-modernism describes a genre of thought with wide-ranging differences within it. I shall just mention one or two aspects which are particularly relevant to the present argument. The post-modernists in international relations see themselves as being in the same tradition as Winch (and hence Wittgenstein), who are referred to respectfully. The international relations post-modernists are largely English-speaking and identify themselves as within this tradition, which is regarded perhaps warily but with respect even by its critics in the general analytical tradition of philosophy written in English. However, they also see themselves as being in a broader Western European tradition of philosophy (in practice largely French and German), where writers such as Lyotard are explicitly part of the tradition. This tradition is looked at much less respectfully by many mainstream British and North American philosophers. However, though in the Winchean tradition, in general the post-modernists are more radical than Winch.

Like Winch, the postmodernists concentrate on understanding and are averse to causal analyses of the sort practised in behavioural political science. However, they, or at least some of them, are concerned with the marginalized groups in society. (This is a theme of Ashley and Walker.) It leads to the view that there are no social events but multiplicities of events – perhaps as many as there are people who have experience of the event either directly, as observers or by report. The marginalized in this perception are as important as anyone else. Indeed, one could fairly easily move from this to arguing that marginality was not meaningful in that it implied a centre to be marginal to. If there is no centre, as would seem plausible for a post-modernist to suppose, then the concept of marginality becomes that which is not often mentioned. I discussed the implication of these views and its possible incorporation into even an empirical point of view in Chapter 3 (pp. 67–69) and return to it in Chapter 9 (pp. 178–180). This issue is one of emphasis rather than a big new development over Winch.

However, a more fundamental point is the more general scepticism of the post-modernists about communication in general. I shall consider this in terms of writing and the writer. The standard view of writing and communication is that it is an attempt by a writer to communicate ideas to a reader. In the case of a scientific paper, the criterion of successful communication is the closeness with which the reader and writer understand each other. Likewise for this book. The closer my readers understand what it going on in my mind, the better I shall have achieved one of my objects. For poetry this may be less true. A poem may stimulate some emotional or aesthetic response which may not be the author's but which the author would accept to be a legitimate use or interpretation of the poem. For the post-modernists, everything is like poetry only more so. They regard what is written as supreme and the author as of no importance. The 'death of the author', envisaged by Roland Barthes in 1968, is a theme of some post-modernism. Authors have no greater claim to view their interpretations of their texts as definitive than has anyone else. There is no notion that text is a means of communication between author and reader. Thus we have an intensely subjective view of the world in which social science in anything remotely like its behavioural form can have no place. Indeed, it is not clear that we can have anything which looks very much like knowledge. Everything is deconstructed and not much is left. Hence we come to know very little about other human beings, as writers successively reduce the range of the knowable. In this, they move a long way from Winch's position. The aim of Winch's position is to understand other people's 'texts' as they see them, thus giving a privileged status to an 'author'. It merely stresses that there may be difficulties of understanding.

We can represent this by means of three diagrams (Figure 6.1). The first depicts the position of the optimist who believes that the communality of human experience is what is dominant and that in general we do know what human beings at other times and places

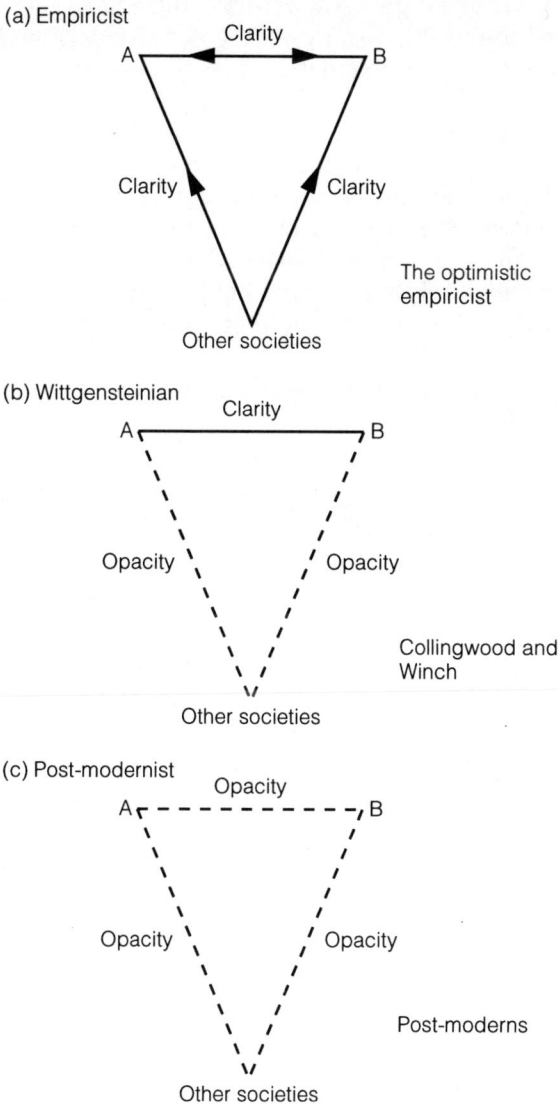

Figure 6.1 Perception and communication about other societies

are up to. This is the tradition of Hume, Freud and the modern social scientists. In a rather different way it is the tradition of the classical theorists such as Martin Wight who laid great stress on historical experience as a guide to general and current experience. He, however, would never be called an optimist. The second represents the position of Winch and Collingwood, who are doubtful about our understanding of other societies but think that communication within our own social group is possible and not over-problematic. Finally there comes the position of the post-modernists, for whom all communication is problematic.

Ideas and social behaviour
Winch is one of the main philosophical opponents of the idea that social behaviour can be analysed in the empiricist mode. His arguments must be addressed by anyone seeking to maintain an empiricist position in the social sciences.

I shall repeat what I think is a central passage which encapsulates his argument that historians and other social scientists use data to

> produce scientific generalizations and theories establishing connections between one kind of social situation and another . . . I have tried to show . . . how this involves minimizing the importance of ideas in human history, since ideas and theories are constantly developing and changing, and since each system of ideas, its component elements being interrelated internally, has to be understood in and for itself; the combined result of which is to make systems of ideas a very unsuitable subject for broad generalisations. I have also tried to show that social relations really exist only in and through the ideas which are current in society; or alternatively, that social relations fall into the same logical category as do relations between ideas. It follows that social relations must be an equally unsuitable subject for generalisations and theories of the scientific sort to be formulated about them. (1990, p. 133)

In this, Winch makes three claims which can be regarded independently. First, he argues that ideas are constantly changing; secondly, that a set of ideas has to be understood in and for itself and causal analysis of ideas is inappropriate (or possibly impossible, it is not clear which); finally, that social relations fall into the same logical category as do relations between ideas. In the next three sections I shall argue against all three of these positions at least in any extreme form, and thus suggest that we can have generalizations in social affairs and causal relations between them. However, I shall take them in what seems a more natural order given my argument.

In this section I shall argue, first, that the analysis of social behaviour involves the analysis of ideas only in a narrow sense. Secondly, I shall argue that in any case causal analysis of ideas is appropriate both in the immediately relevant narrow sense and in a broader sense also. Thirdly, in the next section I shall argue that whether or not rules vary, making generalizations difficult, is an empirical question, not one to be assumed a priori.

First, then, because social concepts are interpreted, does it mean that they are logically the same as ideas as Winch alleges? Consider the simple case of buying and selling a house. The argument runs that it is not just the physical act which is relevant here but also the awareness and interpretation on the part of the actors of participating in buying and selling. It also involves an interpretation and understanding of the concept of a house.[1] Thus, there is a mental event involved. If other social acts of the same nature are involved – such as the comparison of different articles by the consumer and the selection of the most appropriate – then the social actions consist of people behaving in ways which they interpret. There are mental events associated with all the actions and thus an interrelatedness of mental events. I do not dispute this account of an individual buying and selling, or indeed of it as an account of many forms of social behaviour (I do not wish to discuss issues of instinctive behaviour, such as jerking back from a hot surface, which are not important to the argument). I do dispute the significance which is given to it by Winch and many post-modernists in this rather basic sense that ideas are mental events.

However, I shall argue now the second point that it is quite proper to regard mental events (of the sort which interpret some sort of behaviour as 'buying') as being involved in chains of causes and consequences. I shall go on to elaborate on the notions of causation as applied to ideas more generally, though this is not strictly necessary for a minimalist version of my argument.

Consider again the buyer and the seller of the house. At some point the seller asks a price (a concept which involves a mental event, an understanding on the point of buyer and seller) which is refused by the putative buyer. The seller then offers a lower price, which is accepted by the buyer. The reduction in the price by the seller can perfectly properly be described as causing the change in behaviour of the buyer. Indeed, it would seem to be odd to talk of it any other way. Though there is no added principle involved, this is even clearer when referring to groups. The price of apples goes up, which causes people to buy fewer apples. This is not a use of the word 'cause' by analogy; it is a direct and proper use of the word and concept. Without accepting this we are in difficulty in talking of influencing other people. If I wish to influence someone, I do something or say something which causes them to react. All involve mental events. The interaction which involves mental events, which is the nature of social life, involves causal language and causal concepts.

This establishes my basic argument. However, it is useful briefly to elaborate on the way in which we use the concept of cause, which we do, whether rightly or wrongly, when we discuss ideas in the sense of systems of ideas such as ideologies, rather than the more narrowly defined mental events discussed above. We do this in two ways. First, we relate one set of ideas to another set, arguing totally in terms of ideas. Secondly, we relate ideas to circumstances, implying some causal link between the ideas and the circumstances in which they are found. As an instance of the first, we discuss history of music relating some ideas to others or some forms of music to others in at least a quasi-causal manner. Likewise, we discuss the history of science where we argue that certain sorts of ideas can come about only in a certain sequence but that when the point in the sequence is reached, then observations of the world will make the next step very likely. Einsteinian physics could not come until after Newtonian. It required more mathematics and more theoretical physics. To substantiate it, further developments in observation were necessary, themselves requiring developments in observational techniques. If we do not go as far as saying that the preceding ideas caused relativity theory, we are saying that they were necessary conditions for its emergence in some form or another, not necessarily in the mind of Einstein but possibly in someone else's mind or possibly among a group of people.[2] The development of a science is not just a collection of random intellectual developments. This is not to deny that the ideas have to be understood by anyone who is endeavouring to make a theory of them, but there is no reason why we should take seriously Winch's assertions that they cannot be theorized about. It is very unclear why not. More directly, we can discuss, in impeccable causal language, the development of mathematical concepts in the child, or the process of language learning. This is a causal analysis of how ideas change. Indeed, a theory of learning as a whole is a theory of the change of ideas which is expressed, quite properly, in standard causal form.

We also talk of ideas being related to social circumstances as when we relate revolutionary ideas to conditions where income is beginning to increase or of ideas of imperialism coming under conditions where imperialism is profitable. On my interpretation of conceptual communities there is no problem in doing this.

The stability of rules

The third, and perhaps the most serious, issue which Winch raises is the possible instability of the rules which people follow. Winch asserts they are unstable, an issue which now needs analysing.

First, let us consider the relationship between rules, generalizations and preferences. A behaviour rule for person X states that, under conditions p, q and r, X will perform action A. Thus, if the stock of bread in X's house has fallen below half a loaf (condition p), the weather is fine (condition q) and it is coming close to a mealtime (condition r) then X will go to the shop and buy bread. The action and preconditions may, or may not, be verbal acts but they must be discernible in some way to an outside observer. There are usually some understood background conditions such as that X has not just had a heart attack, but such understood background conditions are a part of any explanation. Clearly, this gives us a generalization in the sense that whenever we observe p, q and r we will see X doing A. If X is in some way a typical actor in the group, then, whenever we observe another member of the group faced with the preconditions, we observe them doing A also. We have a generalization. In many cases we can go further in the analysis of X doing A, namely that X does A in order to achieve a goal of G. In the case of the bread-buyer this is the relatively obvious goal of not being hungry. In general, goal G is one of a set of alternatives, H, J, K and so on, which might be chosen by X. These different goals are determined by X's preferences over the available alternatives. To move on from the individual, in the analysis of a business firm the alternatives might be different distributions of commodities. In the analysis of the behaviour of a state, it might be different military postures. Thus, if G was the decision-maker's goal, one can deduce what will be done in circumstances p, q, r, whereas if H were the goal, some other act B would have been carried out. Similarly, if p, q and r were replaced by p, q and r′, the decision maker would do C in order to achieve G. The whole process is part of a deductive system where some of the terms involve observation sentences. (I discuss the status of goals in Chapter 8.) Analysis of this sort is widely conducted in the social sciences, particularly in microeconomics, where it is standard, and widely too in international relations, particularly in the realist tradition. Thus Kaplan (1957) in his analysis of various systems uses not only this sort of procedure but also this sort of language. Not all rules need be stated in terms of the achievement of goals. For example, different acts might be performed if the actors are under stress. The goal in this case might be interpreted as the actor finding some way of coping with the stress and hence posed as a rule (Janis, 1982; Nicholson, 1995).

However, this might be awkward. It is always possible to interpret an act as goal-seeking but it may not always be the most convenient way of analysing the problem.

If the rules are stable, the generalizations about behaviour are stable; if not, then not. Stable, of course, has to be defined in relation to the types of problem one is discussing and the sort of time frame which is relevant. If we are dealing with short-period shifts in alliances over a year or two, we do not need to concern ourselves with long-term changes in attitudes to the use of violence in international relations and the legitimacy of annexation as a tool of policy. However, if we are comparing alliance behaviour in the late nineteenth and late twentieth centuries, clearly we have to. Similarly, in the analysis of international crisis behaviour, the fluctuations in the levels of power or in the underlying economy can be ignored over the period of a few days (though financial variables such as gold flows or exchange rates cannot), but they have to be regarded as variables in a longer-period analysis of power changes. (for example, Organski and Kugler, 1981).

There are three potential sources of instability for rules. By instability, I mean changes in the rules of such frequency that we cannot predict behaviour in the sorts of contexts we would wish to.

First, people might change the rules they adopt in apparently autonomous and uncaused ways. Either there is no rule which governs the change in rules or it is not possible to find out what that rule is, perhaps even in principle. This is not the same as saying that choice is 'free' in the sense of uncaused. One can follow a rule, such as always leaving the house at five past eight in the morning, and still have free will. It is possible to vary the rule even though one may not do so; in fact, one's behaviour might be very predictable. The possibility of change is what makes it a free act, not the frequency of breaking the rule. The second source of instability is if the rule is complex in a complex system such that the initial conditions are hardly ever the same. The rule is stable in itself but the conditions are unrepeatable so it is not helpful as a predictive or even explanatory device. The relevant generalizations barely exist. Centrally there is the question of structural stability. If the initial conditions are repeated but only approximately, then the question is whether the predictions which follow from this follow approximately or whether they result in very different consequences. If the latter, then this is very damaging; if the former, the complexity factor is not such a problem. Unfortunately, in the state of knowledge as it is at the moment, it is hard to be sure. The third possibility is that human beings, following rules, learn about the consequences of doing so. In learning, they modify the rules; that is, they evolve new rules.

This is a version of the first difficulty except that there is the prospect of deducing the theory of rule change, which was left open in the first case.

The question, as I have posed it, is an empirical question. Indeed, as Winch poses it, it is also an empirical question, though he does not stress this. The issues may well be of different importance in different sorts of systems. One cannot determine whether rules are stable or not by abstract analysis alone. It is only by the observation and analysis of systems that one can observe whether rules are stable or unstable. I shall take two examples which incline to opposite conclusions. First, the ability to explain the behaviour of the British economy as a whole has been rather disappointing in the past two decades. In the heyday of the Keynesian revolution, namely, the first quarter of a century after World War II, the capitalist economies seemed to follow the Keynesian rules quite well and there was widespread (though never universal) belief that we had a fairly accurate theory of the aggregative behaviour of market systems. However, this faded. The monetarist replacement fared well as an explanatory system but only briefly. Currently there are anomalies in any theory which attempts to explain the macro-economic system such that none has a commanding position. This is consistent with any of the three options concerning the stability or otherwise of rules. The system may be so complex that the application of the rules is not likely to be helpful; alternatively, learning may have gone on in a way we have not yet fully understood, finally, people may have just changed their behaviour in ways which we cannot explain. None of these reasons may apply. It may be that economists have not found out enough about the workings of the system and a good explanatory theory will in due course emerge. It is always subject to the problem of learning (Ormerod, 1994).

The second example is in the case of small-group behaviour. The rules followed by people in small groups, and hence their behaviour, are more readily amenable to analysis by means of fairly stable rules (and hence generalizations). Group learning takes place within the more confined context of the group, where we have observed many cases of group learning before. Thus we can have knowledge of the rules by which the rules change and can formulate coherent theories of small-group behaviour. The groupthink phenomenon in small groups has been effectively applied to the analysis of decision-making in international crises. This is a theory of how perceptions change under stress. Further, the structural characteristics of groups which are likely to manifest groupthink are also well known. Because of the widespread knowledge of groupthink it is probable that learning has gone beyond the confines of particular groups and that people forming decision-making groups explicitly try to construct them such that groupthink is less likely. However, this can be done only because certain rules are known to apply under certain conditions and are relatively stable. This is the opposite of Winch's contention.

Thus, whether rules are stable or not is an empirical issue. Perhaps they are stable in some circumstances and not in others. Which is which can be established only by empirical investigation, though it is probable that a theory could be formulated, and no doubt some day will be, which will identify social systems that are likely to have stable rules and those that do not. Casual empiricism would suggest that reasonable stability is the norm but there is considerable variation between different sorts of social system.

One extreme view of the stability of rules is that of Stigler and Becker (1977). They hold that human preferences are constant throughout the ages and people choose differently simply because there are different choices available. They also argue that there is an underlying constancy of preference even when there are superficial changes. Thus people choose to wear blue one year and red the next not because of a change in the preference for colour but because in both cases they wanted to be fashionable. The apparent rule shift in fact follows from the constancy of more basic rules. The difficulty with the Stigler–Becker position is that it is tauto-logical. One can always find some higher-level rule which will explain changes in a lower-level rule but this is not very helpful. The practical question is whether rules vary at the level where explanations are being carried out. It would seem that sometimes they do and sometimes they do not.

What if generalizations in social science are impossible?
Suppose Winch is right, or suppose any of the other objections to generalizations in social science and international relations hold up. They are all sufficient conditions, so only one needs to be valid for my whole case to collapse. Crucially, it would mean that prediction about social events would be impossible in both what I shall call the strong sense and the weak sense. By prediction in the strong sense I mean an unqualified statement about the future state of affairs. By prediction in the weak sense I mean a conditional prediction of the form 'If A then B.' If even weak prediction is impossible, then it is impossible to assert 'If I do A, then B.' But this is the core of policy-making. There are doubts about the first sort of prediction, particularly in the social sciences but also in the natural sciences, as we discussed in Chapter 2. However, the inability to carry out conditional predictions would be very inhibiting and fly in the face

of what we think we can do (which is not the same as saying we can in fact do it).

Let us consider the question of the relationship between choice and prediction more closely. Choice, of course, is central to policy-making, for policy-making means choosing to adopt one course of action rather than another. Initially, let us pose the problem in terms of an individual in personal life. Suppose we have a choice between two courses of action, A and B. If they are not to be identical, meaning that the choice is vacuous, A and B will have different consequences. Suppose someone is offered a job in London and another in New York. They make predictions about what life will be like in each of the two places. To make a rational choice, they have to know what the consequences of choosing each of the alternatives will be, at least in a probabilistic sense. If we have no idea what the consequences of a choice will be, we have no basis for making a choice at all, and might as well choose by means of a random device such as tossing a coin. Certainly we do not believe that the future is so opaque and believe that over at least a certain number of things we have some control. If we are not deluded, this means there is some predictability, and also some capacity for generalization.

If the choices involved merely concerned issues in the physical environment such as whether to take a raincoat in case of rain, few problems are raised. However, even in our personal life, our choice normally involves our behaviour among other people, so we are making conditional predictions about how people will respond to our behaviour. To do this we have to make conditional predictions about other people's behaviour. If I wonder whether to put up for the town council, I shall reflect not only on the amount of work involved and the pleasures of power, but also on how my family will respond, how my employer will respond, on the different way people will regard me and so on. In Winch's terms, this means knowing the rules which other people will adopt and hence predicting their behaviour in response to my own. But, as argued elsewhere, the knowledge of a rule itself implies some sort of generalization. That is, the rule can be reinterpreted in terms of behaviour to say what an individual will do under certain sorts of situations. Clearly this can be extended to the actions of organizations. A multinational corporation considering investment in a developing country considers such issues as the reaction of the host government, the possible opposition of some groups within the country, the attitude of other governments, the attitude of potential competitors, of the IMF and so on. The corporation considers the rules which others are likely to follow and is thereby making a prediction about its action.

This discussion has so far assumed that the observer was an actor in the system, and indeed, in any policy-oriented social science this is what is normally assumed. However, now let us assume we are observing the system from the outside. We may not be able to predict the behaviour of the social system in any unambiguous way. However, suppose the system is one in which we could have taken part, either in reality or imagination. In that case, we will be able to say that if a particular actor chooses A, the other actors will choose in response to that in predictable ways; that is, the ways in which we would have assumed had we been in the specific actor's position and chosen A. We assume nothing in addition to this. Thus if we can predict enough to choose rationally, then we can predict enough (in principle at least) to make some modest predictions about the possible behaviour of a social system we are observing. Prediction, as we have argued, is a particularly severe criterion for a satisfactory explanation. While chaos theory is not relevant to the theories which we deal with here, the practical difficulty of knowing all the initial conditions is extremely relevant. The 'zebra principle' comes into its own. Explanation can take place under rather weaker conditions, and so a broader set of situations where explanations though not predictions are possible is likely, though they do depend on generalization. In fact, most of the explanations we indulge in in international relations are not symmetrical with prediction. Successful prediction is a rarity.

The relationship of rational choice and hence rational policy to conditional prediction and hence some form of generalization has been misunderstood by many classical theorists. In the post-1945 years there has been a close relationship between strategic studies and the realist school of international relations which has produced warnings about the dire consequences of failing to preserve the balance of power, of failing to have enough nuclear weapons, or of committing the great sin of the post-1938 (or possibly 1939) twentieth century, appeasement. However, for these to have any meaning at all they must be based on generalization. This is fully understood by the many strategists who take behavioural work seriously and to the chagrin of behavioural critics of the strategists such as Rapoport (1966). However, realists of the classical school who join in just as vigorously with the policy recommendations elsewhere condemn generalization, at least as something which could be systematically studied (Bull, 1969; Northedge, 1976). Unfortunately, they are being inconsistent in doing so. These predictions, conditional though they are, must be based on generalizations presumed to be true, and preferably tested.

Hierarchic understanding

In the Winchean picture it is the perception of the actors which is central and perhaps exclusive in any interpretation of a social situation. However, there is a severe weakness of the position. There are certain sorts of situation where we want to stand externally to the ideas and explain them in a broader context which the actors themselves may not accept or possibly understand.

Let us consider the concept of religious fundamentalism, which is currently an important issue for scholars of international relations. In the case of Christian fundamentalism one can argue that, to understand it, one has to understand the belief structure of those who believe in it. Thus, one needs to know not only the general principles of Christianity but why the believers have adopted this particular form of Christian belief and why they think it appropriate as opposed to non-fundamentalist Christian beliefs (which again must be understood by the observer, at least in broad terms). Merely to understand the belief structure is probably also inadequate. The observer must have some empathy with people who believe very passionately in a religious creed. It is not just an account of the formal belief structure of the creed but an awareness of what it feels like to believe it. It is also necessary to understand what it feels like to belong to a group of people who together follow this sort of creed. It is the sense of a group working together, often against the hostile infidel or heretic, which is a central aspect of many religions. Thus it is the emotional as well as the strictly cognitive aspects of the belief which must also be understood. So far, so good. However, one wants to go further. Islamic fundamentalism has some characteristics in common with Christian fundamentalism. To understand it, one needs to go through a parallel exercise to that of understanding Christian fundamentalism. This is similarly true if the centre of interest is Jewish fundamentalism or Hindu fundamentalism. However, such a study might be based on at least a tentative hypothesis that the belief structure and its concomitant emotional structure are not the only issue under consideration. For many issues in international relations we can reasonably argue that 'fundamentalism' is the appropriate category for study rather than any particular variety of it. Many psychologists would agree. Our study of it may come up with the result that what is important is a dogmatic belief which can be phrased such that it is immune to refutation and which is associated with enthusiastic meetings of like-minded people. The actual cognitive structure of the belief may not be an issue of importance. This approach would of course then lead us to speculate that the more extreme versions of nationalism or political positions might serve the same role and

be properly classified under the same heading as religious fundamentalism. Thus, while we have to have a general notion of what
the belief structure is to work our way round to this position, it may
turn out that its content is relatively unimportant. What is important is that it is the *form* of belief rather than the belief itself which
is crucial. We need to know this form rather than the details, in the
same sort of way that one needs to know what it means to speak and
read a language without actually speaking it – that is, I understand
the concept of speaking Bengali even though I do not myself speak
it. Similarly, I can understand the concept of Hindu fundamentalism without knowing very much about the doctrinal details.

Once we begin to use fundamentalism as a category other issues
become relevant. There appear to be patterns of development of
such beliefs where initially believers are very dedicated and self-
sacrificing. This initial period is often followed by periods where
the opportunists jump on to the bandwagon and mouth the
rhetoric with enthusiasm but their basic beliefs may be more pragmatic. Religious fundamentalism shares this with all revolutionary
movements. Other features which appear to be common are the
rise of charismatic leaders, even in cases where the doctrines are
ostensibly non-hierarchic, and the intolerance of heresy, often leading to schisms and internal warring of great ferocity. These aspects
are left unanalysed in any causal way if we let the content instead of
the form of the ideas to become too dominant in our analysis.

While form is important, there is clearly a basic difference
between the case of language and fundamentalism. The Bengali
speaker and I are in total agreement as to what he or she is doing
when speaking Bengali and we would agree about our mutual level
of ignorance in the face of an Arabic speaker. All three of us would
know what we were doing and claim no privileged understanding of
the process. However, in the case of fundamentalist religion, this
would not be so. Fundamentalists claim to have the one true religion in a way no one claims to have the one true language. Many
Christian fundamentalists would argue that to compare their beliefs
with Islamic fundamentalist beliefs is to miss the point. In their
view, their belief is correct and the other false in a mirror image of
the picture reciprocated by the Islamic fundamentalists. To categorize the two phenomena under the same heading on the basis of
what would be regarded as a few superficial and unimportant similarities would appear to be misguided.

However, even this is not a necessary position. I have argued
above that ideas, being characteristics of people and in some sense
factual, can be discussed in causal ways. The explanation of why
someone holds a particular belief is logically separate from the

truth or otherwise of the belief. Thus, a person holding a particular belief can give an account in social or psychological terms of how they came to be acquainted with the belief and hold it, which is separate from a justification of the belief. A Christian fundamentalist could quite properly argue that living in a Christian society and being brought up in a Christian home was pertinent to their holding the belief, as distinct from the heathen who had no such good fortune. These are explanations of how the holder of the belief holds it but they do not invalidate or prove the belief as such. They are separate categories. Clearly the explanation of a belief can be self-referring. As I have described, one can explain one's own beliefs in terms of causal factors and not just in terms of other beliefs. A Christian fundamentalist might still accept a causal explanation of their belief and admit to similarities between their beliefs and other fundamentalist beliefs without necessarily abandoning the view that the Christian fundamentalist belief was true. Admittedly it is unlikely to be a common view but it involves no logical inconsistencies. An evangelical fundamentalist (and, in most religions other than the Jewish, evangelism is a characteristic of the fundamentalist belief structure) needs a causal theory of belief generation, at both the psychological and social level, if resources are to be most effectively directed towards maximizing conversion. Implicitly, and perhaps sometimes explicitly, such theories appear to be held. The holder of the beliefs would have one extra dimension which the outside observer would not have. The believer would argue that God had revealed himself or some similar sort of argument. The outsider would accept this as part of the belief in the sense of agreeing that the believer *believed* that God had revealed himself. They would not dispute the belief but they would either dispute the fact which was believed or at least remain agnostic about it.

The causes of attitudes are more straightforwardly understood in a general framework of perceptions rather than one in which belief is central. An explanation for someone liking Mozart can be given in terms of being exposed to his music from childhood, of its being associated with emotionally important circumstances, and so on, without its in any way altering or demeaning the passion of that person's appreciation of the music. Further, while one cannot say that Mozart's music is objectively beautiful, it is an objective fact about a particular person that they find it beautiful. That is, a belief is a fact about an individual even if that belief is not itself about anything factual. It is of course also true even if it is about something factual and even if it is a false belief. Thus it can be true (though a disturbing truth for my near and dear) that I believe that there is a pink elephant sitting outside the front door, though the belief itself is false. Again we come back to the notion that belief structures can play a role in a causal argument as they are facts about the people who hold those beliefs.

The argument is not just about belief structure, however, but about the whole nature of the situation in which fundamentalist beliefs are held. Thus, the desire to belong to an enthusiastic group which has this overriding belief in common and works towards a common goal is a feature. This again could be accepted by the sophisticated fundamentalists. They still would argue that the prime mover in all this was God, whereas the external observer would put the causal arrows the other way round and argue that a belief in God, or more particularly a whole structure of beliefs about God, followed from the other social and psychological factors. However, though disagreeing, the sophisticated fundamentalist could understand the outsiders' theories, which is the crucial factor here. Furthermore, they could even accept a lot of the outsiders' theories even if both sides would balk at the last and, for the fundamentalist, the crucial stage. I am not suggesting that this is a common view among fundamentalists. I am arguing that it is a logically possible view and probably held by some though I am unable to cite instances.

This may seem to have reintroduced a symmetry between observers and observed, which is which depending on one's viewpoint. If one accepts, with Feyerabend (1975), that observation in the scientific mode as the source of truth has the same authority as but no more authority than the belief in a particular text as the source of truth, then this is the case. There is no rule that one rather than the other takes precedence in the case of disagreement. However, I find such a position difficult to adopt. Having come down on the scientific side, I assert its privileged position by virtue of the openness of the position. Thus, as argued above, self-criticism about belief is built-in as a central core of scientific methodology.

The point about this argument is that we are seriously impoverished in our understanding of social events if we are too constrained by the viewpoints of the actors. There are many situations where we need to use the concept of religious fundamentalism in order to analyse things, where we regard the forms of fundamentalism as on a par, irrespective of the particular belief structure of any one form. That is, we regard actual belief structure as secondary to the *form* of belief structure. Important questions can then be tackled, if necessary over the indignant protests of those who hold those beliefs.

Religious fundamentalism is one important category of this sort which is not only important as a problem in international relations but also particularly appropriate for the discussion of the general issue. However, there are many cases where it arises. In the analysis of perceptions of narrow sets of things, we find the same sort of problem. In Janis's theory of groupthink, he argues that at certain times of crisis there is a strong pressure among members of the group to agree with each other and to ignore evidence which contradicts the group consensus. There is a tendency to believe and continue to believe in views which the group as a whole find attractive even if this ceases to be a rational belief in the light of emerging new evidence. Deviants from the consensus become excluded from the group or may find themselves giving in to the group pressures and becoming themselves part of the consensus. Janis provides strong evidence for the existence of this phenomenon in many circumstances and also provides the outline of a theory of groups' structures which suggests when groups are liable to such processes and when not. Though the structure of thought in which these perceptions and misperceptions are found is less profound than religious structures the same principle applies. The outsider is looking at the ideas of the subjects and claiming greater knowledge of what is going on, though in the case of groupthink the subjects might later accept that the outside observer had been correct. The analysis implies a hierarchy and the observer is in a privileged position *vis-à-vis* the observed, a view which is anathema to the post-modernists. However, this does not mean that the observed cannot become a self-observer; indeed, this is what is often expected to happen, though after the initial acts of perception have been done.

Notes

1 Though the concept of a 'house' may not be shared. One person may think of it as a barn and the other a house. There may be further complications such as one thinking of it as a 'home' for themselves, the other as an investment. A common understanding does not need to be total, though it is likely in most cases for people to understand the other's concepts as in buying for investment and buying for living.

2 In general with scientific developments one assumes that if Newton, Einstein or whoever had not lived then a 'substitute Newton' or a 'substitute Einstein' would have carried out the same analysis. The state of science as it is today would be essentially the same irrespective of the accident of who had or had not lived (which is not to denigrate the genius of the people who were capable of such vast acts of creativity). In corroboration of this view, and of the view that there is a rough sequence in the way in which different things can be discovered, one can cite the

near-simultaneous discovery of various scientific principles. Likewise in the relevant mathematics. Leibnitz and Newton both discovered (or invented?) differential and integral calculus around the same time (and were involved in an acrimonious dispute about who was the first). However, C. P. Snow (1967) disputes that this was the case with Einstein and relativity theory, and argues that Einstein really was special, which I find surprising.

7
Quantification in international relations

The concept of measurement

The issue of quantification raises more passions among scholars of international relations than its apparently clinical image would suggest. It is the object of intemperate attack and equally passionate defence. Hedley Bull is dismissive while David Singer, on the other hand, regards quantification as central to the social scientific enterprise, as indeed do many of both its critics and its supporters (Bull, 1969; Singer, 1969). As described in Chapter 1, there has been a great deal of work in the quantitative tradition done since the 1950s (and a significant amount before that) which is essentially ignored in the classical tradition. The questions asked by the quantifiers, and the answers they believe they provide, are of obvious importance. Thus there is a lot of evidence to suggest that democracies hardly ever (on some versions, never) fight each other (Russett, 1993; Rummell, 1983, 1985). Analyses of the factors which lead to war in terms of arms races (Wallace, 1979, 1982; Diehl, 1983,1985) or the relationship of the initiation of war to the expected utility of a victory (Bueno de Mesquita, 1981) are all issues of the most profound significance. It may be that the answers are not what they seem and are meaningless in some sense, but one can hardly accuse the quantifiers of triviality in their choice of problems.

This does not mean that one should accept the results of statistical investigations uncritically or necessarily at their face value. Clearly, if one accepts a Winchean account of social behaviour, statistical tests are irrelevant, as Winch denies the possibility of generalization on which they are based. The supposed acts of measurement are merely exercises in manipulation which have no proper interpretation in the real world. For the Winchean, there is no point in pursuing the matter further. The arguments I shall make in this chapter assume that the Winchean position is not accepted. However, even for those who reject Winch, there are non-trivial doubts about the reliability of quantification of some or all of the factors which are relevant for the study of international relations. It would be as foolish to dismiss these doubts out of hand as it is to dismiss the possibilities of successful quantification out of hand. I shall analyse these doubts in this chapter.

It is to be hoped that at least some measures are appropriate in that it enables us to make much stronger statements about the international system than would otherwise be the case. The view that measurement is not possible may be forced on us by analysis (though I think it is not). The view that it is to be deplored, presumably on aesthetic grounds, seems very strange. If quantification turns out to be impossible or very restricted, then, as with the rest of the social scientific approach to international relations, this will be reason for regret, not pleasure.

Quantification can involve one or more of three different activities. All involve either *measuring* or *counting*. We shall discuss some issues involved in the distinction in the next section. An example of counting is the counting of the number of bricks in a pile. This gives a whole number as the answer. An example of measuring is the measuring of the length of a brick, which need not give a whole number. In any case, if it gave a whole number with one measure, such as inches, it would only rarely do so with another, such as centimetres.

To count we first classify things. We put them into different categories or classes where two members of the same class have some relevant characteristic in common. It is more interesting if we classify things according to two criteria and relate them. Thus we can ask if Catholic countries are more likely to go to war than Protestant countries, the classifications being Catholic/Protestant and warlike/non-warlike. (There is no discernible difference. Indeed, according to Richardson (1960b), all religions seem, statistically, to show an equal proclivity for war – apart from some rather ambiguous results as far as the peacefulness of the Buddhists is concerned.) Secondly, we can characterize things by some quantifiable characteristic. We can measure a state's arms level, its power, or its gross national product (GNP). Some of these characteristics involve a measurement such as armaments but others (though very few) involve counting, such as population. We may then compare two countries and say, on the bases of these measures, that one country is more powerful than another, or richer than another, or, by integrating some of the measures into a composite measure, that one country has a higher standard of life per head than another. Finally, we can search for relationships such as the form (if any) of the relationship between GNP and military power or the relationship between the level of one country's level of arms and another country's. This enables us to say such things as if one country increases its arms by 10 per cent, the other will by 5 per cent. More abstractly, we get a 'functional relationship' between the two variables which were measured.

Clearly a study may involve more than one of these activities. Suppose we may investigate the relationship between states, their level of armaments and the likelihood of war. We measure the level of armaments and classify states into highly armed states and those with low levels of arms. This has involved measurement. We then relate states to the incidence of war, where we regard war/not-war as a dichotomous variable. Then we count them. We then check whether a result is significant or not, in that we ask whether any pattern generated could plausibly have come about by chance (the example is a rather simplified version of some work by Bremer (1980), who shows a positive relationship between military capacity and war).

Such ways of looking at international relations stem clearly from within the behavioural tradition. Such questions were not really asked before. However, I shall give two illustrations of how one needs some form of quantification, at least, in order to make certain sorts of statement in international relations which would normally be regarded as relating to questions that, historically, have been regarded as central to the discipline. I take them deliberately from classical realist theory. Anti-quantifiers, such as Bull, imply that classical theory can be developed without measurement. These instances show not. Many propositions asserted by classical analysts effectively imply quantification.

Suppose we assert (i) 'Country A is more powerful than country B'. This implies some degree of measurement, though it could be just an ordinal measure; that is, a measure which ranks things in order of magnitude but does not enable us to say anything about how much bigger one thing is than another. We have made the statement on the basis of some evidence which permits it and justifies it taken on its own. This involves rather weak presuppositions. Suppose we also assert (ii) 'A is more powerful than B which is more powerful than C'. We still need not go beyond an ordinal measure as we have simply joined two statements together which are of the same form. We can, though, from the two statements taken together say that 'A is more powerful than C'.[1] However, if we assert along with (ii) another statement (iii) 'B and C together are more powerful than A' we are implying some sort of additivity which is a stronger mathematical operation than that permitted by ordinal measures alone. It may not be a process of simple addition, but some process of addition, broadly conceived, is required. (Indeed, it could be a multiplicative relationship if the measure of B and C were greater than unity.) This involves a stronger or cardinal measure (I elaborate on these measures later). To legitimately make a statement implying a cardinal measure, we need more information than we did in order to make the ordinal measure.

Is there a way round the problem? Are we really involved in making statements which are meaningful only if we accept the possibility of a cardinal measure? It could be a metaphor (though, if so, it would be a rather misleading one). If it is meant to be a direct statement about the world then there are two possibilities. If the information which permitted (ii) is the same as that which permitted (iii) also then we have deduced (iii) from the same information set as (ii). This deduction must have involved some process of addition. However, it has to involve the taking together of the two quantities to produce another quantity (in this case a larger one) according to some rule. This is the position claimed above. However, we might have required more information in order to make the statement (iii) beyond that required to assert (ii). If so, no deduction need have taken place and we could still be in the realm of ordinal measures. However, this last is a rather weak theory. Statements concerning the balance of power normally require something more.

To elaborate a little. Suppose the set of observations (a, b, c) justify our assertion that (ii) is the case. We shall call it a *minimum observational base* if the removal of any of a, b, or c means we cannot justify the assertion. That is, none of the evidence is redundant. We do not presume that a minimum observational base is necessarily unique. If that same observational base enables us also to assert (iii); then the process involved must involve addition. If it requires (a, b, c, y) in order to make it, then it is a new observation and does not imply additivity.

In the second illustration we show the need for counting. Suppose we assert the following proposition: 'When there is a balance of power, there is less likelihood of war than if there is not.' What is relevant evidence for deciding this? A single spectacular instance on either side might be psychologically impressive but it is logically unimpressive if we are trying to define rational criteria for belief. First we have to define what we mean by the balance of power. Here classical analysts have been very careful to distinguish different usages of the term, though actually to identify a case might still be difficult (Wight, 1966; Bull, 1977). Having picked an appropriate criterion, we should then look for instances of the balance of power and equivalent cases where there was no balance of power. Possibly we might look for these at times of crisis when the system is in any case war-prone. When the instances have been classified in this way we then *count* – I stress the word 'count' – the frequency of outbreaks of war when there is or when there is not a balance of power. Clearly, this is a possible way of going about things. I would argue more strongly that it is a necessary way of going about things if the statement relating the balance of power to the incidence of war (or to anything else involving behaviour in the international system) is to be given any meaning. A direct test of the proposition can be avoided only if the proposition is deduced from an earlier proposition or set of propositions which have been tested. However, the testing of these prior propositions must likewise have been done by counting so counting must have come into the picture at some point.

I am making two claims. First, the proposition about the balance of power and war has meaning only if we can specify observations in the world which would confirm it or refute it. In this case the observations involve counting. These observations may be observations in principle only and not ones which could in practice be carried out. The lack of practicability would not affect the meaning. The further claim concerns whether the proposition is true or not, within some reasonable limits of doubt. That is, questions to which we do not know the answer can be perfectly meaningful. However, if we cannot carry out or have not carried out the sorts of tests suggested above, then we cannot make strong truth claims. Pointing to some historical instances might give some intimations but they are just intimations in comparison to the sort of test specified above.

I stress again that this is a methodological point and that many writers on the balance of power are perfectly aware of this sort of issue. My complaint is against the classical theorists, as defined by Hedley Bull, who deny this is relevant evidence or who make truth claims while denying the procedures necessary to make them.

Quantification is permitted, in classical analyses, given that generalizations are made, which they are. It is required for systematic testing. We have argued the general case in Chapter 6. The basic point is that, if we can generalize, we can count. The serious conceptual point is whether we can generalize or not. On this, the classicists and the behaviouralists are on the same side, however distasteful this might seem to some.

The subject matter of international relations is not uniquely inappropriate for quantitative analysis. It is no more nor less so than other social sciences. Economics is often regarded as lending itself more naturally to quantification, as its subject matter is more often presented in measurable form. However, most of the measures in economics, except for a few narrowly defined concepts involving population, are based on arbitrary assumptions. Merely to note a few makes the point: quantity of money, gross national product, or even the level of profit of a firm (about which economists and accountants are particularly prone to quarrel). Other questions requesting quantitative answers which initially seem unproblematic are clearly not so if one pauses to analyse them. 'What is the population of London?' – it depends what is meant by London. 'How many languages are spoken in the world today?' – it depends on how a language is defined. Answers vary from 4,000 to 10,000 and doubtless, by altering the definition of language, we could extend the range further (Crystal, 1990). The figures would alter not because of a set of new discoveries about hitherto unknown languages but as a consequence of the altering of the definitions. 'How long is the coastline of Britain?' – it depends on a whole set of arbitrary conventions such as where a shoreline, such as that of the Thames estuary, is regarded as the bank of a river or the coast of the sea.

These examples show the enormous ambiguity of measurement when describing social factors. The argument may lead one to rejecting measurement altogether in the analysis of social affairs. This would be extreme, though tenuously consistent. To abandon as meaningless a statement such as 'London is bigger than Oslo' would require an almost perverse unwillingness to draw arbitrary boundaries. However, if such a statement is regarded as meaningful, procedures for establishing it must be specified, however arbitrary these procedures are. They are neither more nor less so than procedures in international relations. The claim that international relations is particularly unsuited to measurement is either wrong or at least needs a great deal more justification.

Most of the analysis in this chapter is conceptual. However, it is important to distinguish between conceptual errors and the problems of acquiring data in the first place. Thus, there is no conceptual problem involved in defining the population as it was in 1066 in what is now the British Isles. We know without difficulty what is meant. However, there is a practical problem in that there are no reliable records and little enough data from which to infer a reasonably accurate figure. We might make guesses from our knowledge of how many people might have lived in villages, towns and so on but the figure is bound to be very broad-brush. This becomes more problematic if one is trying to estimate something like income, whether individual or national income, for a period well in the past. In this case there is both the conceptual problem of defining income in a society which is very different from our own and the difficulty of finding the raw material for constructing an index even when the conceptual or definitional problem has been dealt with. The data we want are likely to be seriously deficient. This is not just an issue with historical statistics. The effort to get an adequate statistical picture of the former Soviet Union was generally agreed to be a nightmare, even for such basic issues as production of steel. Over more complex issues such as armaments, where there was an obvious motive for deception, there was even more doubt. The reliability of data outside a few countries with sophisticated statistical services is often low. Some sorts of historical data are very dubious. Platt (1989) argues that many economic historians have been willing to place excessive faith on data based on few and often unreliable observations. There is no particular value in doing elaborate statistical analyses on data which are wrong or arbitrary; indeed, there is harm in that people might take them seriously.

This does not mean that only perfect data will do, though it does mean that the awareness of major error in the data has to be taken seriously. The central issue is that in any statistical analysis it must be demonstrated how sensitive the analysis is to error, or alternative definitions, and whether the error within plausible ranges will lead to significantly different results. This is of course standard practice and is no novelty for statisticians, whose data often consist of sample data which inherently involve error, though of a precisely defined kind.

Different forms of quantification

Quantification can mean a lot of different things. In this section I shall simply describe some of the distinctions which are particularly relevant for the social sciences in general and international relations in particular. The elaborations and the problems I shall leave for a later section.

The simplest and most basic forms of quantification are *ordinal measures*. These are measures which permit statements such as that X is greater than Y, less than Y or the same size as Y but go no further than that. They 'order' things in sequences, saying that one is first, another second, another third and so on. Thus, one could not say that X was twice as big as Y. Consider the concept of power. We might be prepared to say that A was more powerful than B but not be willing to say that there were appropriate features of the situation which would enable us to assert that A was 20 per cent more powerful than B.

The stronger statement, that A is 20 per cent more powerful than B, involves what are known as *cardinal measures*. Numbers are put to the measures which we can add, multiply, divide and so on. With such a measure we could say that if A is 50 per cent more powerful than B and B is twice as powerful as C then A is three times as powerful as C. Further, we could say that A is as powerful as B and C put together. All this would be impossible with a purely ordinal measure. This is the strongest form of cardinality. A weaker form of cardinality is exemplified by the expected utility analysis. Clearly, a cardinal measure implies an ordinal one, though not conversely. Cardinal measures are stronger than ordinal both in that more powerful deductions can be made with them and in that they require a larger information base in order to be derived. In some cases this may be conceptually as well as practically impossible.

Forms of quantification can be divided into two general categories: those which involve the operation of counting and those which involve the operation of measuring. Counting assumes the existence of units which are in some sense the same for the purposes under review. I shall assume the operation of counting to be understood. Counting can be done exactly (in principle). Thus the number of people in a room can be determined exactly as, say, 10. It is not approximately 10. Similarly, I know that I have exactly 32 great-great-great-grandparents. However, a definitional question arises here. It is possible that one great-great-great-grandparent doubled up and fulfilled the role on either side (I have no idea in my own case, though this must happen frequently in communities which are stable over time). Thus, if we are referring to the specific individuals concerned, all I can say is that *at most* I have 32 great-great-great-grandparents, though if I refer to the role and not the individual who occupies it the original statement holds. Even in such a straightforward matter as this, definitional issues appear and we have to be very careful about the question we wish to answer. However, I can be sure that, on either definition, I have exactly the same number of great-great-great-grandparents as my siblings.

Measurement is done along a continuum. Against a crude measure, a piece of wood may be a metre long. A more refined measure may make it 1.02 metres and a more refined measure yet may make it 1.01972 metres and so on. There are limits beyond which one cannot determine the length of a piece of wood. It is a comparative measure in that there is a measuring instrument. Weighing is similarly a measure. Counting and measurement clearly involve rather different processes. In international relations we use both. We count population, for example, and we measure gold stocks (in the form of weighing). These are two relatively straightforward examples. Unfortunately for both forms of quantification there are many practical problems concealed in the innocuous phrase above: 'in some sense the same'.

While in the natural world many measures are comparatively simple and straightforward, in international relations most things are complex and involve mixtures of things. Thus we want to measure such things as the levels of armaments of a country (in a way which makes them comparable with the level of arms of others) or the gross national product of a country, in total or perhaps per head. These are complexes of different attributes and not just the aggregate of a single attribute such as the quantity of coal produced (though even this is complex if we take into account the different qualities). They are measured by *index numbers*. In essence we are adding potatoes and meat to get a quantity of food in some way which can be justified. It is, in fact, the celebrated 'index number problem' to which earlier economists devoted so much attention.

Let us consider the problem in a particular fairly narrow but relevant case: the size of an air force. We could simply list the numbers of aircraft of each type, the numbers of personnel and so on and leave it at that, as the International Institute for Strategic Studies does. This would make overall comparisons difficult, for example, if one wanted to use the data in the analysis of an arms race. If we want to have some idea of the overall power of the airforce then we want to add up the different types of aircraft. The simple addition of a high-tech fighter with a small communications aircraft to call it 'two aircraft' would be formally correct but very misleading. We therefore 'weight' the various items according to their importance, counting the fighter as, say, equal to four times the communication aircraft in some sort of 'standard aircraft unit'. This is where the problem lies: on what basis do we determine the weights? In the case of armaments it is customarily got round in terms of costs. If a fighter aircraft costs four times the communications aircraft then it is deemed to be four times as important. This has the merit of simplicity, particularly for aggregates. Nevertheless, it is very arbitrary. Clearly, we plausibly could adopt some very different sets of weighting and get very different answers. Even with items close together, like different sorts of aircraft, the arbitrary element is significant. In comparing an infantry battalion with a squadron of aircraft in order to add them together, the range of plausible figures is much larger. In practice, total-value figures are the commonest in making 'measures' of the level of armaments, and the index number problem is not discussed to the same degree as it is in the case of economics. However, it is there, and the conceptual problem underlies many of the measures which we use in international relations.

Frequently we want to use a measure where a measurement of the basic variable we are interested in is difficult or impossible. In this case we use *indicators* to stand in for the underlying measure. Thus we might use the infant mortality rate or number of telephones per head to 'indicate' the standard of living. Likewise, we might use the proportion of the population in the armed forces as an indicator of militarization. Richardson (1960a) used 'warfinpersal' (a curiously ugly term for a stylish if unusual writer). It is defined as the number of people involved in warlike activities, including munitions work, divided by the average wage as a measure of the economic input into warlike activities. It has the merit of weighting people according to their salary, as the colonel counts for several times the mess-waiter. This, we hope, is an appropriate indicator of their military importance. Indicators stand in for factors such as these where there are some difficult problems of definition of the underlying factor. They are also used where the underlying variable can be clearly and unambiguously defined and where it is in principle possible to measure it. However, it may be infeasible in practice for cost or ethical reasons, or when the process of measurement contaminates the phenomena.

I shall now discuss rather briefly two measures which have been used in international relations to show their nature.

First, consider the use of content analysis as a measure of affects such as hostility (North *et al.*, 1963). Content analysis is the systematic analysis of written texts to determine characteristics of style such as the use of certain grammatical forms, of particular words and so on. It has been very successful, and generally accepted as such, in determining such things as disputed authorship. More controversially, it has been adapted as a device for measuring such things as hostility. A 'dictionary' is made up by different scholars in which various terms and phrases are weighted for their degree of hostility. A text is then scored and its hostility index determined. We then have a measure of the degree of hostility of the sender at the time of the message and can plot changes of hostility with successive measures. This has been done in the analysis of crises and in particular was used in the first systematic analysis of the 1914 crisis using social scientific methods. At first this might sound bizarre. However, let us reflect what is done in conventional historical analysis. Historians will often refer to a response as being angry or hostile and tensions as things which can be raised or lowered. An ordinal measure, at least, is being applied here. The historian is making a judgement about the mental state of the actor. Content analysis merely systematizes the judgement. At its weakest, a content analysis of a set of documents to determine their relative hostilities has added nothing to, but subtracted nothing from, a conventional judgement. However, by systematizing the judgements it may make finer relative judgements possible. Further, it forces the judges to be clearer about the basis of their judgements. Notice, nevertheless, what we are trying to do. It is asserted that actors in the international system are expressing hostility. The hostility may be an expression of their actual mental state or it may be what they want the recipient of the message to perceive as being their mental state. In either case, however, an event is taking place. The purpose of the measure is systematically to observe this event.

Secondly, consider the well-known analysis of the initiation of war by Bueno de Mesquita (1981). He applied a modified form of an expected utility model to decision-makers. It did not imply a strict maximization of expected utility by the decision-makers but it was argued that war would not be initiated unless the expected utility of fighting a war was greater than that of not fighting one from the point of view of the initiator. The model was tested over the period from 1815 onwards. Clearly it was not feasible to get direct measures of expected utility. The von Neumann and Morgenstern concept of utility is a measure in principle (von Neumann and Morgenstern, 1944). It can be measured in practice (indeed, it has been) but only under narrow experimental circumstances, which are the only contexts in which measurement is feasible. However, by defining it in the way they did, von Neumann and Morgenstern showed that it is a meaningful concept. It is infeasible in practice to carry out such a measurement procedure in most circumstances where it would be of interest. However, because it can be shown to be a meaningful concept, we are entitled to use indicators. The relevant variables in the initiation of war case are the probability of success (and hence of failure) and the utility of success. The probability of success is the subjective probability held by the decision-makers of the initiating power – clearly difficult to discover even if we are dealing with contemporary events; impossible, unless one were very lucky to find some appropriate documents, in any historical case. Such a probability may well not be explicitly formulated as such in any case. However, it is plausible that the probability is thought of as concerning relative power. Thus the indicator of probability was measured in terms of relative power measured according to industrial capability, and the distance of the fighting from the home base (which reduced power, the further away it was). The utility was effectively a measure of agreements with other states and was a measure of relative utility. This was indicated by the similarity of alliances. If two states had identical alliances there was no advantage to be gained even by a successful war. If there was a close, but not exact, match between two states' alliances there would be some small gain in utility by moving them to an exact match. A war might then be fought but not unless the probability of winning (as measured above) was very high. If there was little similarity on two states' alliance patterns then state A would greatly increase its utility by fighting and hence might initiate a war even if the probability of war was not very high. The expected utility would still have to be positive, however.

The problem of 'sameness' in international relations

If we generalize, we assert that two factors are related to each other (or we may, of course, deny it in a situation where there was some earlier presumption of a relationship). If we generalize we are implicitly involved in some form of quantification. More formalized quantitative studies put this on a more rigorous basis.

The basic issue about measurement is whether two items or events can be put in the same class as each other because they share common characteristics. For example, we use the common noun 'state' to mean entities which share common characteristics of importance, and have few qualms about putting India and Iceland along with Colombia in the same set of things we regard as states. We become uneasy only in the case of some very small states such as St Kitts and Andorra, wondering whether the characteristics they lack of statehood are not too serious for them to be similarly put in the same set. Our uneasiness is reflected in that we call them micro-states. The uneasiness is calmed as we realize that they are small in number and that practically any problem in international relations (except perhaps for a few legal ones) can be considered without worrying about the classification. 'State' is comparatively easy, for these purposes at least. We also use 'crisis' to denote various events. This indicates that there is something in each of the individual events which it shares with the others and does not share with non-crises. This something is relevant to the analysis of what are deemed to be interesting forms of behaviour. Similarly, we use terms such as an 'alliance', a 'war' and an 'empire'. We also ascribe qualities to some things such as the 'size' of a war or the 'hostility' of a particular interaction, where normally we are willing to use such phrases as 'more hostile than'. We assume that there are statements which can be made about two crises which are true about both and are true because these are statements about crises in general. If we can make statements of this sort, then we are starting off in the direction of measurement. Only if we follow the line of Peter Winch, where no generalization is possible, will this not be the case.

To carry out tests we need to be able to categorize, which, nevertheless, most international relations theorists of most schools of thought feel able to do. None of the categories above should have caused very much unease. I shall illustrate what we hope to do but also some of the difficulties. This is not a textbook on statistics. I shall devote just one paragraph to outlining the nature of the problem. The propositions we are interested in come in two forms which are better seen as ends of a spectrum. On the one hand we have yes/no dichotomies where we ask whether two factors are related or not. Thus, if we ask whether alcohol relates to road accidents or not we examine people who have been in accidents (or their corpses) and see whether the proposition that drivers with more than some level of alcohol in their blood are more likely to have accidents than those without is true or not. This results in a two by two table of the following form:

	Alcohol < x %	Alcohol > x%
No. of drivers in accidents	p	q
No. of drivers not in accidents	r	s

p, q, r and s are numbers of instances in each category. What we are looking for is a pattern. If alcohol has no relationship then the proportion of drivers in accidents with less than x% alcohol in their blood will be about the same as those with more than x%. Thus p/r will be approximately equal to q/s. If it is the case that alcohol affects the accident rate then q/s will be high in comparison to p/r. Even if this were the case, it is possible that it could have occurred for-tuitously, particularly, for example, if the number of cases were few in number. We therefore estimate what the probability of getting a particular pattern would be by purely chance processes. The sorts of 'confidence limits' we normally adopt are that a particular relationship should be really the case with 95 per cent certainty or, if we are ambitious, 99 per cent certainty. The basis of making these calculations is the theory of probability, which I shall not call into question here. This sort of analysis is widely used in social affairs.

In the example above, the categorization was relatively easy. We could redefine what is meant by 'accident' and alter the threshold level of alcohol in the blood, but the basic concepts are clear.

However, now let us consider an example from international relations. Wallace used the same technique in analysing the relationship between arms races and wars. By taking states which had been involved in arms races with each other and which were then involved in a serious diplomatic incident, he examined how many resulted in war and how many did not. The resulting table was as follows:

	Serious International Disputes	
	Preceded by arms race	Not preceded by arms race
Followed by war	11	2
Not followed by war	4	63

Source: Wallace (1979)

These seemed very convincing figures which could not plausibly have come about by chance. Arms races disposed states towards war.

However, this analysis was severely criticized by Diehl (1983, 1985) on the grounds that the definitions of 'war' and 'arms race' were inappropriate. The problem is not so much in defining warfare but in defining the notion of a single war. This is disturbing, as war, however regrettably, is a central concern in international relations.

'How many wars were there between 1815 and 1945?' appears to be a perfectly proper question which one might hope had a clear-cut answer. As long as we deal with situations like the Franco-Prussian War (1870) where there were two participants fighting in a fairly steady military campaign, there is no great problem. It would be counted as a single member of the set of wars. However, if we look at World War II we immediately see that there is a problem. Clearly the war between Japan and the USA was only tenuously connected with the war between Germany and the Soviet Union, though they are both described as being aspects of World War II. The USA and Britain, as far as Europe was concerned, had related interests, though by no means identical ones, while their interests in the Pacific were not always too close. Perhaps New Zealand and Australia had as near identical interests as any pair of states. The problem is not difficult if we take extreme definitions. Thus we describe a war as a single war if there is fighting where participants are divided into two groups such that all the enemies of any country A are either the enemies of B or are neutral. There are no triples such that each is fighting both of the others. This would allow us to call World War II a single war. Alternatively, we can count every pair of dyads as a separate war. Thus Britain versus Germany is one war, Britain versus Italy another and so on. On this account, World War II is just a general cover name for a very large number of wars. We run across the problem of who should be counted a combatant and when – was there a war between France and Germany after the occupation in 1940?

When something which initially appeared homogeneous such as a war turns out to be heterogeneous, we break it down into different subgroups or, in this case, different sorts of wars. That is, we provide a typology. This comes about if we think that, though there was some basis for categorizing wars together, and there were some true statements which could be made of them all, by subdividing them many more interesting statements could be made within the subgroups which would not be true of the category as a whole. Vasquez (1993) presents an interesting typology of wars which he uses to good effect. Wars are divided according to a number of characteristics. There are wars between equals (wars of rivalry) and wars of inequality. There are complex wars with more than two actors, and dyadic wars. Wars are also categorized according to whether they are total or limited, both in goals and resources. Clearly a breakdown of a class reduces the generality of a theory but it makes up for this in being able to make more powerful and interesting statements about the subclasses.

I took the problem of defining the unit 'a war' partly because of its centrality in international relations but partly because it illustrates the problem in an extreme form. The definition of the classes is not for the most part so awkward. There are no such major problems over the definition of crisis. There are different alternatives which mean that different events find themselves classified differently, but in the analysis of crises this has not led to any great difficulties, at least so far. There is no reason to suppose that the issue of categorization and the definition of events as the same is any worse in international relations than anywhere else. This does not stop it being a problem, however.

Correlations and functions

Our aim with statistics is to test hypotheses. It is not the only way but it is an important way. When we have factors which can be put into two, or a limited, number of categories we see whether the distributions of categories could reasonably have come about by chance. These problems have been central in this chapter so far. We move ahead now and discuss those situations where the factors of interest are measurable, such as arms levels. These features may be countable characteristics such as number of wars and number of frontiers (these are positively related; Richardson (1960a) was the first to show this in rigorous form). More often they are measurable, such as changes in arms levels and the incidence of war.

The aim of any social scientist is to formulate causal laws about behaviour. The most the statistical data can do is confirm any hypotheses presented. In themselves the statistics make patterns (or fail to do so) which are consistent with the hypothesis and constitute tests of the hypothesis. Initially we want to know if there is a relationship between two variables. Do they increase or decrease together or inversely with each other? If so, then we say the two variables are 'correlated'.

Ideally we can get some mathematical relationship between them, usually of a simple nature such as a straight line known as a 'regression line'. This is by far the commonest, as it is the simplest, and characterizes most international relations applications that get so far. However, there is no reason to suppose that life is linear, and more complex relationships such as quadratic relationships (relationships which normally have one turning point) are also fitted to data if it appears justified. Unfortunately, while correlations are frequently reported in the international relations literature, the patterns beyond this are so indistinct as to be consistent with a large number of relationships. In most cases a linear relationship is the simplest of many which could plausibly be fitted. Once again, one measures the reliability of such a relationship by calculating how likely it is that it could come about by chance.

Correlations are not unadulterated, flawless facts which confirm or otherwise the speculations of the social scientist. Among the myriad of problems, there are two of particular importance. The first I illustrate by a (fictitious) example. Suppose a motor insurance firm carries out an investigation and finds that students are more prone to automobile accidents than the rest of the population. In other words, the correlation between the state of being a student and the likelihood of having an accident is positive. Clearly, there should be a student premium to compensate the insurance company against the higher risk. However, further investigation reveals that drivers between the age of 18 and 25 have higher accident rates than the average. It is quickly noticed that a very high proportion of students fall into that age group. It may be noticed then that the accident rate of students is actually lower than that of the average for the 18 to 25 age group. Compared to this new reference class, the correlation has become negative. Now suppose that the statisticians find that over a lifetime university graduates have more accidents than non-graduates. On this revised, but clearly relevant definition of accident-proneness in automobiles, the correlation has once again become positive. But then the risk of having an automobile accident is negatively correlated with the number of children people have, while university graduates have fewer than the average; standardizing for this new variable means that the correlation has once again turned negative.[2] The question is where we should stop in the search for new variables in order to locate the 'correct' reference group. There is no clear-cut rule for this. In the fictitious case of road accidents there is at least a wealth of data in the sense of a very large number of cases, where the categorizations such as accident, graduate, age and so on are tolerably unambiguous. The insurance companies must have such data; they have probably carried out the sort of investigation I have outlined (and probably with different results). In international relations there are far fewer data and, more relevantly, the categorizations are much less clear-cut. The sort of manipulation of readily accessible data as envisaged above is less easy. If a correlation turns out to be in an unexpected direction, the first step for an econometrician, cliometrician, polimetrician[3] or whatever is to look for another variable to correct it. But this somewhat sullies the austere obedience to rules which ideally one would like to see in the dispassionate empirical investigator.

The second problem concerns the form of the relationship between two variables – we assume just two for simplicity of argument. The easiest initial assumption is that two sets of observations when taken at the same time lead to a correlated result – road accidents and alcohol consumption would be obvious cases. However, for many variables one would expect a time-lag between the causal variable and the caused variable. Thus, we would expect the reaction of one state to another state's increased level of arms to be lagged. The problem is, then, how long is this lag? It could be a 'simple lag' where the level of arms of one country is directly related to the level of arms of the other at some specified interval in the past. However, if we have no prior expectation of what that interval is, we might test for a number of different intervals, thus increasing the likelihood of finding one set of data which fits. Further, the lag might not be a simple lag but a 'distributed lag'. That is, the preceding year's arms may have a lot of effect, those of the year before that have some effect but a smaller one, and the year before that have a smaller influence still. By an adjustment of the weighting of different periods, and by some appropriate adjustment of the time-lags, the possibility of finding an acceptable correlation out of one lot of data is increased. A lack of correlation over simultaneous data can be dismissed in favour of an acceptable correlation coming over, say, a distributed lag.

The problem is compounded when we realize that there are numerous manipulations of the data which might appear justified. Absolute figures may not seem justified but, where proportional changes appear relevant, a logarithmic measure may seem appropriate. If the variables do not appear to move together in a general sense then they might be fitted into some other pattern such as the quadratic function. If the investigator is still disappointed, rates of change may be given priority over absolute levels. The difficulty is that, with sufficient ingenuity, some pattern or another can probably be found in any set of data to which a mathematical function of some sort can be fitted. Either we can select different sets of data according to time or we can manipulate the relevant functional form to give us a wide range of options. We need only one correlation for us to claim our proposition is vindicated. This is reminiscent of geocentric astronomers and their epicycles.

While the flexibility in the analysis of data is disconcerting, there is not infinite flexibility. Some sets of data may resolutely refuse to yield any sort of pattern of interest however vigorously they are manipulated. However, it is true that the possibility of a spurious correlation is increased when there is a wide range of possibilities. We return to this issue in the final section of this chapter.

Inasmuch as such exercises are relationships between numbers there is no problem involved in seeking correlations. 'Are there patterns in the distribution of numbers or not?' is a question which can be answered (or not) according to some unambiguous set of procedures. However, there must also be some reason for the numbers to be related for it to be of any scientific significance. That is, somewhere or another there lurks the philosophically treacherous problem of causation. 'Spurious correlation' is where some set of figures are closely interrelated, but there is no reason to suppose that there is any causal relationship, either direct or indirect. Thus, in the UK, there is a very close quadratic relationship between cumulative rainfall and the price level (Hendry, 1993), though hardly anyone would want to impute any causal significance to this. There are many such examples. Extreme cases such as this are not particularly troubling as they are unlikely to mislead. However, lots of social variables are interconnected, and sorting out causal relationships merely on the basis of correlations between sets of numbers is a hazardous procedure. Causal assertions come prior to any attribution of significance to a purely statistical relationship.

Conclusions

As quantification in international relations normally involves probabilistic relationships and not deterministic ones, we have spoken of patterns, tendencies, and so on. Relationships are not of the form that whenever A is present so is B. We are making the weaker but none the less significant statement that if A is present there is more likely to be a B than if A were not present. A few counter-examples of As without Bs does not invalidate our proposition. The data involve groups of events, not individual events. In quantification, we have an extremely valuable tool if in fact the claims for it are justified. If the claims turn out to be spurious then, once again, this is a cause for lamentation, not rejoicing.

Statistical tests of significance all depend on some comparison with the chance hypothesis. Could a given pattern or relationship have come about by chance? The rules of chance, so to speak, are those given by the calculus of probability. The calculus itself is not in much dispute but its interpretation is. Thus, is probability just something which is applicable to classes of events or can it be interpreted in terms of individual events? As the controversies are not directly relevant to the problems of this chapter, I have not discussed them. It is important to make clear that the appropriateness of probability theory underlies all inferences which are made on the basis of statistics.

The underlying concern about the use of statistical data in the testing of hypotheses in international relations (and much else in the social sciences) is the inordinate flexibility with the measures and with the terms. In almost any situation we can look at three ways of altering the problems slightly to encourage the data to confirm our hypotheses. We can redefine the concepts (such as power); we can redefine the relevant data, such as by choosing a different indicator or altering the time lag; or we can modify the hypothesis, such as by transforming the data into logarithms. All can be redefined to portray a slightly different system. Unfortunately, this carries with it the danger that a system can be found, somewhere or another, in which almost anything one could think of would be confirmed. This is where there is a danger in relying too heavily on the hypothetico-deductive method as exemplified by physics. In physics, very precise mathematical relationships can be specified. The evidence which would confirm or refute a specific generalization can be clearly stated. The range of data consistent with a particular hypothesis is clear and narrow. In the case of the social sciences, predicted relationships are much more general. They consist of statements such as 'X and Y will increase together' without its being possible to specify anything more than a very general functional relationship. Coupled with the possibilities of being able to redefine X and Y, the range of potentially confirming instances is very large, while the number of potential falsifiers is correspondingly small.

The question does not look much more tractable whether we pose it as an issue of verification, as is done above, or as an issue of falsification (which is what we would expect, at least on my interpretation of verification and falsification). Thus, suppose we want to claim that there is a lagged relationship between two variables such as the arms levels of two countries suspected of being in an arms race. We examine the data over different intervals and find that, for a weighted average of a nine-month lag and twelve-month lag there is a good correlation, but for all other periods the correlation is poor. The poor correlations would not falsify the theory; the good one would confirm it. We seem to have come round to an asymmetry between falsification and verification which is the obverse of Popper's when considering such propositions as 'All swans are white.' One good result confirms, but any number of bad results do not disconfirm. Does this mean that systems can be made which are consistent with all possible theories? Dismaying though this conclusion would be from a scientific point of view, it would at least solve the problem of why social scientists disagree so much on what would appear to be scientific questions.

The answer is negative. I have shown that systems involving quantification can be very flexible and hence not very vulnerable to refutation. However, I have not shown they are tautological, which would mean that even in principle they would be invulnerable or untestable. The degree of exclusion of hypotheses by evidence can be relatively small but it is not zero. In practice our approach would not be as crudely inductive as was implied in the example given above. We may have a very precise theory about lags, in which case only one time interval would do. We could not shop around, in the manner implied, and find whatever lag happened to suit the hypothesis. Even if the theory about lags was imprecise, but nevertheless involved the proposition that there was a lag of some sort, this would still exclude a good correlation on simultaneous data as grounds for confirmation. Thus while we have too much flexibility for comfort, it is not infinite flexibility. The real difficulty lies in social science theory. We do not, and perhaps cannot, have theories sufficiently tightly specified as to exclude all but a narrow set of results as confirmations of our theories. This is not a difference in principle between social science theories and theories in natural science, but it is an enormous difference in practice. On top of the basic holism of Quine's approach, where evidence confronts all theory and can be accommodated by some redefinition of some term within it somewhere, social scientists are also faced with a sort of pragmatic holism where even neighbouring hypotheses can be adjusted without much cost. However, this version does not necessarily imply Quine's, nor is Quine's necessarily particularly relevant to this much lower-level argument. This is not to say that statistical evidence tells us nothing in that any correlation, however good, could be defined away and any failed correlation could be brought to life with another set of definitions or manipulations of the data. The manipulations become increasingly implausible in that the assumptions on which they are based become more and more bizarre. When a good result comes out on the basis of what appears to be an arbitrary definition (as, for example, the results following from Singer and Small's definitions of such concepts as bipolarity in 1968), then it is usual to test the result on the basis of other definitions. Only when it is shown to be robust on a number of different definitions does it gain much credence. Likewise, one does not transform a set of raw data into logarithms without offering some reason for doing so. While one might be designing the theory to fit the facts, one has to provide a theory, nevertheless. Further, in a subsequent exploration of the same theory, the logarithmic procedure must still be adhered to (or a *very* good reason offered for why not). These constraints and procedures are not infinitely flexible, even if they are more flexible than one would like. This leads to an approach which requires the robustness of results in the face of alternative measures and definitions when these are plausible. Oddly enough, practising statisticians are aware of this.

Notes

1 To make this assertion, it is necessary to assume that power has the property of 'transitivity'. We can illustrate this with reference to height. If A is taller than B, and B is taller than C, then A is taller than C. Transitivity might be supposed to apply to power in general, though there may well be contexts and definitions where it was not a justifiable assumption. Any cardinal measure has this property.

2 The first part of this paragraph is a simplification of Leamer's argument in 'Let's take the "Con" out of econometrics' (1983). The rest is a modest extension of the argument.

3 An econometrician is someone who tests economic hypotheses by statistical means, a cliometrician is someone who tests historical hypotheses by statistical means while a polimetrician is someone who tests political hypotheses by statistical means. The groups are clearly not mutually exclusive. Those who test hypotheses in international relations have no special name of their own.

8
Rational choice theory and international relations

Rational choice theories of behaviour
A common mode of analysis in the social sciences is the so-called
rational choice approach, though this is not the most fortunate of
names, as will become clear. It is an active mode in international
relations. The basic proposition in this programme is that social
behaviour can be seen in terms of actors pursuing goals. The actors
can be individuals or social groups of some sort such as business
firms, states, or any group which can be described as having a
collective goal. This would exclude a grouping such as 'children
under 5' or 'sufferers from influenza' though it would include a
group such as a society for research into influenza. The actors are
presumed to follow certain goals which are attributed to them and
the consequences of pursuing these goals are worked out in various
circumstances. The context of a choice may be impersonal such as
when an actor chooses between two gambles. This is the province
of 'expected utility theory' (see 'Utility in the Glossary). It may,
however, be a situation where several decision-takers interact with
each other where all the actors are assumed to be pursuing goals.
This is the province of the 'theory of games' (see 'Games, theory
of' in the Glossary). Rational choice analysis leads to deductions,
sometimes complex, which imply that various sorts of behaviour
will occur which are not at all obvious from the initial assumptions.
Whether the correct goals were attributed to the actors or not is
determined by whether the conduct deduced from those goals takes
place. The goals themselves cannot be observed directly, a point of
some significance to which we shall return.

Rational choice analysis is particularly widely used in economics,
where it started. This is especially so in micro-economics, which is
the analysis of the behaviour of individual economic actors. In its
simplest form, businesses are assumed to maximize profits while
consumers are assumed to maximize utility. Profits can be directly
observed but utility cannot. These assumptions are the basis of the
analysis of markets. It is clearly very simple and would be unlikely
to provide a full account of the market system but it is an excellent
start. To move on from this, and to circumvent the anomalies which
the very simple picture of the world provides, more complex sets of

goals can be assumed, perhaps the most famous extension being Herbert Simon's concept of 'satisficing' (Simon, 1982). Though emanating from economics and being a part of the standard equipment of the economist, this style of analysis has now penetrated almost every field of the social sciences from the structure of families (Becker, 1976) to political theory (a good example is Taylor, 1987). Its protagonists claim its widespread effectiveness and it is hard to argue that as a research programme it has not already achieved considerable success. Gary Becker, an economist, unsurprisingly, argues that the 'combined assumptions of maximizing behavior, market equilibrium and stable preferences, used relentlessly and unflinchingly . . . provide a valuable unified framework for understanding *all* human behavior' (emphasis in the original). While Becker's view may be extreme, his general attitude would find a lot of support.

International relations theorists have used rational choice theory very effectively. It is now a commonplace, particularly among scholars of strategic studies. Informally this has been true ever since analysts first looked at power as something which states pursue and involved themselves in analyses of such phenomena as the balance of power. More formal and explicit use of rational choice theory came rather later with the interpretation of the theory of games in international contexts, most notably with Schelling (1960) and, rather more critically as far as its applications were concerned, Rapoport (1965, 1974). The problems and paradoxes implicit in the nature of conflict became made explicit in games such as chicken and prisoners' dilemma (see 'Games, theory of' in the Glossary), and their awareness of them has served to trouble scholars of international relations ever since. The interpretation of issues in international relations in terms of concepts derived from the theory of games has proceeded apace ever since with the work of Brams (for example 1985), Niou *et al.*, (1989) Wagner (for example 1986) and a host of others. Its impact has been enormous. More general applications of an explicit expected utility model have been made, particularly by Bueno de Mesquita (for example, 1981) with ambitions not just to explain but predict.

Realism and pluralism are both decision-centred approaches to international relations and it is comparatively easy to interpret them, as many have done, in terms of the rational choice model. Classical realism takes the state as the unit and attributes to it a particular utility function: the maximization of power. This is a rather poorly defined utility function as it is not clear what power is: for the moment we neglect this point, crucial though it is. In many people's view, realism leaves a lot of features of the international system poorly explained. The pluralists argue that the failure of the realist programme lies in wrongly identifying the decision-making unit for large numbers of relevant issues. However, they are still working within the same general research programme, which can readily be described as a rational choice programme, but are looking for more appropriate units than states alone as the units which take decisions. Pluralists may or may not argue that the states' utility functions are incorrect in the sense of not properly describing conduct, though this is not necessarily the case. Vasquez (1983), mentioned above as a severe critic of realism, is involved in the first sort of critique rather than the second. The claims of big differences between the pluralist and realist research programmes, which go as far as claims that they are incommensurable, are misconceived. They are rather close from a methodological point of view, both being aspects of the rational choice research programme. Politically, and from policy-making points of view, the differences are considerable – they involve different theories after all. However, this is a totally separate thing from the methodological differences, which are few.

It is widely, though not universally, accepted that rational choice theory is a powerful technique. It is also very often misunderstood. Some advocates claim a lot for it, though they are not quite as naive as sometimes is implied. My main concern here is with the conceptual nature of rational choice theory, though its role in international relations and social theory in general needs some attention. In the next section I shall elaborate the structure of rational choice and goal-directed theories. A discussion of their relationship to hermeneutics follows. In the final section I discuss the problem of goals and consciousness.

The structure of goal-directed models
The various concepts involved in a goal-directed model are *actors* who have *preferences* over the possible consequences of conditions which might arise. Actors, therefore, are people or groups who would prefer condition A to condition B to condition C where a condition may be a collection of commodities available to consumption or, if the actor is a government, the condition may be the government of another country, a set of alliances or some set of trade arrangements. These preferences can be referred to as the *goals* of the actors (Figure 8.1) where it is assumed that they seek to achieve these goals as effectively as possible. There is an *environment*, which might be inanimate or consist of other actors; initially we shall assume the first. The environment and the goals indicate which *acts* must be carried out in order to achieve the *consequences*. There are also *rules*, which are derived from the goals that dictate the choice of

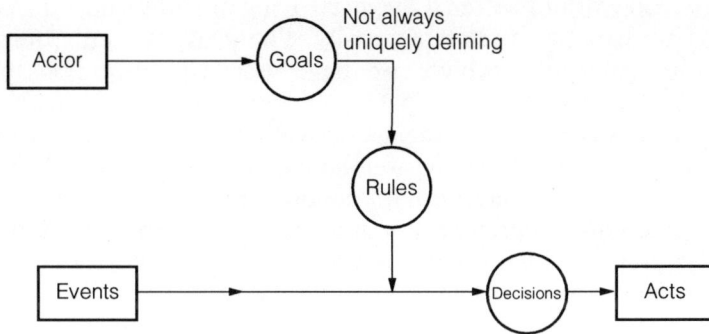

Figure 8.1 The process of decision: a single actor

the act under certain conditions; that is, specified states of the environment. Thus a rule is 'under conditions E(1), E(2), E(3), choose A(*x*)'. The rule is derived from the goals and does not add any further factors to the analysis. It is an interpretation of the rule in the context of the particular environment. Thus the 'maximin rule' in the theory of games (see 'Games, theory of' in the Glossary) is a rule in this sense where the general goal is 'maximize utility' (or benefits, or whatever the units are in the context of the game) given that the environment is one of a zero-sum game with known pay-off matrix and a known opponent. Where the environment is inanimate or in some classes of games such as two-person zero-sum games the goals lead directly to a unique rule. However, in non-zero-sum games this is normally not the case and we cannot derive a clear rule of choice from the goals alone.

First, however, we want to see where this model touches the world of empirical observation. Take first the concept of a rule. In order for a rule to be a proper rule, 'choose A(*x*)' has to be distinguishable from 'not choose A(*x*)' in terms of an action and hence something which is observed, or, at least, is observable. Likewise, the environment is external to the actor, who must be able to distinguish between, say, E(1) and E'(1). If the actor can make this distinction, the observer can do so also. There may be practical difficulties, but not issues of principle. One act of choice on its own can be recognized only as conforming to the rule or not. However, a sequence of confirming observations can lead to the judgement that an actor is acting consistently with the rule. So far, this is all impeccably empirical and strictly analogous to any other empirical statement. The consequences are likewise observable events. However, the goals are not. These are characteristics of the individual which we cannot know about directly other than by the actors' own reports. How would we tell if they were lying or had made a mistake? In fact we can do so relatively easily. The goals and environment determine the rules which, we have asserted, have potentially observable consequences. That is, the rules are derived from the goals in the strict sense of logical derivation. Thus, if a sufficiently large number of instances of following the rules are observed (which in practice may be fairly small), these will determine the goals. The goals, therefore, are analogous to the theoretical terms such as gravity which appear in the natural sciences. Indeed, it is appropriate to regard them as theoretical terms as they are conceptually the same. They are not observation terms even in principle. However, they do play a central role in an empirical theory such that, while they are not directly observable, they have implications which are. Further, without them the theory would be inordinately detailed and cumbersome. Though in principle we could start off with the rules, they would need specifying for all possible environments, which would be very cumbersome. The simpler deductive theory involving goals is much to be preferred.

While rational choice theory can be used for both normative and explanatory analysis we are mainly concerned with the latter. We shall discuss the normative issues in a later section ('A rational choice research programme', p. 165). In an explanatory theory, the need is to use the goals which people in fact have. Within the context of the theory, there is no judgement about the desirability of these goals from a moral or other standpoint. This does not absolve us from moral judgements at some stage but these are external to the theory itself.

In order to develop a rich body of theory, we need to set only some minimum restrictions on the goals and the rules. These are effectively two. The first is that the actors are optimizing agents in some sense. That is, in the light of the information they have, they choose the course of action which most effectively achieves their goals. Thus, suppose there were a choice between a glass of beer and a glass of orange juice where the chooser clearly prefers the beer. There are two alternative choice situations. In the first the chooser is allowed to select the preferred drink (in which case the beer will be chosen, which is a rather trivial implication). In the second a coin is tossed and whether the beer or the orange juice is selected depends on whether the coin comes down heads or tails. The chooser would be supposed to adopt the first principle of allocation as it would always deliver the beer whereas the second one only might deliver the beer.

The second principle of rational choice is that preferences should be transitive. Thus, If A is preferred to B and B is preferred to C then it should also be the case that A is preferred to C^1. This may seem innocuous though it can be less so when the alternatives consist of a complex set of constituents. However, while standard. rational choice theory requires these restrictions, I shall argue in the final section that the rational choice research programme does not.

So far we have been concerned with an actor choosing in a non-strategic environment. Initially it would seem that the introduction of another actor as a part of the environment in which the decision-maker acts would make little difference. We can represent it in Figure 8.2 by adding in the extra box. However, a difference arises in relating rules to goals. In the impersonal case it was assumed that a set of unique rules could be deduced from a set of goals and a given environment. Clearly, this is not logically the case but in practice there seem to be no serious problems involved as far as the questions social scientists study are concerned, either in international relations or anything else. This is not so when more than one actor is involved. Sometimes, as in the zero-sum game mentioned above, the goal of maximizing utility does yield a unique rule. However, in many non-zero-sum games this is not the case, including some games such as prisoners' dilemma and chicken which are directly relevant to conflict situations and play a large role in various parts of international relations theory. It is well known that the 'obvious' maximizing rule in prisoners' dilemma leads to perverse conclusions, at least as far as common sense is concerned. In the case of chicken, there is no clear rule of choice of any sort, whether leading to perverse results or not. These are not curious examples dreamt up to confuse us; the problem is very common in non-zero-sum games. This difficulty is central to the analysis of conflict. In the early days, it was assumed that somewhere or other it would be possible to devise plausible goals which would determine unique rules which would yield 'solutions' to these sorts of strategic situations. Now the approach is more centred on trying to redesign situations such that some unique rules might give appropriate solutions.

Clearly the goal-directed analysis involved in rational choice theory is different from the form of causal analysis described earlier in which a set of antecedent conditions in conjunction with some general laws determined (possibly statistically) a consequence. However, it is not as far from this form of causal analysis as might appear superficially.

It is sometimes objected that the achievement of goals is the 'cause' of the actions, which reverses the normal temporal order in which cause either precedes or is simultaneous with effect. However, this is not the case. It is the formulation of goals, not their

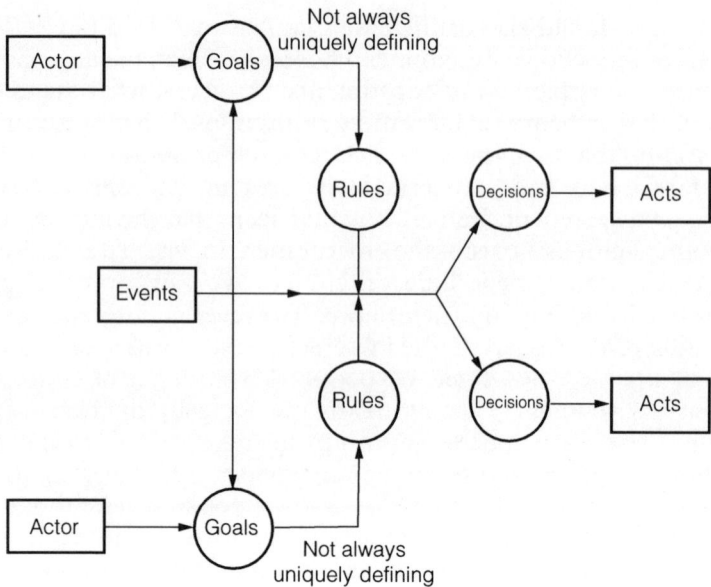

Figure 8.2 The process of decision: two strategic actors

achievement, which is the causal factor where the formulation of the goal takes place prior to any action. Thus, when the appropriate conditions present themselves, the rule can be said to cause the act and the set of consequences which follows on from them.[2] The goal might, indeed, be thought of as a basic characteristic of the actor involved. However, there is a further, legitimate question of where goals come from. It may be that there is some sort of deep conditioning from which specific goals emerge in the appropriate circumstances. However, this is not very helpful. If we say that the underlying goal of every action is to maximize utility, we are guilty of tautology. It is useful to consider goals only if they are posed in such a way as to yield specific decision rules (or, of course, show that such rules do not exist, as in many non-zero-sum game cases). Partly, of course, goals can be derived from higher-level goals. A general goal of 'maximize security' can yield a lower-level goal 'preserve the balance of power' when integrated with realist assumptions about behaviour in the international system. This lower-level goal will then be interpreted in terms of the behaviour rules appropriate to the particular circumstances of the moment. However, there is some point at which we stop. It is possible to argue that certain sorts of goals are to be found in some sorts of societies and not in others. The goals appropriate to economic agents in medieval society are not the same as those appropriate to modern capitalism. A micro-theory of one is unlikely to be of much explanatory power for the other except in a very general sense. Some of this might be explained by differences in the circumstances but not all. People wanted different sorts of things in thirteenth-century Britain than they do in modern Britain. In principle, at least, we can have a theory of goal generation which specifies the circumstances in which certain sorts of goals will be followed. This will be a theory in the causal form described in Chapter 2.

Rationality and rational choice theory

What often concerns people is the rather tendentious choice of the word 'rational' in the phrase 'rational choice theory'. In its use as an explanatory theory, all that is meant by rationality is the efficient pursuit of consistent goals. This is clearly a very restricted concept of rationality and it is known as 'instrumental rationality'. It is clearly a perfectly proper concept as far as the explanation of behaviour is concerned, as the explanation, consistently with the general view expressed in this book, should be separated from its evaluation. Nevertheless it is an unfortunate use of the word, and one which can lead to confusion. The word 'rational', for many people, has a connotation of approval (though for others a connotation of disapproval), but this is not intended in this sort of analysis. Rationality means little more than efficiency. This is not to deny that rational can be used in many other contexts also to mean other things. Perhaps the most important of these is 'expressive rationality', used to mean not the direct pursuit of goals as such but behaviour exhibited by people when expressing some quality about themselves such as that they are brave or caring or honourable (Hargreaves-Heap, 1989). Instrumental rationality is much more limited but it is the usage to which we shall restrict ourselves here. It is perhaps unfortunate that the whole field is called rational choice theory, which is almost an incitement for it to be misunderstood. 'Goal-directed theories' would be better. However, the term is so deeply engrained that there is nothing much we can do about it.

Instrumental rationality does not necessarily imply self-interest except in a vacuous sense. The goals can be interpreted to include altruism or any other quality. The goals can be interpreted to include a broad range of things. Thus, an individual's goal might be to identify with a group, either a small group such as a family or a large one such as a tribe or a nation. Apparently altruistic conduct when looked at from a narrowly individual standpoint might appear to be easily explicable in terms of a desire to belong to some group or gain its members' approval, though this is not to exclude the possibility of true altruism. In classical decision theory, this is all described rather blandly as actors optimizing the utility functions which embody their preferences.

The concept of instrumental rationality can lead to some curious apparent paradoxes unless we are careful to remember the limited sense in which we use the term rationality. Thus, about every dictator, whether Napoleon, Stalin, Hitler or whoever, there is a debate over whether they were rational or not, at least in this sense of instrumental rationality. The debate over the origins of World War II between A. J. P. Taylor and Hugh Trevor-Roper (later Lord Dacre) is illuminating in this respect. Trevor-Roper argued the traditional case that Hitler had a long-range plan which was stated in its essentials in *Mein Kampf*. This plan might have defied the principles of broad rationality but it was a coherent scheme. The carrying out of the plan was instrumentally rational until the later part of the war when its chances of success became slim.[3] Taylor regarded Hitler as a short-period opportunist, like other statesmen, who was guided by a general plan only in the vaguest way, again like any other statesman. However, he could still have been instrumentally rational except inasmuch as he allowed his racial policies to influence his behaviour. In a similar way Saddam Hussein can be regarded as having been instrumentally rational though unlucky. He gambled on the quite plausible hypothesis that Iran would be defeated quickly but the gamble failed. Similarly, he gambled that nothing would be done when he invaded Kuwait, but again the gamble failed. Both were arguably good bets from Iraq's self-interested point of view and hence instrumentally rational. This is not to say they were moral acts; quite the contrary. However, he lived in a realist world where morality was nothing to do with the issue. Machiavelli and Clausewitz were clear in their instrumental rationality, though not in so many words, on the basis of a certain set of preferences, namely the self-interest of states or rulers.

So far the analysis of rationality has assumed that the actors had full information and were making choices in the full knowledge of what the consequences of these acts were. This is clearly not so. It can quite easily be the case that an act which is rational under the state of information which an actor has, would not have been so had the actor been aware of other issues. Consider a military example. Suppose the decision-makers whose viewpoint we are taking believe that the enemy's tanks have a range of twice that which in fact they have. Clearly, the tactics they adopt will be different from those they would have adopted had they been correctly informed. The rational choice theorist, in pursuit of an explanatory theory, considers the information the actor in fact has and not that which the actor might have under ideal circumstances. The state of information may not always be easy to find out, though it is, in principle, something which is identifiable. However, information is not normally something which is given as part of an unalterable environment. One can acquire information and thus improve decision-making. The army in the above example could have improved its intelligence and found out the true range of the enemy's guns. Unfortunately, information does not come free. By spending more resources we get better information and hence improve decision-making. The problem is that we can know by how much we improve the decision-making only after we have spent the resources. It may be that the improvement will not be sufficient to compensate for the search for information which made it possible. Thus, we have a classic problem of information under uncertainty. There are no neat solutions to this issue, though it is a well-recognized issue in decision theory (Savage, 1972).

A more fundamental objection levied at rational choice theory is that, even in its instrumental form, it seems to endorse a 'Western' view of rationality and hence is inapplicable to societies which do not accept this. This would limit its applicability historically and to other societies. This is a broader objection than that other societies have different information. It is an argument that the whole belief structures of people will mean that they process information in a totally different way. Suppose it is believed that a rain dance will bring about the appropriate level of rain for a crop and is there-fore a necessary part of the growing and harvesting procedure. Given this belief, it is also rational, in the instrumental sense, to carry out the dance. If our purpose is to explain behaviour, and we are rigorous in this ambition, then we simply accept the belief structure and explain the behaviour accordingly. It is analo-gous to the acceptance of goals as defined by the actor. Our initial job is to observe, not to criticize. I shall abandon this strict explanatory mode in the section beginning on page 165. However, belief structures other than those of standard Western scientific beliefs can be incorporated into our explanation of people holding other belief structures provided we can understand what they are.

Goals and understanding

Goals produce rules which determine actions; that is, behaviour. Superficially, this looks similar to the arguments of Peter Winch in his interpretation of Wittgenstein for the social sciences (Winch, 1958). According to Winch, human beings follow rules and a knowledge of human behaviour involves understanding these rules. Winch goes further, and argues that knowledge of human behaviour comprises knowing these rules as the sole form of relevant knowledge, which is a much stronger claim than is being made here. Just as I have argued that a proper behaviour rule must come with principles identifying whether the rule has been followed or not, Winch and Wittgenstein argue that knowing a rule involves knowing what it means to break a rule. Though not quite the same, these are clearly closely related positions. Have we argued ourselves back into a Wittgensteinian position after apparently playing with empiricism so far?

There are three responses. First, it is true that goal-directed models require 'understanding'. It is not just an optional extra. The second response, however, is that this does not bring us full circle to the Wittgensteinian position. The argument made earlier as to why this does not preclude scientific reasoning still holds in this context. Thirdly, while Winch seems to hold that the understanding of rules is the only permissible form of knowledge of human behaviour, this sort of exclusivity is not implicit in rational choice theory. I shall elaborate these arguments, which are particularly pertinent in this context. However, they effectively bring us back to the case argued in Chapter 6. The understanding of what goes on in people's minds is a necessary condition for the analysis of social behaviour but it is not a sufficient one.

As far as the first response is concerned, it has been argued throughout this book that some, though by no means all, of the 'facts' we are dealing with in the social sciences involve an understanding of the events in the terms which the actors themselves understand those events. The approach used in rational choice theory raises no new issues as far as this factor is concerned. Thus, it is not possible to use, say, a model of profit maximization without understanding what profits are, in at least the same general sense as the person who is following this rule. Likewise, if we use a goal-directed model in international relations to analyse the formation of alliances, the problems of arms control, or the issues raised in the co-operation among states, then we must pose the questions involved in terms which the actors can understand as well as the analyst. There can be exceptions to this, as we discuss below, but in general the application of the rational choice or goal-directed approach involves understanding. Indeed, for the most part, it is hard to see how the approach could be of use without some concept of understanding.

As far as the second response goes, while Winch and Wittgenstein argue that the following of rules disqualifies social behaviour from dealing with generalizations, rational choice theorists do the opposite and exploit the rule-guidedness of human behaviour to derive theories. Rational choice procedures are effective inasmuch as there is reasonable stability of behaviour. The stability of behaviour can be interpreted here as stability of rules but these in their turn are dependent on preferences. If preferences are volatile and further do not vary in a consistent and predictable way, then the rules will vary rapidly and behaviour be hard to predict. However, as argued earlier, this is an empirical matter which, one might surmise, would be different for different aspects of human behaviour.

Rational choice theory is not normally represented as an exclusive way of analysing social behaviour, though some analysts, such as Becker (1976), might get close to arguing it. It is more normally presented as an important methodological tool, but not as an exclusive epistemology. In this again it differs from a covert Wincheanism though in this case at a more pragmatic level.

All these points were made in respect of all forms of the scientific analysis of social behaviour. They become particularly clear as they relate to rational choice theory but the principles are not different from any other aspect of the social sciences. The rational choice approach can be embedded without difficulty into the general empiricist philosophical approach.

The awareness of goals

In rational choice theory, the actors need not be conscious of their goals. In everyday conduct we do not usually reflect deeply on our decision procedures but they can be described in rational choice terms without difficulty. However, even though we rarely reflect on them explicitly, if pressed we, and decision-makers in general, would be able to articulate them. In more important decisions it is probably more normal to reflect on the principles involved. The political decisions which are at the core of international relations are important and are therefore more likely to be taken in the context of some thought-out schema. This would seem to be the most natural assumption. Exceptions could be studied as interesting cases because they are exceptions.

However, the potential awareness of goals is not a necessary assumption. Actors may be following more complex sets of goals than those of which they are explicitly aware. There are two very different ways in which this can be important.

First, there are the cases where the proximate goals of which the actors are assumed to be aware lead to a behaviour in the system as a whole which is hard to predict and of which the decision-makers are likely to be at best only dimly conscious. The best-known of these sorts of theories in international relations is 'neo-realism' as developed by Kenneth Waltz (1979) and discussed in Chapter 5.

The second form of problem is where the motives of the actor are unconscious and where the conscious motives are superimposed on the unconscious. Sometimes the conscious motives are implications of the unconscious; sometimes they are inconsistent with them. Though, in my view, considerations of unconscious motives have great potential applications in international relations as well as in other social sciences, their applications, so far, have been limited. However, partly because of their potential significance, but mainly because of their conceptual significance, we should consider them here.

An important case in international relations theory where the proximate goals and the long-term consequences of action are different is contained in neo-realist theory. Central to the neo-realist argument is that each state is constrained by the behaviour of the system as a whole. The central unit of analysis is the system as a whole rather than the individual units in the system. In Waltz's depiction of neo-realist theory (Waltz, 1979), he regards it as a 'holist' analysis as distinct from a 'reductionist' analysis (see pp. 11–12). Though the behaviour of the system is determined by its actors together, the behaviour of individual actors is determined, or at least narrowly constrained, by the system. If survival is the primary goal of actors, their behaviour must follow the rules. If survival is not the primary goal, they will not survive in what is primarily a competitive and conflictual system. Survival need not be a conscious goal, or at least not an articulated one, though it probably would be if a state were under threat. However, the goal might be so embedded in the underlying value system of the decision-makers that it is taken for granted while they concentrate on more immediate and obvious goals.

This does not of itself mean that actors need be ignorant of the structure of the international system as a whole. They (meaning now the governments of the state) know their goal is self-preservation and choose accordingly in the light of the constraints which are imposed. Even in specific acts of policy this is clearly the case. Thus when states are admonished for selling arms to undesirable states, a typical defence is that if they did not do so, another state would. The withdrawal of one actor from this form of systemic behaviour will not alter the behaviour of the system. A rich state can acquire arms and that is that. However, one can also argue that, even if the governments are not explicitly aware of the basic constraints which are put on their behaviour, they will in effect follow the rules, as the consequences of not doing so will be adverse. Thus, the withdrawal of those Western European states from their respective empires in the post-1945 period was only a little due to any sense that self-determination was a good thing. They had little option. The genuine decisions were over detail. Otherwise it was a question of one part idealism to nine parts compulsion. Another instance of the principle is the way in which, in democratic societies, opposition parties come into power and follow foreign policies very similar to those of their predecessors. Likewise, when women have become heads of government, which has happened on a number of occasions since World War II, any difference in policies, which at least some feminists might have hoped for, has been indiscernible. This essentially systemic view of the behaviour of the world does not mean that everything is totally determined. Some states in some conditions may have a very constrained set of choices consistent with survival. At other times, states might have broader alternatives. Thus the increased hostility towards the USSR with the coming of the Reagan administration was a choice – it need not have happened. Similarly, Iran after the Islamic revolution fundamentally changed its foreign policy, especially with regard to the West and in particular the USA. It could presumably have kept its old policy and would have done if the former regime had remained in power.

That there are constraints on behaviour clearly does not necessarily imply that the actors are ignorant of this and unaware of the goals they are following in either the short or the long term. However, it is often the case that certain goals are claimed as being the 'real' goals and the apparent deviations from them are explained away as exceptions due to anomalous circumstances. However, the so-called deviations are so frequent as to become the norm and the 'true' goals which in fact explain behaviour are different from the asserted, and possibly believed in, goals. That this phenomenon exists can scarcely be denied. How common it is is an empirical matter which can be determined by observation, but such an investigation has not been carried out in international relations.

The concept of 'unconscious goals' of which the actors are unaware is a different type of issue.[4] The concept is well accepted in individual psychology, at least in those schools of thought which take the unconscious mind seriously, such as the psychoanalytic schools of Freud and other schools deriving (though often acrimoniously) from the psychoanalytic. Mainstream international relations has tended to veer away from such discussions, though debates on genocide, nationalism (especially violent nationalisms), religious fundamentalisms and so on are unlikely to be explicable solely in terms of conscious goals (though see Bloom (1990) for a recent counter-example). We discussed this earlier in Chapter 6. Though they are not important in current international relations, I would expect these sorts of approaches to expand. Largely as a consequence of the attacks by Karl Popper (1968) and Hans Eysenck (1985), they are sometimes held to be beyond the pale of proper empiricist analysis. While this is not the place to counter this view, one can make a good case for arguing that theories based on the unconscious are amenable to empirical test. Some of the tests which have been made on the Freudian theory, for example, are genuine tests (Kline, 1972; Fisher and Greenberg, 1977[5]). Conceptually, the unconscious can be treated as a theoretical concept in the sense discussed in Chapter 2. If one allows this, unconscious goals can become theoretical concepts also, in the same way as conscious goals. There need be no basic difference. Unless there is no such thing as an unconscious mind, and hence unconscious motives, it would seem curious if we could not analyse them in some ways, though this does not mean that psychoanalysis as it is construed in any of its current variants has got it right. Our procedure, of assuming goals and deducing consequences, can proceed as in the rest of rational choice theory.

There is a possibility also of an intermediate level of awareness. To cite again the concept of 'groupthink', people are motivated not only by a desire to solve the problems ostensibly before them but also by desires for group consensus for its own sake. However, this latter aspect of their feelings usually hampers their consideration of the problem before them and leads to irrational decisions, in terms at least of their stated goals. While in the grip of groupthink, they would probably deny it and in this sense it is unconscious. However, it is not very deeply so and people can become aware of it after the event without great traumas. Further, they can be forewarned of it before the event and take steps to avoid it. Both can be said to have happened in Kennedy's administration with respect to the Bay of Pigs fiasco and the Cuban missile crisis. In Freudian terms, the goals involved in groupthink would be said to lie in the pre-conscious where they can be relatively easily be brought to the surface. The unconscious is a different matter. In the Freudian view, only difficult and perhaps painful analysis can bring matters from the unconscious to the conscious.

There are some problems raised about the conscious articulation of goals which do not require bringing in the concept of the unconscious mind. Further, issues are raised about the observer's perceptions of the goals where these perceptions are separate from those of the actor. Thus, goals determine the rules which are applicable to a given environment and dictate the acts. Given the goals and environment we deduce the acts. This does not mean we can go backwards along the logical trail. It is an elementary proposition from logic that, if G and E imply A, it does not follow that A and E imply G. However, it is A and E which we observe and it is possible that together they do not imply a unique G but only either G or G'. Does this matter? If G and G' always imply the same set of A and E then they are identical and it makes no difference which formulation we adopt, as one can be restated in terms of the other. More significantly for the practising social scientist, G and G' may imply the same consequences for all the cases which interest us empirically while implying other things elsewhere.

For example, suppose an entrepreneur is interested in power within a state. The first step for achieving such power might well be to achieve great wealth. Thus the goals of maximizing wealth and maximizing power will yield the same predictions in a wide variety of situations. However, there is some point where the two diverge and it is at this point that the social scientist must beware. This example is of some interest in the world today and has often been of some interest in considering the media, where there is a possible conflict between maximizing profits and maximizing power and influence.

Milton Friedman pushed this argument to its limit (1966). He argued that it does not matter whether our assumptions about goals or the context of goal-directed behaviour are realistic or not provided they give the same predictions. He gives the example of skilled billiard players. Their behaviour as they play billiards could be accurately explained by assuming they were solving various sets of differential equations and hitting balls accordingly. Few, if any, billiard players in fact do so. However, according to Friedman this does not matter. Our job is to predict the movement of the billiard balls. This is accurately done by assuming that the billiard players act *as if* they had solved the relevant differential equations even if we can be fairly confident that the assumption is false. As, for Friedman, prediction is all, he dismisses one's feelings of discomfort about knowingly having a false statement in a scientific theory. This might be a good pragmatic solution to a problem. It is undeniably helpful, if we wish to make predictions easily, to use a rule which gives good predictions in the area of primary interest even if it would lead to false predictions in irrelevant areas. However, the social scientist should be aware of the dangers. The issue is one of empirical interest and is not strictly a scientific issue at all. What does not interest an observer at one point in time might become of paramount interest at another.

A rational choice research programme and policy
Rational choice theory is not a set of principles embedded in stone but an approach to social behaviour which is adaptable and

developing. What is central to the approach, the 'hard core' in Lakatos's terminology, is the conception of human beings as pursuing goals. In this sense it can best be seen as a scientific research programme in Lakatos's sense rather than a static body of theory. Indeed, it has been suggested that the forms of interactions which are the province of game theory would be better called 'drama theory' in that this is a more appropriate metaphor (Howard, 1994). Whether or not this is a useful terminological device, to view the rational choice approach as a developing research programme is more fruitful than seeing it as a static theory.

What are the problems involved in regarding rational choice analysis as a fruitful framework for explaining decision and choice behaviour?

There is a practical problem involved in describing conduct as the pursuit of goals. The general procedure is to assume some set of goals which seem *a priori* plausible and observe whether people's actions are consistent with such choices. This may or may not be done directly. It is normal, however, to be involved in some deductive chain before an actual testable result comes out. An assertion that actors maximize expected utility is tautological. Any choice, no matter how bizarre, can be seen as the consequence of a bizarre set of preferences. We need to be more specific and hypothesize the optimization of some variable where it is possible to imagine what the consequences of not optimizing it would be. This has to be specified independently of the observation of the choice itself (or, more commonly, set of choices). Thus, we might argue that an actor is maximizing money outcomes. This then is a perfectly testable proposition in that we can specify what sorts of choices by the actor would be consistent with this goal. Indeed, some critics argue it is bound to be wrong as long as people make such simplistic assumptions.

Even if we have avoided tautology at the initial stage by refusing to adopt an open-ended utility, we can still slip into a tautological procedure if we are not careful. Suppose a particular set of assumed goals does not predict correctly, then we can assume that either the choice of decision-making units or the choice of the utility function was incorrect. Somehow we can always come to a point where conduct is explicable in terms of an individual or a group making choices in the pursuit of goals. We need to specify externally to the general programme what the actors are, and specify what factors go into the utility functions for such theories to become non-tautological.

Further, we have to decide at what point the procedure itself and not just the particular nature of the utility function is at fault.

Almost any class of theories can be made tautological if we are willing to define its terms sufficiently broadly. This is the implication of Lakatos's analysis. Rational choice does not differ in principle from other forms of theorization in this respect. Though it is always the case that we can describe all forms of conduct as the optimization of some goal or another, if the procedure gets more and more cumbersome, requiring more and more convoluted assumptions about goals, then in time it will be seen as a degenerative programme. This will happen if preferences vary rapidly over time and are transitory. Reasonably stable preferences, or at least rules about how preferences alter, are required if the procedure is to be reasonably effective. The key to testable theories lies in its being possible to be reasonably abstemious with our definitions. The effective use of rational choice theory depends on striking a balance between tautology on the one hand and excessive naivety on the other.

There are many unanswered problems within rational choice analysis but problems, nevertheless, of a sort whose solution may add to the domain of the theory rather than constrain it. Conspicuous is the problem of preference. The stable preferences which Becker identified as a crucial requirement of a successful rational choice research programme do not appear to hold on many definitions of preference. However, rule-guided alterations in preferences might be a very fruitful form of theory to explore. The case of crisis decision-making and groupthink illustrates this. Decision-makers may pursue their goals as they perceive them at the time in a perfectly efficient manner but come to regret it later. The Bay of Pigs was a clear case of this but many other crises exhibited the same post-crisis tristesse. That is, the goals and preferences of the decision-takers became temporarily warped by the stress of the crisis (Nicholson, 1992). This is not explicable in terms of constant preferences. However, this is not a case of tautologically adjusting the preference in order to get the facts to fit the theory. Janis (1982) has offered a theory of such preference change which we have merely incorporated into the rational choice theory. This is a perfectly proper development of a scientific research programme in which the positive heuristic is appropriately adjusted to defend the hard core.[6]

Whether rational choice theory will prove in the long run to be a progressive research programme in either the social sciences in general or international relations in particular can be said with confidence only when it has been explored further. So far, it seems to be doing well and the contributions to certain aspects of strategic thinking at the very least have been very helpful. It may, of course, stop at this point. All we can say is that we have a research programme which straddles the social sciences, with international relations as a prominent feature, and which looks at the moment to be a progressive one.

So far we have stayed carefully with the view that rational choice theory is explanatory and not prescriptive. Thus, the goals of an actor were accepted for what they were without comment. However, description and explanation are often pursued as preludes to prescription while the name 'rational choice theory' suggests a normative interpretation. Thus it seems natural to consider some normative interpretations of the work.

There are three possible questions which can be analysed using goal-directed models in the rational choice manner: first, 'Is this how people in fact behave?'; secondly, 'Is this behaviour rational?'; and thirdly, 'What should I recommend that the actor should do (or what would I do myself) in order to be rational?' The first is an empirical question which we have already addressed. The last two are normative questions. It is important to distinguish between them as the name suggests that it is the last two which are of central interest.

We can ask the second question either in the narrow sense of instrumental rationality or a broader sense in which we are prepared to make judgements about the nature of the goals and beliefs on which the rationality is based. Elster (1983) distinguishes usefully between the 'thin theory of rationality', which is instrumental rationality, and the 'broad theory of rationality'. The second brings in judgements about the goals themselves and the belief structures on which they are based. Thus, on the broad theory of rationality, we can call certain sorts of beliefs irrational. This moves from the detached non-judgemental view of rationality but it gets closer to the more common concept of rationality.

Let us return to the rain dance. On the belief structure of the people who perform such a dance, this is rational in the instrumental sense. However, the theory on which such a custom would be effective is not a part of modern meteorology and it is most unlikely that evidence would confirm that it was a useful procedure.[7] Thus, if we go back a step and regard some belief structures as more rational than others, the procedure becomes irrational if related to the more rational belief structure. While it is fashionable in certain circles to treat non-scientific beliefs with deference, I adopt a more robust approach. If the aim is to produce rain, a rain dance will not suffice (nor will anything else) and one might as well accept the fact. It can be argued that the rain dance does no harm either and people might as well enjoy it. This is a perfectly acceptable argument provided they do not delude themselves. However, some procedures are harmful. If propitiating the rain god involves sacrificing six virgins, then there is every reason to try to stop the procedure. Similarly, if complex religious ceremonies intended to induce rain involve diverting resources from an irrigation project, there is a similar reason for trying to persuade people that their viewpoint is mistaken and, in the terminology of this book, irrational.

Once we move from the explanatory to the normative the need to understand the goals of the actors and the conceptual framework in which they operate becomes clearer. For example, suppose we are concerned with groups which use terrorism as a political tool. It is conventional for their opponents to regard them as either mad or wicked. However, from the point of view of the terrorists they are freedom fighters, or fighters in a holy war or whatever. Thus, to execute a captured terrorist might have the very opposite effect from that which the authorities desired in that it creates a martyr and brings new people into the movement. Without some conception of the belief structures of the terrorists, opponents will have little chance of understanding the appropriate ways of either defeating or negotiating with them. This does not preclude viewing their beliefs as mistaken or even wicked but it does involve understanding them.[8] However, once again we are in the area of explanation in terms of understanding in order the better to act more effectively in the world. The need, however, is to distinguish between the two.

Notes

1 This also applies to the concept of 'indifference'. A and B are said to be indifferent if, in a choice situation, a decision-maker does not mind which of the options is selected. The transitivity rule then states that, for all alternatives to which A is preferred, then B is similarly preferred to them and similarly all alternatives which are preferred to A are likewise preferred to B.

2 This does not preclude free will. The rules (and goals) are what people in fact follow. Thus, every morning I have a cup of coffee; this is a very simple form of rule which I follow and which could be confirmed by anyone sufficiently interested. I have perfect freedom to break this rule and very occasionally do, but it is a very good predictive principle.

3 What really was dubious from an instrumentally rational point of view was fighting both the USA and USSR at the same time. If Hitler could have pacified the West and concentrated on attacking the Soviet Union, he might well have succeeded in many of his aims.

4 I discuss these issues in greater detail in Nicholson (1983, Chapter 13) and Nicholson (1992, Chapters 6 and 7).

5 For further discussions of the issue of the scientific status or otherwise of psychoanalysis see Sherwood (1969) and Farrell (1981).

6 Many important problems concerning the complexities of preference are

raised by Sen (1977) and Elster (1979, 1983). I shall not elaborate on them further here.

7 In the drought of 1976 in Britain, there were many prayers for rain. These were based on the same sort of principles as a rain dance. There was, to my knowledge, no clear correlation between the incidence of prayer and the incidence of rain.

8 Michael Walzer's (1977) discussion of terrorism, particularly in terms of resistance movements in World War II, makes this point clear.

9
Values, policy and international relations

Policy and the separation of fact from value

The classic empiricist position is to argue that facts (and theories) are separate from values and, in particular, moral values. Thus, if we have a picture of the world consisting of theories established by empirical observations, this is separate from our values about the world and whether we are pleased that this is the case or not. The Earth goes round the Sun and not vice versa. No matter what our ethical viewpoint, we should accept this as true. The truth or falsity of particular theories has nothing to do with moral values. This view reached its limit with the logical positivists, who held that all statements other than the analytical or empirical statements of science were meaningless, but in the more moderate version of Popper we get science *demarcated* from moral values and metaphysics (which, unlike the logical positivists, he did not hold to be meaningless but merely different). This separation of fact from value is objected to by many, explicitly among some Marxist writers and critical theorists and implicitly among some in the classical tradition such as Martin Wight. Critical theorists argue that science is a social phenomenon which grows up under certain social conditions and reflects the values and power structure of the society in which it is practised. The very concepts which are used reflect the values of the society involved. I accept some of this argument. However, I shall argue that it not only can be but must be separated from the issue of whether a statement is true or false. I shall reconcile it with the traditional empiricist view, which I broadly accept. However, I shall show that there are some complications, rather than qualifications, which the more extreme versions of empiricism neglect.

Many, perhaps most, international relations theorists are motivated by a desire to improve the working of the international system, judged by many to be poor. Immediate policy application of theories may not be the issue but there is a long-run desire to understand the system in order to improve policy. This involves values. A choice (which is what a policy is about) involves selecting one set of consequences over another, but this means evaluating them not just factually but morally. What, then, is the relationship between facts, broadly construed to include theories, and moral and political values?

Values and value-free statements

The central issue in this debate relates moral judgements to scientific statements. Should moral judgements affect our judgement of what is true or false? Clearly, people do let their values influence their views on what is true or not but that is not the question here. The question is whether it is possible to separate judgements of truth from judgements of value.

It is easy to confuse the logical status of a statement as a scientific, factual statement and the context in which it is uttered. However, to do so is a mistake and it is important to distinguish between the two. I can best illustrate by giving an example. Suppose I were to have given a lecture on the ballistics of missiles at the time of the Nazi regime in Germany. I could hardly claim that it was a morally neutral act. However, the lectures themselves would have consisted of scientific statements most of which would have been highly confirmed by the data. There would be no moral statements mentioned: everything said would be totally value free. This essentially makes my point. A particular statement as such can be value free. However, where and to whom I choose to utter that statement involves value considerations. The act of asserting it involves value judgements inasmuch as it can be the case that people will act differently in the light of the information conveyed. This may seem like pedantry but it is not. If I am trying to find out what *is* true or false I must try to do so without being influenced by what I *would like to be* true or false. Similarly, as a social scientist in my professional capacity, I should try to be clear how far one can rationally believe in anything I assert to be true. However, there may be contexts where I feel that I should not tell the truth or, as in the case of ballistics in Nazi Germany, should simply refrain from saying anything. This, of course, raises a whole plethora of moral problems about telling the truth. Is omitting to say something true, knowing that this will affect someone's conduct, the same as telling a lie? However, these moral problems are not the subject of this book. I merely endeavour to show where the relationship between the nature of a statement which is true and the context in which that statement is made are separate issues.

In many cases, of course, the moral implications of the context are trivial, as they are for practically all articles published in academic journals. Many issues have no policy implications. Perhaps more commonly, the implications are unclear and it becomes a matter of faith that they will suggest no malign policies at some stage in the future or in conjunction with other pieces of knowledge about the international system. However, in a discipline such as international relations and the study of war, one is always poised on the edge of something which might have policy relevance. Suppose someone is interested in the issue of passive resistance. The person is a pacifist who believes that it is immoral to engage in active combat, with the aim of killing people. Passive resistance, however, is deemed a morally acceptable alternative. One may very well find out various strategies which make for more effective passive resistance. However, if this were to be discovered by a putative invader, they would be helped in finding out more effective ways of combating this passive resistance. The basis of the work would be on impeccably scientific principles of social psychology without a moral statement involved. However, it is a profoundly moral issue to whom one conveys this work.

Morals and the choice of subjects: feminist and Third World approaches

The most stringent positivists accept that the choice of a subject to research is a value judgement. If we choose to study war, it is because we are interested in war. This interest may come from a desire to stop it, because we are fascinated by it, because we want to fight it more efficiently, or because of some mixture of motives. But, however scientifically we study the issue, the initial choice of the issue was an extra-scientific choice. It can be seen as the purely personal choice of researchers as to which topic they should work on. Indeed, this is an important issue facing the researcher, and one which may have a profoundly moral aspect. The same is true for the natural scientist. This quickly leads on to the realization that which bits of science are developed and which not depends on the interests of the investigators. However, the pursuit of science requires resources both in terms of support for the scientists and of equipment. Social science is relatively cheap compared with some aspects of the natural sciences. There is no need for vast, expensive particle accelerators. Social science is not free, however. Libraries, computers and so on require expenditure and scholars require incomes. Surveys can be quite expensive. This means that the direction of research is influenced by the availability of resources. Those fields which are favoured by the owners of resources develop while the less favoured ones stagnate. Thus research which might have military implications has flourished in this century, particularly since World War II. Until it reaches the engineering stage, the research itself is value free, but the development of one set of subjects at the expense of others is not.

There are other and more subtle ways in which the direction of research can be influenced. International relations has grown up as an 'Atlantic' discipline, mainly pursued by white middle-class males most of whom are fluent in English even when it is not their native language. While the range of political attitudes among researchers is broad, from hard-line nationalist right-wingers to liberal internationalists to hard-line Marxists, nevertheless the view of the world is largely as seen by moderately privileged members of privileged societies. This has not gone unnoticed. Certainly since the 1960s such scholars as Johan Galtung (Galtung, 1976–80) have stressed this point, and the whole literature on dependency theory has been clear about this issue. A common pattern in the development of a domain of interest, such as environmental problems, is that an issue is raised initially in the context of the wealthy countries. It is then realized that it does not look quite the same from the perspective of poorer countries. This is followed by an effort to blend in the concerns of both poor and rich. Probably this is inevitable given the greater resources of richer countries which are available for thinking and research. However, it means that there is an inbuilt bias as to how problems are developed. This bias may or may not be corrected by the guilt this induces in the comparatively wealthy investigators who then feel the need to plead rather ostentatiously the cause of the poor, at least as they perceive it.

An example of this process was when a variety of computer models were developed following the 'Limits to Growth' work of Forrester and Meadows (1972), which aimed to analyse the future pattern of world resources (Meadows *et al.*, 1982). They suggested a pessimistic future as pollution rose and non-renewable resources fell. Significant falls in the output of the world economy and hence people's incomes, including those of the West, looked likely around a third of the way through the twenty-first century. Some Latin American scholars, with impeccable academic credentials, adopted an explicit Third World perspective and developed the 'Bariloche model', which was another computer model of the same general genre but working from a different basis (Meadows *et al.*, 1982). They pointed out that the conditions which were foretold for the West and which the original modellers dreaded were already in existence in Latin America (and other parts of the world for that matter). A problem looks more pressing if one suffers from it already than if one merely hopes to avoid it in the future (when it may not happen). The Bariloche scholars themselves were members of the elites in their respective societies (and indeed in the international scholarly society), so even they are not suffering from the problem in any direct sense. However, it is inevitable that scholars of the social world are detached to some degree from the problems they study. The poor, by definition, do not have the resources to carry out investigations into the causes of their poverty. Again, I stress that the studies internally do not involve value statements. The theories used are in themselves value free; the mathematics involved is devoid of moral content. The questions asked, however, are not.

The other major bias in the asking of questions is that international relations, as with practically every other branch of the study of society, has neglected the issue of gender. Until recently, writing has been 'gender blind' and theories were 'androgynous'. This has meant that significant questions have gone unasked. For example, wars are actually fought almost entirely by men, for whom violence seems to have a particular attraction, particularly when they are young. *Lysistrata and the Trojan Women,* where the women end by going to war, is effective because it is implausible. As war is such a central issue in international relations it seems odd for its strongly masculine nature to have gone unnoticed until recently. As Cynthia Enloe (1989) has pointed out, the view of woman as helpmeet to the man, mopping the tired warrior's brow and encouraging him to further acts of valour, is unusually strong in perceptions of the military, and yet it has been largely neglected. Outside international relations, the male obsession with violence seems to continue: crimes of violence in all societies are overwhelmingly committed by men. Terrorism, on the other hand, seems to be practised by women on a similar basis to men, an issue which in itself needs examination. Thus questions have gone unasked partly because of the nature of the group who have normally asked questions in the area.

Another relevant question is why women, when they reach high political office, behave so much like men. Thatcher of the UK, Bandaranaike of Sri Lanka, Gandhi of India, Meir of Israel, Bhutto of Pakistan – the list now goes on – are hardly symbols of the classic feminine virtues. One could not have told they were women from an analysis of their policies alone. This may be because the structure of the internal political environment means that only by being man-like (or, as some feminists might say, of the masculine gender but the feminine sex) will they achieve such positions, or because the structure of the international system such that choice is so highly constrained that there is not much an individual decision-maker can do. This is the structuralists' view of the system.

Many feminists would argue that the issue of feminism is more than an issue of unasked questions. The whole set of concepts are implicitly gender based. Discussion of this area can easily move on to the 'separate truths' type of argument for which I have already shown scant sympathy.

The consideration of the unasked questions raised by feminists is parallel with those raised over the Third World. What seems interesting to scholars depends to some extent on where they come from in society. There is an understandable tendency to examine issues which are seen as problematic from that perspective. However, this is not to say that such questions cannot be posed. Many people are devoid neither of goodwill nor empathy and the vigorous supporters of such theories as dependency theory are themselves from the élite. I return, however, to my main theme that the choice of the questions posed is a moral judgement but the mode of answering those questions is not, it is a scientific procedure.

Critical theory and 'conservative' empiricism

Many theorists view their theories as agents for change rather than tools of description. The empiricist account of the behaviour of the world is based on what is the case or has been the case in the past. This has led some critics to argue that it is conservative, implying a commitment to the *status quo*. It will be clear that I disagree with this view but first I shall briefly examine some theories which stress change.

Marx and Freud were both prominent in stressing that their theories were tools of change. They expressed this in similar ways. Thus Freud, in the introduction to one of his more detailed case studies, 'Little Hans', writes, 'Psychoanalysis is not an impartial scientific investigation, but a therapeutic measure. Its essence is not to prove anything, but merely alter something' (Freud, 1909). This is the clinician speaking who appears to disparage theory in a way which is scarcely borne out by his voluminous theoretical works and his frequent claims to be a scientist. Marx writes in similar vein in his Theses on Feuerbach: 'The philosophers have only interpreted the world, in various ways; the point, however, is to *change* it' (Marx, 1950). This statement was thought to characterize Marx's work so clearly that it was put on his tombstone. Though the domain of Marx's and Freud's work was very different, there are some remarkable similarities in style. Despite their apparent disdain for theory, both were prolific theoreticians. Marx was heavily involved in political action while Freud always had an extensive clinical practice, which makes it clear that, in both cases, their concern with practice and change was not just abstract. (The capacity for work of both was prodigious, though this is a separate issue.) The view of theory as being essentially critical of what is being theorized about as distinct from being essentially descriptive, as with the empiricists, has been taken up by several scholars in the Marxist tradition known, unsurprisingly, as 'critical theorists'. The origins and centre of this are in the Frankfurt School, one of the particularly prominent writers being Habermas (for example, Habermas, 1988). To a degree, Habermas's position was taken against Marx, though in a Marxist tradition. The tenor of Marx's work is deterministic and, indeed, it could be argued that there is something of a contradiction between his view that he was changing the world and the view that its path was already preordained in ways which were foreseen by Marxist theories. Habermas did not accept a determinist view. There are choices and it is up to theory to elaborate these choices. Theory, however, is a tool for change. The change is in the direction of 'empowerment' and 'emancipation' where this is meant to be the broadening of the choices of more people. There is an odd resonance with the vocabulary of some of those who advocate a full-blooded market economy, who likewise talk in terms of broadening choice (Friedman, 1962). The social and political perspectives of Milton Friedman and Jürgen Habermas could hardly be more different.

Many social scientists in international relations and elsewhere, who would otherwise see their views as very different from those of the critical theorists, would argue that their motive for working in the field was similarly a commitment to change. Kenneth Boulding is a clear case of someone holding this viewpoint (for example, Boulding, 1962). Their choice of topics is determined by this commitment. In particular, scholars working in the peace research tradition would emphasize this, peace research being the overt study of the conditions which promote peace. The peace research tradition is very broad and includes some who explicitly would call themselves critical theorists. It also contains many who follow the empirical social science tradition. Their choice of topic is determined by their values but the structure of the theory itself is independent of these values. Further, in order to promote change most effectively, it is argued that it is necessary to develop an explanatory theory of the structures in which change is desired. If one has a good account of the behaviour of the system, then one can specify the changes in behaviour which will be required in order to get a particular sort of change, with a greater hope of being correct. To have a good description of measles is not an endorsement of the moral worth of having measles any more than an analysis of poverty is an endorsement of poverty. In the natural sciences, good (in the sense of effective) engineering depends on good (in the sense of accurate) physics. The branches of physics which are best developed will often have engineering implications of a sort the sponsors are interested in (often the military), but the two activities are separate in principle if in practice intertwined. It is perhaps easier to think of pure science which is detached from its engineering applications than it is of pure engineering, which, at least in its more novel areas such as, today, the development of computers, involves as much science as engineering in the sense that the novel characteristics of the external world are being investigated. If critical theory is intending only to give an account of the motives of the researchers, it is interesting but nothing to do with our present concerns. In this case, peace researchers and many social scientists of an empiricist persuasion all become critical theorists and the category becomes more or less redundant. If the critical theorists argue that their theory is different because of their commitment to change, then the activity becomes highly suspect unless they are claiming to be designers, dependent on the scientist for the background theory and interested only in the results of that theory. However, this last does not seem to be an obvious reading of the genre.

Multiple benefits, multiple losses

In Chapter 6 we pointed out that an event such as a battle (or a famine or a public holiday) or an institution such as a pub, a theatre, or a factory looks very different to different people. Likewise, whether some new state of affairs which is projected by an act of policy is beneficial depends on how a person is affected and, when two people are affected similarly, upon their tastes, their view of the world and so on. This is a point properly stressed by the post-modernists (for example, Ashley and Walker, 1990b). However, the general point is an old one and one which troubled welfare economists in the earlier part of the century (Pigou, 1952; Van de Graaff, 1957). I have argued above that the motive behind most people's engagement with international relations is ultimately policy, however abstract their current analyses may be. They hope that their work will enable a more informed set of choices to be made so that the future behaviour of the international system will be different from what it would otherwise have been. This involves the moral judgement that the forms of international system that one hopes will come about are better than the ones which would other-wise obtain – in itself not a very profound remark. However, almost any act of choice means that some people will benefit and some people will lose. This is not a logical truth. It is possible for some act of policy to benefit everybody but such acts are rare. This raises a number of issues of which I will mention three. First, whom does a policy affect? Who benefits and who loses? Secondly, how do people who are affected perceive the relevant situations? Thirdly, on what basis do we compare the values of the benefits of one group to the losses of another?

The question of who benefits from some act of policy is not as straightforward as appears at first sight. There are two aspects to this. First, it is very easy, in any sort of analysis, to overlook some group which is affected. This is either because they are missed out altogether or the plausible collective interest of some subgroup is not noticed. Secondly, the preferences of a group, whether earlier neglected or not, may not be as clear-cut as they may superficially seem.

In the earlier analysis of the battle we showed that the view of the war differs radically according to the position of the actor. Descriptions of war often concentrate on the strategic, but ignore the interests of those over whose ground a battle is fought. Among those whom we accept as being affected, how do we group them in order to consider common interests? Everyone is individually affected by events; some people hate war but others are excited by it. However, some aggregation of individuals is legitimate and inevitable if we are to avoid intolerable complexity. Groups such as women have been neglected, as feminists have pointed out. But women can be sub-divided into poor women with lots of children who may be affected in one way and wealthy women from the élite who may be affected in other ways. Thus, 'women' may be an appropriate category for some purposes, 'poor' for others and so on. Further, it often appears to be the case that some event is obviously bad, such as war. But a formerly unemployed worker taken on by an aircraft factory, particularly in a country which is not likely to be directly attacked, clearly benefits from it. Most people would make the judgement that this is not worth a war, but it is foolish to deny that some people gain. To fly a bomber in 1944 was dangerous and unpleasant but perceived by many as glamorous, to be bombed by a bomber was simply dangerous and unpleasant; to make a bomber in Seattle was to be secure, physically and economically. This issue is constantly and properly raised in connection with the arms trade. Who is affected by some act of policy is in principle a scientific judgement. The difference in effects among different people is also factual and can in principle be determined. However, it is not an easy task.

The second issue derives from the first. Are we sure that people in fact perceive the benefits and drawbacks of a situation in the same way as we do? How those affected value their position, whether they like it or not, is also a factual matter. However, this raises some difficult problems which are ethical as much as practical. People may prefer a more traditional society which is materially poor to a more affluent society on the Western model. However, given a moderately affluent version of a Western model, as opposed to exchanging a rural slum for an urban slum with unemployment, most people seem to opt for the affluent. This involves strains and stresses on a society, and the concept of what people want becomes very ambiguous. This is shown in problems of family planning. On the surface it would seem that the long-term wealth of the society in general and themselves in particular would clearly benefit materially from their having small families. However, this is not always the case. A large family in a place where there is high mortality may be necessary to guarantee support in old age – a concept which is easily comprehensible to practically everyone. Even apart from this, people often have complex attitudes towards reproduction which are a mixture of cultural, religious and unconscious attitudes combined in a way which makes a ready analysis difficult. Such ambiguities are neglected both by the hearty modernizers who assume that an air-conditioned or centrally heated apartment is the acme of civilization, and the romantic traditionalists who swoon over insanitary and overcrowded slums in which they would personally not dream of living, except perhaps briefly to show their solidarity with the poor.

Given that, for almost all conceivable acts of policy, there are winners and losers, how to weight the one against another? This brings us into the field of ethical philosophy which it is not my purpose to enter. However, the problems do not disappear by using such blanket phrases as 'emancipation', 'liberation', 'modernization' or whatever. Discussions of policy involve both science and ethics and both sets of issues must be faced.

The empiricist's view of ethics and policy

I have asserted that most scholars in the field of international relations, including those in the empiricist tradition, view the discipline as a way of improving the world. This assertion is made on the basis of casual observation, though I think it probable that a systematic survey (which I should have done first to be totally consistent) would broadly confirm it. It is incorrect to say, as Hedley Bull (1969) at least implies, that empiricists are uninterested in moral questions. They wish to demarcate moral questions from scientific questions, and not confuse the two. This is not the same as arguing that moral questions are not important, or indeed crucial, as far as issues in international relations are concerned.

The empiricist is committed to the view that the cumulative growth of knowledge about the international system is possible and, though this need not necessarily follow, most would argue that it is occurring. It is a consistent but rather discouraging position to hold that such knowledge is possible but that none, so far, has been achieved. Most people would argue that the greater the knowledge of the international system or any other system, the greater the possibilities of controlling its behaviour. Again this does not directly follow from the belief in cumulative knowledge. If the international system is totally deterministic then there is nothing we can do. Policy is irrelevant as choice is ineffective.

Suppose, however, we do believe that choices are possible in the international system, which will in fact make a difference to its behaviour, and we can predict in a better than random manner what the consequences of such choices will be. How can we be sure that those who are in a position to control the international system by policies based on our theories will behave in ways which will meet with our approval? The scientific principles we discover may be used to pursue policies which we believe to be misguided or even immoral. I argued this above in the case of passive resistance, and it has certainly been the concern of many natural scientists working on subatomic physics. The boundary is sometimes very fine. One could work on bacteriological warfare to find adequate defences or to produce more sinister weapons; the actual scientific work is much the same. This problem has troubled some international relations scholars, particularly those working in the peace research tradition. Richardson was concerned that his arms race model would be used malignantly and wondered whether to suppress it (Ashford, 1985). Rapoport was deeply concerned about the strategic uses of the theory of games as applied to problems of nuclear war (Rapoport, 1965). Thus, even if one accepts that greater knowledge of a system implies greater control it does not imply that this control will be applied benevolently. This further assumption is a totally political one about who one hopes will be in the position of doing the controlling. The answer does not seem to be clear. However, there does not seem to me to be much reason for believing that bad science applied by malignant people will do much good either. Nazi theories of racial superiority helped no one (except, presumably, the sadists who were provided with an opportunity to gratify their tastes). The most one can do is pursue those parts of the scientific endeavour which seem most likely to lead to benevolent policy conclusions and do this in as rigorous a manner as possible. The road to perpetual peace is vague and unclear but it is most unlikely that it will be advanced by romantic confusion.

Glossary: some terms used but not explained in the text

Chaos theory

An outline of chaos theory is contained in the text (pp. 37–43). A slight amplification is relevant. The question arises because of the properties of certain non-linear differential equations (see under **function (in mathematics) and equation**). These have the properties described in the text, namely that their trajectories from closely neighbouring points diverge markedly for all points in the system. This in itself is a purely mathematical result and as such is abstract and has no necessary interpretation in the real world. It is necessarily true (assuming there are no mistakes, which are now unlikely given the number of mathematicians who have worked over the field). The significance of the mathematical result outside mathematics is that these sets of differential equations do turn out to be appropriate models for various processes in the real world, such as the pendulum system described in the text. Thus there is a direct parallel between the mathematics and the real world (I do not explore the nature of these links here. For a discussion of the problems see Körner (1960)). It is this which is at the centre of chaos theory. It is a relationship between the mathematics and what it describes. In the debate on Lighthill's admirable article on the subject (Lighthill, 1986), he makes one unfortunate response. To P. Mathias's comment that historically the indeterminate in science has proved on further investigation to be determinate, Lighthill responded that chaos theory was different, as it was a purely mathematical result and (error apart) was true. However, this establishes only that it is true mathematically. It is possible, though very improbable, that the chaotic mathematics may turn out to be inappropriate models of the physical systems and that a closely related but non-chaotic system might turn out to be the appropriate model. This is an empirical issue and not a logical issue as Lighthill incorrectly thought.

Reading: There are a large number of popular books on chaos theory and its development. A clear and reliable one is by Stewart (1989), a mathematician who has made frequent highly successful excursions into the popular exposition of mathematics. Lighthill

(1986) is a little harder going but admirably clear and quickly goes to the centre of the issue. He does not attempt to prove the results. I found this paper clarified issues which everything else had left obscure.

Empiricism
Empiricism is the view that knowledge of the external world comes from experience. There is no a priori knowledge. The approach advocated in this book is broadly empiricist. (See also **Positivism**.)

Epistemology
Epistemology is the study of the theory of knowledge, normally now construed as being about belief in the external world and hence in science. Why we should believe in generalizations in social science (or not, as the case might be) is an epistemological question. This book is mainly about epistemological questions (see also **methodology** and **ontology**).

Function (in mathematics) and equation
We can read the expression $y = f(x)$ as 'y is a function of x'. This means that as x varies, y also varies according to some rule, though the actual rule is unspecified in this very general form. One of the simplest functions is the *linear function* or *linear equation* where $y = mx + c$. In this, y and x are 'variables', meaning they can take on many values, while m and c are 'constants' and have fixed values. We call x the independent variable, meaning that it can take on any value, while the values of y, the dependent variable, are given by the equation and the values of x. If we plot y against x on a diagram, the result will be a straight line, hence the name. A *non-linear equation* is any other sort of equation. Thus, $y = x^2$ is a quadratic equation which is downward-sloping for negative values of x and upward-sloping for positive values of x. The equation $xy = k$ gives a rectangular hyperbola. Functions come in many, many forms and can have many, many variables. They are most useful as models of the real world when they are simple or can be manipulated into simple forms.

Mention has been made of *differential equations* (see also **Richardson model**). A differential equation is one where the rate of change of some variable is related to the absolute size of the variable. Thus, the rate of growth of a tree of a certain species might be related to its height. Let y be the size of the tree. We read the expression dy/dt as 'the rate of growth of y [the size] with respect to time'. We can write this as $dy/dt = f(y)$. We might go further and relate the rate of change to the rate of the rate of change (in some contexts 'acceleration'). The rate of the rate of change is written as d^2y/dt^2 and an equation might be

$$a.d^2y/dt^2 = b.dy/dt = f(y) \text{ and so on.}$$

Non-linear differential equations are represented by expressions such as $a.(d^2y/dt^2)^2 + b.dy/dt = f(y)$. Differential equations are central tools in much of physics.

Games, theory of (game theory)

Associated terms discussed: solution, zero-sum game, non-zero-sum game, prisoners' dilemma; matrix, pay-off matrix; maximin strategy, minimax strategy.

A 'game' is any conflict in the strategic mode; that is, where each participant follows some clear-cut goals and knows the rival to be doing the same thing. Players are supposed to be instrumentally rational (see p. 157). Chess is a good example. I make a move knowing that my opponent will respond to the move and, in formulating that response, bear in mind my own response to that response and so on. The word 'game' is unfortunate as it implies some basic lack of seriousness about the content. Strategic conflicts include everything from nuclear war to chess, or, indeed, noughts and crosses.

Important distinctions in the theory of games are between *two-person* and *n-person games*. In n-person games, where there are more than two parties, coalitions can be formed, increasing both their complexity and applicability. A further crucial distinction is between *zero-sum games* and *non-zero-sum games*. A zero-sum game is one where the gains of one are the losses of another, as in a game of cards for money. A non-zero-sum game is one where the amount to be divided varies according to the strategies used. Thus, in a court case over a bequest, the parties involved can hire some lawyers, pay them a large fee and have less to divide. Alternatively, the legatees and would-be legatees can arrange things among themselves, divide the whole lot and not pay any fees. In the latter case it is possible for all the legatees to be better off.

The aim of the theory is to find a *solution* to a game. In a two-person game this is a pair of strategies such that, if player A plays the solution strategy, the best response of B will also be the strategy to which A's solution strategy is the best response so far as A is concerned (the example below should make this clearer). Thus neither party has any incentive to move. Such a point is known as a *Nash equilibrium*. Not all games have solutions; some important ones from the point of view of application do not. However, all two-person zero-sum games have solutions in this sense.

We can illustrate the zero-sum game with a simple example of a game with no name – it is not sufficiently interesting to have one. The two players, A and B, each have three strategies; they lay down one of three cards. A(1) is the laying down of the ace of spades, A(2) is the laying down the ace of clubs and A(3) is the laying down of the ace of hearts. B(1) is the laying down of the king of spades, B(2) the king of clubs and B(3) the king of hearts. Now consider the table or *matrix* below which shows the payments for any pair of strategies. A payment from B to A is represented by a positive number while a payment from A to B is represented by a negative number. The matrix shows that, if A plays A(1) and B plays B(1) then B pays A £3. If A(2) is played against B(1) then A pays B £2. This matrix is known as the *pay-off matrix*.

A particular zero-sum game

		B's choice set			
		B(1)	B(2)	B(3)	minimum of row
	A(1)	3	0	-1	-1
A's choice set	A(2)	-2	-1	5	-2
	A(3)	2	1	3	1
Maximum of column		3	1	5	

What is the recommended 'rational' way for the players to play the game? For A we suggest looking at the first strategy in order to find the worst which could happen if this were played. This is the minimum of the row, namely payment out of £1 represented as –1. We recommend that this is done for each row and the minima for each row put in a list as is shown in the far right-hand column of the table. The player is then recommended to choose that strategy which gives the best of these worst outcomes. This is known as the *maximin strategy*. In this case, A(3) ensures that A does no worse than gain £1. This might seem a very pessimistic or overly prudent approach to the game but we can show why in this case the prudence might be justified. Consider B and recommend the same principle, though in this case the aim is to maximize the minimum or get the biggest negative outcome. The maximum for each of the columns is shown in the bottom row of the matrix. The smallest of these values is 1, which for B represents a loss of £1, and the player is recommended to choose the *minimax strategy* of B(2). A(3) against B(2) leads to a pay-off of £1 from B to A. We can show this is a solution as defined above. If A(3) is played then B cannot profit from moving away from B(2) as it will involve an even greater payment being made. Likewise, if B(2) is paid, A can get only a reduced payment by moving. Thus, this apparently pessimistic pair of strategies, generically known as 'maximin strategies', turns out to be the best the instrumentally rational actor can do.

The way of finding a solution for all two-person zero-sum games requires the use of 'mixed strategies'. (This extension is not necessary for the arguments of this book: see Rapoport (1974) or Nicholson (1992) for simple accounts.) However, even with mixed strategies, many non-zero-sum games do not have solutions. Further, the solutions of some games, even when they have them, have some curious properties.

This is so in the well-known *prisoners' dilemma*, a simple case of which I give below. The first number is the payment to A and the second the payment to B from some common fund.

A game of prisoners' dilemma

B's choice set

		B(1)	B(2)
A's choice set	A(1)	(3,3)	(1,4)
	A(2)	(4,1)	(2,2)

It can readily be seen that A(2) gives a better result than A(1) whether B plays B(1) or B(2) and similarly for B. Thus it seems obvious that A(2) and B(2) will be played by instrumentally rational players giving a value of (2,2). Further, (2,2) is the solution point, being a Nash equilibrium as defined earlier. Neither A nor B can benefit themselves by moving away from it. However, it is not as advantageous to either party as (3,3) so, though it is a solution, it lacks appeal. This apparent paradox is less acute if it is played repeatedly. However, it has involved many people in many hours of thought, work and worry, though its analysis has helped in our understanding of conflict.

Another famous game which has been applied to international situations is *chicken*.

A game of chicken

B's choice set

B(1)   B(2)

A's choice set   A(1) (3,3)   (1,4)

A(2) (4,1)   (0,0)

(3,3) would be the result of playing maximin strategies, though (4,1) and (1,4) would be solution points. There is a temptation to play aggressively and get a solution point as the rival can respond only by inflicting damage on themselves. However, both might do this in a game involving simultaneous play. In a repeated game this might be worth while. If one replaced (0,0) by (−100,−100) the dilemma becomes greater. International crises are sometimes modelled by chicken with severe mutual defect outcomes.

Reading: Locus Classicus: Von Neumann and Morgenstern (1944). Axelrod (1984) gives a now very famous analysis of the prisoners' dilemma and its applications. Nicholson (1992) and Rapoport (1974) give good general discussions while Rapoport (1966) gives a detailed discussion of two-person game theory. Binmore (1992) provides an excellent discussion of many issues involved in game theory.

Groupthink
Groupthink is the name applied to a form of behaviour sometimes exhibited in small groups under stress. Members of the group appear to feel a strong pressure to conform and stifle doubts about the group consensus while excluding people who challenge it. This leads to such characteristics as selecting information which confirms the group consensus while ignoring that which does not. This leads to perverse decision-making as the evidence on which decisions are made is highly slanted. The phenomenon was observed and studied by Irving Janis, a social psychologist, in business contexts. In a very influential book (Janis, 1982), he applied the principles to the analysis of governmental decision-making in international crises, both to situations where groupthink had occurred and to those in which it did not.

Reading: Janis (1982) presents an extremely readable account of the concept applied in international contexts. Smith (1985) puts forward another interesting application in international relations. Nicholson (1995) relates groupthink directly to rational choice theory.

Hermeneutics
The analysis of meaning. Adherents of the hermeneutic approach consider only the meaning of utterances and acts to be the appropriate material for social analysis. It is thus closely related to the Winchean approach. However, some degree of hermeneutic understanding is involved in most analyses of social affairs.

Idealism (in philosophy)
Idealism as a philosophical doctrine is the view that what exists is ideas and that the supposed external world is merely a reflection of those ideas. It contrasts with philosophical **realism**.

Idealism (in international relations)
Idealism is applied to a school of thought in international relations, popular in the inter-war years, whose adherents held that states' behaviour could be made more peaceful as they recognized their long-run self-interests. The school believed that states could achieve peace by banding together in collective security arrangements to combat aggression. It was associated with support of the League of Nations. Idealists of that era still regarded the international system as being primarily a system of states, as did their **realist** opponents. However, they thought that wider and more benevolent sets of behaviour were possible within the context of a states system. Idealism can be used more generally to describe any approaches to international relations which stress the possibilities of change in the international system to make it more peaceful. Idealism is used here in the sense of 'idealistic' and contrasts with realism. However, the contrast between idealism and realism in international relations has nothing to do with the contrast between idealism and realism in philosophy. It is generally agreed that the terms as applied in the different fields have little to do with each other. Charles Reynolds disagrees, particularly in Reynolds (1992). See also Nicholson (1993) for a criticism of Reynolds's argument.

Methodology
Methodology is the study of the methods by which one investigates the external world, or, in the instances we are primarily interested in, the social world. Thus, the underlying principles of statistical

analysis and their bases in probability theory are methodological studies. The boundary between methodology and epistemology is often blurred. In 'The methodology of positive economics', Milton Friedman (1966a) discusses issues which here are regarded more as epistemological.

Newton's laws of motion
Newton deduced three basic laws of motion which can be stated as follows.

The First Law of Motion: Every body tends to continue in a state of rest or in uniform motion in a straight line unless it is compelled by an externally applied force to change that state.

The Second Law of Motion: When two bodies are exerting forces upon each other, the magnitude of the two forces is equal and the directions are opposite.

The Third Law of Motion: The rate of change of the momentum of a body is proportional to the forces acting upon it and it has the same direction.

Ontology
Ontology is the branch of metaphysics which deals with what things exist. In Quine's version it is the enquiry into what things must exist in order for it to be possible to hold on to a given theory. Thus the 'existence' of goals and theoretical concepts is an ontological question. (See also **epistemology**).

Pluralism
Pluralism is an approach to international relations in which it is argued that there are other significant actors in the international system besides states. Organizations such as the United Nations (UN) and the International Monetary Fund (IMF) are actors in their own right and are not just deputizing for states (though the degree to which they are is an issue of dispute). Other international non-governmental organizations (INGOs), such as religious organizations like the Vatican or voluntary organizations such as Greenpeace or Amnesty, are often significant actors if they can mobilize resources. Of great importance are multinational corporations (MNCs).

Positivism
Positivism is originally associated with the French sociologist Auguste Comte in the first half of the nineteenth century and reached its apogee with the Vienna Circle and logical positivism in

the inter-war period. It is an extreme form of **empiricism** in which only statements expressing knowledge derived from experience, along with logical and mathematical statements, are held to be meaningful. The term is used rather casually among social scientists to mean any sort of scientific approach to social behaviour. Hence, Friedman talks of 'positive economics' with approval while 'post-positivism', in the mid-1990s, is the term of approval of those who think (in my view incorrectly) that they have exposed the follies of 'scientistic analysis'.

Probability
Probability is a measure of the degree of risk. It is conventionally measured between 0 and 1. If an event is certain, such as that indicated by the statement 'it will rain in London between 1 January and 31 March in the year 2000', we define its probability as 1. If the statement is represented as E, then $P(E) = 1$. Likewise, if statement F is 'It will snow in Cairo on 1 July 2000', then $P(F) = 0$. Both these numbers denote certainty. Empirically we can never be absolutely certain (there may be a nuclear war or startling changes in the climate), hence we might more prudently say the the probabilities are 'nearly 1' and 'nearly 0'. If a statement G is 'Sonny Boy will win the next Derby' we will give it a probability somewhere in between. We might say $P(G) = 0.5$, which is an assertion of great uncertainty. It is a formal statement of what is informally referred to as 'fifty-fifty' (which implicitly takes 0 to 100 as the range of the measure and is then often referred to in percentages) or, in the language of odds, as 'evens'. This assumes that Sonny Boy is eligible for the Derby and is not an elderly donkey.

Much statistical inference is based on the notion of whether some pattern or another could plausibly have come about according to the rules of probability. This is best seen in very stylized contexts such as the tossing of two coins together. Each coin has a probability of ½ of coming down heads. If coin A comes down heads it in no way influences (that is, is totally independent of) coin B, which still has a probability of ½ of coming down heads. Thus there is a probability of ¼ of their both coming down heads (that is, ½ times ½). This concept of independent events is central in this sort of analysis. We can use this analysis to say that over a sufficiently large number of occasions we will get the following results:

Two heads:	about 25 per cent
Two tails:	about 25 per cent
One head and one tail:	about 50 per cent

Suppose we now want to analyse a real-life situation. We want to test whether spouses' voting habits between Labour and Conservative are independent of each other where the probability of anyone voting Labour or Conservative is equal. We would compare their voting habits against the random pattern generated above. Pure chance would mean that about a quarter of couples would both vote Conservative, a quarter both vote Labour and about half would disagree. If the proportions were markedly different (as I would expect), then spouses' voting habits would be interdependent. One can work out the degree of interdependence by elaborating the model.

The *probability calculus* is the more formal statement of these rules. We can state them in terms of two independent events like the tossing of two coins above. Call the two events (such as 'heads' being the result of the tossing of a coin) A and B. The probabilities of the events are $P(A)$ and $P(B)$ respectively.

Rule 1 $0 < P(A) < 1$ and $0 < P(B) < 1$

This simply states that probability is measured between 0 and 1.

Rule 2 $P(A \text{ and } B) = P(A).P(B)$

This states that the probability of the two events occurring together (such as two heads) is the two individual probabilities multiplied together. Thus on about half the number of occasions, the first coin will come up heads. On about half these occasions, the second will also come up heads. Hence both will come up heads on about a quarter of the total occasions.

Rule 3 $P(A \text{ or } B) = P(A) + P(B) - P(A \text{ and } B)$

The probability of at least one head coming up is the sum of the probabilities for each coin. However, the probability of two heads coming up will have been counted twice – once for each coin – so it has to be taken away once to avoid this double counting.

There are some occasions where the interpretations of probability are fairly conventional and straightforward. Thus, in the case of tossing a coin we can measure the probability either from considerations of symmetry or by observing a sequence of throws. Such situations are referred to as risk. However, in the case of Sonny Boy above, there is no objective way of measuring probability. Some allege it has no meaning in this sort of context. Others claim that people either do or should formulate *subjective probabilities* (or, in Savage's (1972) terminology, *personalistic probabilities*), which are manipulated in the same way. This school is known as the Bayesian school of probability theory.

Applications: The theory of probability can best be seen as a theory of rational belief in the face of uncertainty. However, there is a lot of evidence that people in decisions under risk violate the principles of the probability calculus.

Reading: There are many good expositions of probability theory, one example being Allen (1962). Savage (1972) is to be recommended for a Bayesian point of view, while I introduce the notions in the context of international relations in Nicholson (1989). Cohen (1972) discusses how people do in fact behave under conditions of uncertainty, which does not always correspond with how they ought to behave according to probability theory.

Realism (in philosophy)
Realism is the view that the world exists independently of our perception of it.

Realism (in international relations)
Realists argue that the international system is characterized by three basic characteristics: (a) the primary actors are states; (b) 'interest in terms of power' (Morgenthau, 1948) is the primary goal of states' behaviour; and (c) internal and external politics are almost independent of each other (in some versions, the third principle can be deduced from the first two). Peace can be achieved only by recognizing the realities of power and adjusting to them by such devices as the balance of power. Realism is used in the sense of facing reality without illusions though some might hold that this prejudged the issue. Earlier theorists of international relations from Thucydides, through Machiavelli, Hobbes and Clausewitz were almost automatically realists. However, the shock of World War I made people sceptical of the peacemaking properties of the balance of power and led to ***idealism***. This in its turn was queried with the rise of Nazi Germany and the expansionary policies of Japan. Realism returned with E. H. Carr in 1939 and carried on after World War II with writers such as Morgenthau. The later critiques of realism, from around 1960 on, maintained that it was scientifically flawed, in that it did not adequately describe an international system in which there were many actors other than states (such as economic actors). This contrasts with the critique of the idealists that it was morally flawed. See *idealism*, *pluralism*, *structuralism* in the Glossary and *neo-realism* on pp. 91–92.

The Richardson Model of an arms race

The simple Richardson Model
This can be represented algebraically as follows. Denote A's desired level of arms by X the actual level by x and Y, and y for B's desired and actual level. a, b, and c are constants, the first two reflecting the sensitivity of the desired level to the actual level and c representing some 'grievance' coefficient. A's desired level of arms is given by

$$X = ay - bx + c \tag{A1}$$

and B's desired level by

$$Y = dx - ey + f \tag{A2}$$

When A is at the desired level, $X = x$ and equation (1) which relates the desired level of A's arms to any level of B's can be written in standardised form as:

$$y = x(1 + b)/a - c/a \tag{A3}$$

Similarly (2) becomes:

$$y = xd/(1 + e) + f/(1 + e) \tag{A4}$$

Suppose that all the coefficients a, b, c, d and e are positive and that

$$(1 + b)/a < d(1 + e) \tag{A5}$$

This is the condition for B's security line to slope less steeply than A's so that A's line cuts B's from below. This condition gives the stable version of the Richardson model in which armaments all move towards the equilibrium point, as illustrated in Figure G1.

Suppose now that

$$(1 + b)/a > d/(1 + e) \tag{A6}$$

A's line now cuts B's from above as is shown in Figure G1.

This is the condition for the unstable version of the Richardson Model in which the level of arms goes away from the equilibrium point. This conclusion is counter-intuitive but follows directly from the assumptions.

The differential equation model
Richardson posed the model in terms of differential equations. The two-state case is set out here for direct comparison with the above model.

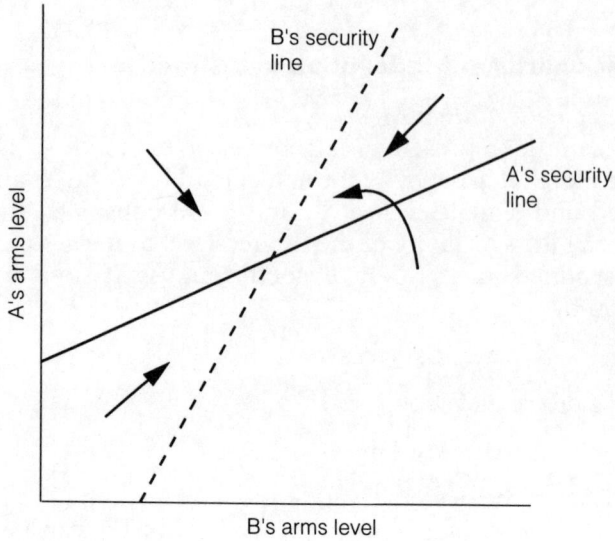

Figure G1 The Richardson Model: the stable case

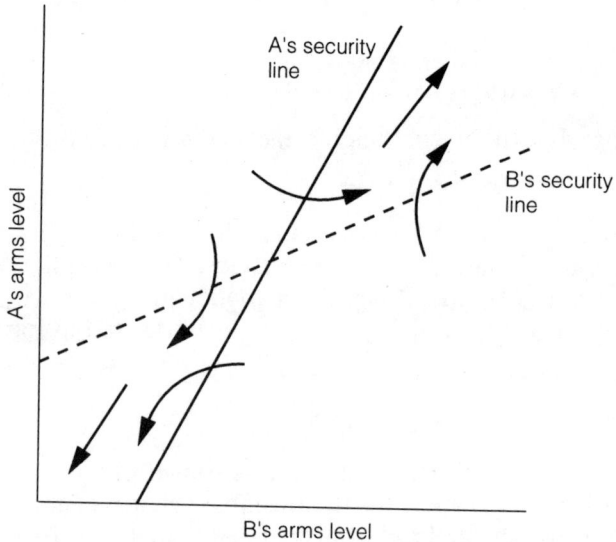

Figure G2 The Richardson Model: the unstable case

The differential equation which describes B's rate of rearmament is

$$dy/dt = lx - \beta y + h \qquad (A7)$$

and for A's

$$dx/dt = ky - \alpha x + g \qquad (A8)$$

$dy/dt = O$ gives B's security line and $dx/dt = O$ gives A's.
$dy/dt = dx/dt = O$ is the equilibrium point.

The model is stable if $\alpha\beta > 1.k$ and unstable if $\alpha\beta < 1.k$ See Nicholson (1989) for a more detailed discussion of the relationship between the two models.

Reading: There are many expositions of the Richardson model to compensate for its earlier neglect: a good one is in Rapoport (1974). The model is widely discussed in the literature. An excellent general view of Richardson's overall contribution to the study of war and peace is given by Rapoport (1957). I have described a simple version of the Richardson model in Nicholson (1992) and in greater technical detail in Nicholson (1989). My version, though slightly less precise than the 'classical' model, has the expository advantage of doing without differential equations. Locus Classicus: The original version of this model with a detailed discussion is found in Lewis Fry Richardson's *Arms and Insecurity* (1960a) which is one of the most original works in international relations ever written.

Solar system: theories
The solar system (or planetary system) is the set of planets, comets and other bodies which go round the Sun, most attention being paid to the planets. The Sun itself is one rather ordinary star in a universe of many millions. The motions of the planets (whose name means 'wanderer') have always been a centre of interest. While, as viewed from the Earth, the stars kept a fixed position with regard to each other, the planets constantly move with respect to other astronomical bodies. Explanations of the pattern of their movements was an enduring source of interest for astronomers.

The traditional view was that the Earth was flat, as common sense would seem to indicate, and that the Sun, Moon and stars went round the Earth in regular motions, likewise in accordance with common sense. The solar system was geocentric. The planets were a problem, but some account of their movement could be given by means of *epicycles*. Suppose P (for planet) is a point on the circle C(1) with centre E (for earth) as illustrated in Figure G3.

P goes round along the circle's trajectory. Suppose we now have another circle, perpendicular to the first, whose centre is P as illustrated in Figure G4. If the point Q goes round the point P in a regular motion while P continues to go round E, Q's motion will look very complex and probably erratic from the point of view of E, though in fact it is quite simple and orderly. Just what pattern it will transcribe depends on whether C(2) goes round faster or slower than C(1) and by how much. This is known as a system of epicycles, and can be made more and more complicated by putting a further epicycle around $C(2)$ and so on. By a sufficiently complex system of epicycles, almost any pattern of movement can be accounted for. The movements of the planets were described in this form by the classical geocentric astronomers.

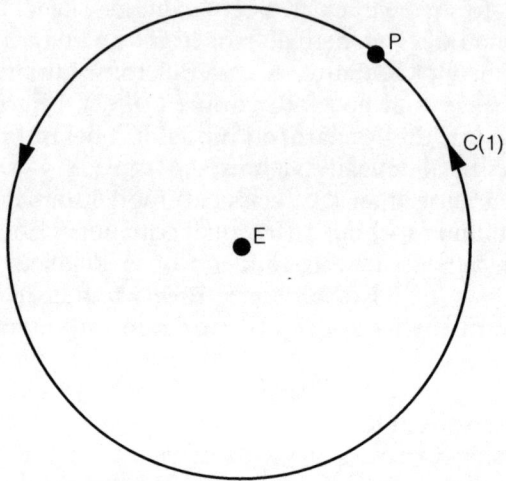

Figure G3 A planet with a circular trajectory

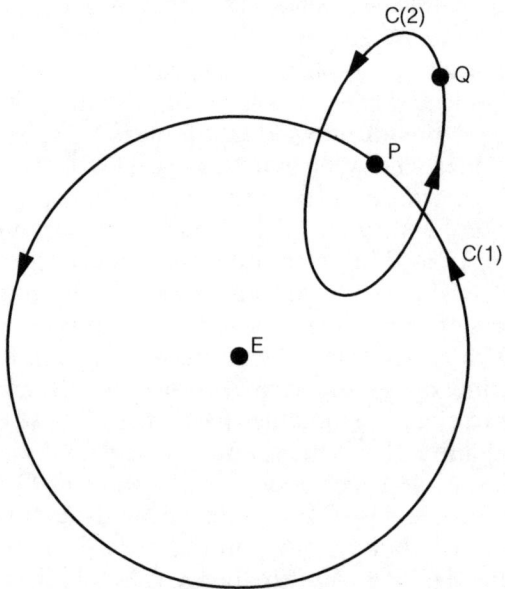

Figure G4 An epicycle

Nicolaus Copernicus proposed an alternative system in which the Sun was the centre of the solar system (and the Universe, but we shall not touch on that here). The planets, of which the Earth was one, went round the Sun in circular orbits. Unfortunately, the predictions about the positions of the planets were little better than those of the geocentric theory. Further, it was against the teaching of the Catholic Church, of which Copernicus was a devout member, though there was sympathy in some clerical quarters including, though somewhat unreliably, the future Pope.

Johannes Kepler modified the Copernican system in very major ways. He argued that (a) the planets went round the Sun in elliptical orbits with the Sun at one of the foci, though it took him some time to realize that an ellipse was the appropriate curve; (b) the speed of the planets was not constant but proportional to the area covered by the ellipse shown by the areas A and B, where S is the Sun; and (c) the squares of the times of the revolutions of the planets are proportional to the cubes of their mean distances from the Sun. (This law was formulated in 1619, a little later than the others.) Kepler's scheme is illustrated in Figure G5.

This revised version of the heliocentric theory gave magnificently accurate predictions and (except for the modifications required by the theory of relativity) is substantially the theory held today.

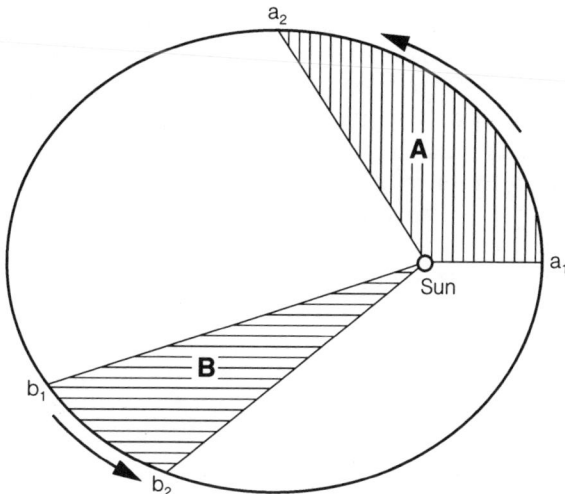

Figure G5 A planet with an elliptical trajectory

Reading: Hanson (1962) gives an excellent account, likewise Thomas Kuhn in *The Copernican Revolution* (1957). See also Munn (1973).

Structuralism

Structuralists hold that the structure of the international system (or any other social system) determines behaviour and that the choices of actors are essentially constrained by the system. Thus, the industrial revolution or the colonial expansion of the European powers would be explained by the social/political/economic factors of the day rather than in terms of any individuals involved. The issue can, of course, be posed as 'How much does structure matter?' rather than in all or nothing terms. Marxist theories, and theories directly inspired by Marxism, are the structuralist theories most commonly discussed. Core explanatory concepts are then class and the economy or, more recently, gender. However, it is a mistake, as is often implied, to assume that structuralist theories are necessarily Marxist or are particularly closely related to Marxism. (See also p. 83 of the text.)

Utility

Associated terms: utility function and expected utility.

Utility is the attractiveness of some state of affairs to an individual. Consider the preferences of an individual. Suppose that individual prefers A (say a car) to B (say a sailing boat). This can be is represented by A (P) B, where (P) denotes the phrase 'is preferred to'. We can express this as A has a higher utility (for the individual, from now on understood) than B. This now can be represented as $u(A) > u(B)$, where $>$ now stands for 'is greater than'. Though the language is now quantitative, in fact the second expression says no more (and no less) than the first.

A *utility function* is defined for a decision-maker where the arguments of the function – that is, the utility-giving variables – appear in a particular mathematical function. Thus, abstractly, $u = u(x, y)$. Suppose we have two sets of values for x and y, namely (x_1,y_1) and (x_2,y_2) where we find $u(x_1,y_1) = u(x_2,y_2)$, meaning that the decision-taker has difficulty in deciding which is preferred. The two bundles of utility-giving entities are said to be *indifferent*. The functional form $u(x,y)$ can be specified from observation for any sets of indifferent bundles even if the relationship between a set of values of the variables preferred to another set of values can only be specified ordinally.

The *expected utility model* is a method of defining some sort of measure for utility in the context of a conceptualization of decisions taken under risk. Suppose that the individual is offered a choice between two gifts, a choice of B for certain or A dependent on a coin falling heads up. Thus, there is a probability of 0.5 of a prize of a car but also a probability of 0.5 of remaining in the same position, the utility of which will be denoted by u(0). Let us suppose that the individual is undecided which to take. We can say then that, as compared with the current position, the utility of the gamble is equal to the utility of B for certain. That is

u[A with probability 0.5 and 0 with probability 0.5] = u(B)

From this it is a short step (but one which needs justifying, though not here) to affirming that

(0.5)u(A) + (0.5)u(0) = u(B)

Rearranging gives

[u(A) − u(0)] = 2[u(B) − u(0)]

This states that the increase in utility of moving from the original position to position A is twice that of moving from the original position to B. My justification is only a hint, though it can be found in any textbook on decision theory or the theory of games. Briefly, it can be shown (though again not here) that if an individual has consistent preferences and makes decisions in accordance with the principles of the probability calculus, then the measure follows. The result is initially surprising and somewhat impressive. There is no real meaning to zero utility in the same sense as there is meaning to the concept of zero weight. We have an arbitrary zero in much the same sense as the arbitrary zero in temperature scales such as the Celsius scale. The measure is a measure of the ratios of *intervals* and a minimum of three points is required to make it meaningful. Strictly, it is just a measure of utility in the context of risk-taking situations. It has no necessary interpretation outside those.

The expected utility model was first formulated in its present form by Von Neumann and Morgenstern (1944); some sort of measure was needed if the theory of games was not going to be restricted to a very narrow range of situations. It has been very extensively used in all branches of the social sciences.

Reading: Locus Classicus: von Neumann and Morgenstern (1944). A rigorous analysis is given by Savage (1972). There are innumerable expositions, including my own which is in the context of international relations (Nicholson, 1989).

Bibliography

Allen, R. G. D. (1962) *Basic Mathematics* London: Macmillan.

Allison, Graham T. (1971) *Essence of Decision: Explaining the Cuban Missile Crisis* Boston: Little Brown.

Appleyard, Bryan (1992) *Understanding the Present: Science and the Soul of Modern Man* London: Pan Books.

Archibald, C. G. (1966) 'Refutation or comparison'. *British Journal for the Philosophy of Science*, 17(4): 279–96.

Arrow, Kenneth (1963) *Social Choice and Individual Values* New York: Wiley.

Ashford, Oliver M. (1985) *Prophet or Professor: The Life and Work of Lewis Fry Richardson* London: Hilger.

Ashley, Richard K. and Walker, R. B. J. (eds) (1991a) 'Spreading the language of exile: dissidence in international studies'. Special issue of *International Studies Quarterly* on postmodernism, 34(3).

Ashley, Richard K. and Walker, R. B. J. (1991b) 'Spreading the language of exile: dissident thought in international studies'. *International Studies Quarterly*, 34(3): 259–68.

Axelrod, Robert (1984) *The Evolution of Cooperation* New York: Basic Books.

Ayer, A. J. (1970) *Language, Truth and Logic* (First published 1936) London: Gollancz.

Banks, Michael H. (1985) 'The inter-paradigm debate in Light'. In M. and A. J. R. Groom (eds) *International Relations: A Handbook of Current Theory* London: Pinter.

Becker, G. (1976) *The Economic Approach to Human Behavior* Chicago: University of ChicagoPress.

Binmore, Ken (1992) *Fun and Games: A Text on Game Theory* Lexington, MA: Heaston.

Blackburn, Simon (1994) *The Oxford Dictionary of Philosophy* Oxford: Oxford University Press.

Blaug, M. (1992) *The Methodology of Economics or How Economists Explain* Cambridge: Cambridge University Press.

Bloom, William (1990) *Personal Identity, National Identity, and International Relations* Cambridge: Cambridge University Press.

Booth, Ken and Smith, Steve (eds) (1995) *International Political Theory Today* Cambridge: Polity Press.

Boulding, Kenneth (1962) *Conflict and Defense: A General Theory* New York: Harper & Row.

Braithwaite, R. B. (1953) *Scientific Explanation* Cambridge: Cambridge University Press.

Braithwaite, R. B. (1955) *The Theory of Games as a Tool for the Moral Philosopher* Cambridge: Cambridge University Press.

Brams, Steven (1985) *Superpower Games: Applying Game Theory to Superpower Conflict* New Haven: Yale University Press.

Brecher, Michael; Wilkenfeld, Jonathan and Moser, Shelia (1988) *Crises in the Twentieth Century* (2 vols) Oxford: Pergamon Press.

Brecher, Michael and Wilkenfeld, Jonathan (1989) *Crisis, Conflict and Instability* Oxford: Pergamon Press.

Bremer, Stuart, (1980) 'National capabilities and war proneness'. In J. D. Singer (ed.), *Quantitative International Politics* New York: Free Press.

Bremer, Stuart (ed.) (1987) *The Globus Model: Computer Simulation of Worldwide Political and Economic Developments* Frankfurt am Main: Campus Verlag.

Brown, Chris (1992) *International Relations Theory: New Normative Approaches* Hemel Hempstead: Harvester Wheatsheaf.

Brown, Chris (1994) 'Critical theory and postmodernism in international relations'. In M. Light and A. J. R. Groom (eds) *International Relations: A Handbook of Current Theory* London: Pinter.

Bueno de Mesquita, Bruce (1981) *The War Trap* New Haven: Yale University Press.

Bueno de Mesquita, Bruce (1992) *War and Reason: Domestic and International Imperatives* New Haven: Yale University Press.

Bueno de Mesquita, Bruce; Krasner, Stephen J. and Jervis, Robert (1985) 'Symposium: methodological foundations of the study of international conflict'. *International Studies Quarterly* 29(2): 119–54.

Bull, Hedley (1969) 'International theory: the case for classical approach'. In K. Knorr and J. N. Rosenau (eds) *Contending Approaches to International Politics* Princeton: Princeton University Press.

Bull, Hedley (1977) *The Anarchical Society: A Study of Order in World Politics* London: Macmillan.

Buzan, Barry (1987) *An Introduction to Strategic Studies* London: Macmillan.

Carr, E. H. (1939) *The Twenty Years Crisis 1919–1939* London: Macmillan.

Chalmers, A. F. (1982) *What Is This Thing Called Science?* Milton Keynes: Open University Press.

Chalmers, A. F. (1990) *Science and Its Fabrication* Milton Keynes: Open University Press.

Cioffi-Revilla, Claudio (1990) *The Scientific Measurement of International Conflict* Boulder: Lynne Rienner.

Clausewitz, C. (1984) *On War* (M. Howard and P. Paret, eds. First published 1833) Princeton: Princeton University Press.

Cohen, John (1972) *Psychological Probability, or, The Art of Doubt* London: Allen & Unwin.

Collingwood, R. G. (1946) *The Idea of History* Oxford: Clarendon Press.

Crystal, David (1990) *The Cambridge Encyclopedia of Language* Cambridge: Cambridge University Press.

Dawkins, Richard (1989) *The Blind Watchmaker* London: Penguin.

Der Darien, James and Shapiro, Michael (eds) (1989) *International/Intertextual Relations: Post-modern Readings in World Politics* Lexington: Lexington Books.

Deutsch, Karl, W. (1963) *Nationalism and Social Communication* Cambridge: MIT Press.

Deutsch, Karl, W. (1964) *The Nerves of Government* New York: Free Press.

Diehl, Paul (1983) 'Arms races and escalation: a closer look'. *Journal of Peace Research*, 20(3): 205–12.

Diehl, Paul (1985) 'Arms races to war: testing some empirical linkages'. *Sociological Quarterly*, 27: 331–49.

Dowding, Keith and King, Des (eds) (1995) *Preferences, Institutions and Rational Choice* Oxford: Oxford University Press.

Dray, W. H. (1957) *Laws and Explanations in History* London: Oxford University Press.

Edelson, M. (1984) *Hypothesis and Evidence in Psychoanalysis* Chicago: University of Chicago Press.

Elster, Jon (1979) *Ulysses and the Sirens: Studies in Rationality and Irrationality* Cambridge: Cambridge University Press.

Elster, Jon (1983) *Sour Grapes: Studies in the Subversion of Rationality* Cambridge: Cambridge University Press.

Enloe, Cynthia (1989) *Bananas, Beaches and Bases: Making Feminist Sense of International Politics* London: Pandora Books.

Eysenck, H. J. (1985) *The Decline and Fall of the Freudian Empire* Harmondsworth: Viking.

Farrell, B. A. (1988) *The Standing of Psychoanalysis* Oxford: Oxford University Press.

Feyerabend, Paul K. (1975) *Against Method: Outline of an Anarchistic Theory of Knowledge* London: New Left Books.

Fisher, S. and Greenberg, R. P. (1977) *The Scientific Credibility of Freud's Theory and Therapy* Hassocks, Sussex: Harvester Press.

Forrester, Jay W. and Meadows, Dennis H. (1972) *Limits to Growth* New York: Universe Books.

Frankel, J. (1988) *International Relations in a Changing World* Oxford: Oxford University Press.

Freedman, L. (1981) *The Evolution of Nuclear Strategy* London: Macmillan.

Freud, Sigmund (1955) 'Analysis of phobia in a five-year-old boy'. In *The Complete Psychological Works of Sigmund Freud,* vol. 10, London: Hogarth Press. (First published 1909).

Friedman, M. (1962) *Capitalism and Freedom* Chicago: University of Chicago Press.

Friedman, M. (1966a) *Essays in Positive Economics* Chicago: University of Chicago Press.

Friedman, M. (1966b) 'The methodology of positive economics'. In *Essays in Positive Economics* Chicago: University of Chicago Press.

Friedman, M. and Schwartz, A. J. (1963) *A Monetary History of the United States 1867–1960* Princeton: Princeton University Press.

Gallie, W. (1964) *Philosophy and the Historical Understanding* London: Chatto & Windus.

Galtung, Johan (1971) 'A structural theory of imperialism'. *Journal of Peace Research*, 13(2): 81–94.

Galtung, Johan (1976– 80) *Essays in Peace Research* (5 vols) Copenhagen: Ejlers.

Gardiner, P. L. (1952) *The Nature of Historical Explanation* Oxford: Oxford University Press.

Gardiner, P. L. (ed.) (1974) *The Philosophy of History* Oxford: Oxford University Press.

George, Donald A. R. (1990) 'Chaos and complexity in economics'. *Journal of Economic Surveys*, 4(4): 397–414.

Gochet, Paul (1968) *Ascent to Truth: A Critical Examination of Quine's Philosophy* Munich: Philosophia Verlag.

Groom, A. J. R. and Light, Margot (1994) *Contemporary International Relations: A Guide to Theory* London: Pinter.

Guetzkow, Harald and Valadez, Joseph J. (eds) (1981) *Simulated International Processes: Theories and Research in Global Modeling* Beverly Hills: Sage.

Habermas, J. (1988) *On the Logic of the Social Sciences* Cambridge: Polity Press.

Hanson, Norwood Russell (1958) *Patterns of Discovery: An Inquiry Into the Conceptual Foundations of Science* Cambridge: Cambridge University Press.

Hargreaves-Heap, S. (1989) *Rationality and Economics* Oxford: Blackwell.

Hawthorn, G. (1991) *Plausible Worlds: Possibility and Understanding in History and the Social Sciences* Cambridge: Cambridge University Press.

Hempel, Carl G. (1965a) *Aspects of Concept Formation in Empirical Science* Chicago: University of Chicago Press.

Hempel, Carl G. (1965b) (first published in 1948) 'The function of general laws in history'. In Carl G. Hempel *Aspects of Concept Formation in Empirical Science* Chicago: University of Chicago Press.

Hendry, D. F. (1993) *Econometrics: Alchemy or Science? Essays on Econometric Methodology* Oxford: Blackwell.

Herman, Charles F. (ed.) (1972) *International Crises: Insights from Behavioral Research* New York: Free Press.

Hollis, Martin (1987) *The Cunning of Reason* Cambridge: Cambridge University Press.

Hollis, Martin and Smith, Steve (1991) *Explaining and Understanding in International Relations* Oxford: Clarendon Press.

Howard, Nigel (1994) 'Drama theory and its relationship to game theory'. *Group Decision and Negotiation*, 3: 187–206

Howard, Nigel; Bennett, Peter; Bryant, Jim and Bradley, Morris (1992) 'Manifesto for a theory of drama and irrational choice'. *Journal of the Operational Research Society*, 44: 99–103.

Huth, Paul (1988) *Extended Deterrence and the Prevention of War* New Haven: Yale University Press.

Janis, Irving (1982) *Groupthink* (2nd edn) Boston: Houghton Mifflin.

Kaplan, Morton A. (1957) *System and Process in International Politics* New York: Wiley.

Kaplan, Morton A. (1969) 'The new Great Debate: traditionalism vs. science in international relations'. In K. Knorr and J. N. Rosenau (eds) *Contending Approaches to International Politics* Princeton: Princeton University Press.

Keegan, J. (1976) *The Face of Battle* London: Cape.

Kline, Paul (1972) *Fact and Fantasy in Freudian Theory* London: Methuen.

Knorr, K. and Rosenau, J. N. (eds) (1969) *Contending Approaches to International Politics* Princeton: Princeton University Press.

Körner, S. (1960) *The Philosophy of Mathematics* London: Hutchinson.

Kuhn, Thomas (1957) *The Copernican Revolution: Planetary Astronomy in the Development of Western Thought* Cambridge: Harvard University Press.

Kuhn, Thomas (1962) *The Structure of Scientific Revolutions* Chicago: University of Chicago Press.

Lakatos, Imre, (1970) 'Falsification and the methodology of scientific research programmes'. In I. Lakatos and A. Musgrave (eds) *Criticism and the Growth of Knowledge* Cambridge: Cambridge University Press.

Lakatos, Imre and Musgrave, Alan (eds) (1970) *Criticism and the Growth of Knowledge* Cambridge: Cambridge University Press.

Lapid, Yosef (1989) 'The third debate: on the prospects of international theory in a post-positivist era'. *International Studies Quarterly*, 33(3): 235–54.

Latsis, S. (ed.) (1976) *Method and Appraisal in Economics* Cambridge: Cambridge University Press.

Leamer, E. E. (1983) 'Let's take the 'con' out of econometrics'. *American Economic Review*, 63: 31–43.

Light, Margot and Groom, A. J. R. (eds) (1985) *International Relations: A Handbook of Current Theory* London: Pinter.

Lighthill, James (1986) 'The recently recognised failure of predictability in Newtonian dynamics'. In J. Mason, P. Mathias and J. H. Westcott (eds) *Predictability in Science and Society* London: Royal Society and the British Academy.

Louch, A. R. (1966) *Explanation and Human Action* Oxford: Blackwell.

Machiavelli, N. *The Prince* (First published 1532, numerous editions)

Magee, B. (1982) *Popper* London: Woburn Press.

Manning, C. A. W. (1975) *The Nature of International Society* London: Macmillan.

Marx, Karl (1950) 'Theses on Feuerbach XI'. In Karl Marx and Friedrich Engels *Collected Works* London: Lawrence & Wishart (and in numerous other editions).

Mason, John; Mathias, P. and Westcott, J. H. (eds) (1986) *Predictability in Science and Society* London: Royal Society and the British Academcy.

Masterman, Margaret (1970) 'The nature of a paradigm'. In I. Lakatos and A. Musgrave (eds) 1970, *Criticism and the Growth of Knowledge* Cambridge: Cambridge University Press.

Meadows, Donnella; Richardson, J. M. and Bruckman, G. (1982) *Groping in the Dark: The First Decade of Global Modelling* New York: Wiley.

Miles, J. (1984) *Physica*, D11, 309–323.

Morgenthau, Hans (1960) *Politics Among Nations: The Struggle for Power and Peace* (6th ed. rev. by K. and W. Thompson. First published 1948.) New York: Knopf.

Most, Benjamin A. and Starr, Harvey (1989) *Inquiry, Logic and International Politics* Columbia: University of South Carolina Press.

Moul, William B. (1988) 'Balances of power and the escalation to war of conflicts between unequals 1815–1939: some evidence'. *American Journal of Political Science*, 32: 241–75.

Munn, Allan M. (1973) *From Nought to Relativity: Creating the Physical World Model* London: Allen & Unwin.

Nardin, Terry and Mapel, David R. (1992) *Traditions in International Ethics* Cambridge: Cambridge University Press.

Neufeld, Mark (1995) *The Reconstruction of International Relations Theory* Cambridge: Cambridge University Press.

Nicholson, Michael (1983) *The Scientific Analysis of Social Behaviour: A Defence of Empiricism in Social Science* London: Pinter.

Nicholson, Michael (1989) *Formal Theories in International Relations* Cambridge: Cambridge University Press.

Nicholson, Michael (1992) *Rationality and the Analysis of International Conflict* Cambridge: Cambridge University Press.

Nicholson, Michael (1993) Review of *The World of States* by Charles Reynolds (1992). *Acta Politica*, 27: 471–74.

Nicholson, Michael (1995) 'Rational decisions in international crises: a rationalisation'. In K. Dowding and D. King (eds) *Preferences, Institutions and Rational Choice* Oxford: Oxford University Press.

Niou, Emerson; Ordeshook, Peter C. and Rose, Gregory F. (1989) *The Balance of Power: Stability in International Systems* Cambridge: Cambridge University Press.

North, Robert, Holsti, O. R., Zaninovich, G. and Zinnes, D. M. (1963) *Content Analysis* Evanston IL: Northwestern University Press.

Northedge, F. S. (1976) *The International Political System* London: Faber & Faber.

Olson, William C. and Groom, A. J. R. (1991) *International Relations Then and Now* London: HarperCollins Academic.

Organski, A. F. K. and Kugler, J. (1981) *The War Ledger* Chicago: University of Chicago Press.

Ormerod, Paul (1994) *The Death of Economics* London: Faber & Faber.

Pigou, A. C. (1954) *Economics of Welfare* (6th edn) London: Macmillan.

Platt, D. C. M. (1989) *Mickey Mouse Numbers in World History* London: Macmillan.

Popper, Karl R. (1959) *The Logic of Scientific Discovery* New York: Harper & Collins.

Popper, Karl R. (1968) *Conjectures and Refutations: The Growth of Scientific Knowledge* New York: Harper & Collins.

Power, Eileen (1946) *Mediaeval People* London: Methuen.

Quine, W. V. (1960) *Word and Object* Cambridge: MIT Press.

Quine, W. V. (1961a) *From a Logical Point of View* New York: Harper & Row.

Quine, W. V. (1961b) 'Two dogmas of empiricism'. In W. V. Quine *From a Logical Point of View* New York: Harper & Row.

Raiffa, H. (1982) *The Art and Science of Negotiation* Cambridge: Harvard University Press.

Raiffa, H. (1992) *The Pursuit of Truth* Cambridge: Harvard University Press.

Rapoport, Anatol (1957) 'Lewis Fry Richardson's mathematical theory of war'. *Journal of Conflict Resolution* 1: 249–99.

Rapoport, Anatol (1965) *Strategy and Conscience* New York: Harper & Row.

Rapoport, Anatol (1966) *Two-Person Game Theory* Ann Arbor: University of Michigan Press.

Rapoport, Anatol (1974) *Fights, Games and Debates* Ann Arbor: University of Michigan Press.

Reynolds, Charles (1973) *Theory and Explanation in World Politics* London: Martin Roberston.

Reynolds, Charles, (1981) *Modes of Imperialism* Oxford: Martin Robertson.

Reynolds, Charles R. (1989) *The Politics of War: A Study of the Rationality of Violence in Inter-state Relations* Hemel Hempstead: Harvester Wheatsheaf.

Reynolds, Charles R. (1992) *The World of States: An Introduction to Explanation and Theory* Aldershot: Edward Elgar.

Richardson, Lewis Fry (1960a) *Arms and Insecurity* Pittsburgh: Boxwood Press.

Richardson, Lewis Fry (1960b) *Statistics of Deadly Quarrels* Pittsburgh: Boxwood Press.

Richardson, Lewis Fry (1993) *Quantitative Psychology and Studies of Conflict* (Collected Papers, vol. 2) Cambridge: Cambridge University Press.

Rosenau, Pauline (1990) 'Internal logic, external absurdity: post modernism in political science'. *Paradigms* 4(1): 39–57.

Rosenau, Pauline (1992) *Post-modernism and the Social Sciences: Insights, Inroads and Intrusions* Princeton: Princeton University Press.

Rummell, Rudoph J. (1972) *The Dimensionality of Nations* Beverly Hills and London: Sage.

Rummell, R. J. (1983) 'Libertarianism and international violence'. *Journal of Conflict Resolution*, 27(1): 27–72.

Rummell, R. J. (1985) 'Libertarian propositions on violence within and between nations'. *Journal of Conflict Resolution*, 29(1): 419–55.

Runciman, W. G. (1983, 1989) *A Treatise on Social Theory* (vols 1 and 2) Cambridge: Cambridge University Press.

Russell, Bertrand (1948) *Human Knowledge: Its Scope and Limits* London: Allen & Unwin.

Russett, Bruce (1993) *Grasping the Democratic Peace: Principles for a Post-Cold War Period* Princeton: Princeton University Press.

Ryan, Alan (1970) *The Philosophy of the Social Sciences* London: Macmillan.

Ryan, Alan (ed) (1973) *The Philosophy of Social Explanation* London: Oxford University Press.

Savage, Leonard J. (1972) *The Foundations of Statistics* New York: Dover.

Schelling, Thomas C. (1960) *The Strategy of Conflict*, Cambridge: Harvard University Press.

Schrodt, Philip A. (1981) *Preserving Arms Distributions in a Multi-polar World: A Mathematical Study* Denver: Monograph Series in World Affairs, University of Denver.

Sen, A. K. (1977) 'The theory of rational fools: a critique of the behavioural foundations of economic theory'. *Philosophy and Public Affairs*, 6: 317–44.

Shapiro, Michael (1992) *Reading the Post-modern Polity* Minneapolis: University of Minnesota Press.

Sherwood, Michael (1969) *The Logic of Explanation in Psychoanalysis* New York: Academic Press.

Simon, H. A. (1982) *Models of Bounded Rationality* Cambridge: MIT Press.

Singer, J. David (ed.) (1968) *Quantitative International Politics* New York: Free Press.

Singer, J. David (1969) 'The incomplete theorist: insight without evidence'. In K. Knorr and J. N. Rosenau (eds) *Contending Approaches to International Politics* Princeton: Princeton University Press.

Singer, J. David (1980) *The Correlates of War: Testing Some Realpolitik Models* New York: Free Press.

Singer, J. David (1993) *Resort to Arms: International and Civil Wars 1816–1980* Beverly Hills: Sage.

Singer, J. David and Small, Melvin (1968) 'Alliance aggregation and the onset of war'. In J. D. Singer (ed.) *Quantitative International Politics* New York: Free Press.

Smith, Steve (1985) 'Groupthink and the hostage rescue mission'. *British Journal of Political Science*, 15(1): 117–23.

Snow, C. P.(1967) *Variety of Men* London: Macmillan.

Stewart, Ian (1989) *Does God Play Dice? The Mathematics of Complexity* Oxford: Oxford University Press.

Stigler, G. and Becker, G. (1977) 'De gustibus non est disputandum'. *American Economic Review*, 67: 76–90.

Sylvester, Christine (1994) *Feminist Theory and International Relations in a Postmodern Era* Cambridge: Cambridge University Press.

Taylor, A. J. P. (1965) *English History 1914–45* Oxford: Oxford University Press.

Taylor, Charles (1964) *The Explanation of Behaviour* Atlantic Highlands NJ: Humanities Press.

Taylor, Michael (1987) *The Possibility of Cooperation* Cambridge: Cambridge University Press.

Thagard, Paul (1992) *Conceptual Revolutions* Princeton: Princeton University Press.

Trigg, R. (1985) *Understanding Social Science: A Philosophical Introduction to the Social Sciences* London: Oxford University Press.

Van de Graaff, J. (1957) *Theoretical Welfare Economics* Cambridge: Cambridge University Press.

Van Fraassen, Bas C. (1980) *The Scientific Image* Oxford: Clarendon Press.

Vasquez, John A. (1983) *The Power of Power Politics* London: Pinter.

Vasquez, John A. (1987) 'The steps to war: toward a scientific explanation of the correlates of war findings'. *World Politics*, 40(1): 108–45.

Vasquez, John A. (1993) *The War Puzzle* Cambridge: Cambridge University Press.

Vasquez, John A (1995) 'The post-positivist debate: reconstructing scientific inquiry and IR theory after Enlightenment's fall'. In K. Booth and S. Smith (eds) **International Political Theory Today** Cambridge: Cambridge University Press.

von Neumann, J. and Morgenstern, O. (1944) *The Theory of Games and Economic Behavior* Princeton: Princeton University Press.

von Wright, G. (1971) *Explanation and Understanding* Ithaca: Cornell University Press.

Wagner, Harrison (1986) 'The theory of games and the balance of power'. *World Politics*, 38(4): 546–76.

Walker, R. B. J. (1992) *Inside/Outside: International Relations as Political Theory* Cambridge: Cambridge University Press.

Wallace, Michael (1979) 'Arms races and escalation: some new evidence'. *Journal of Conflict Resolution*, 23: 3–36.

Wallace, Michael (1982) 'Arms and escalation: two competing hypotheses'. *International Studies Quarterly*, 26(1): 37–56.

Waltz, K. N. (1979) *Theory of International Politics* Reading MA: Addison-Wesley.

Walzer, M. (1977) *Just and Unjust Wars* New York: Basic Books.

Webb, Keith (1995) *An Introduction to Problems in the Philosophy of Social Science* London: Pinter.

Wight, Martin (1966) *Diplomatic Investigations* London: Allen & Unwin.

Wight, Martin (1979) *Power Politics* Harmondsworth: Penguin.

Wight, Martin (1991) *International Theory: The Three Traditions* London: Leicester University Press.

Wilkinson, David (1980) *Deadly Quarrels: Lewis F. Richardson and the Statistical Study of War* Berkeley: University of California Press.

Winch, Peter (1990) *The Idea of a Social Science and its Relation to Philosophy* (2nd edn) London: Routledge.

Wittgenstein, Ludwig (1953) *Philosophical Investigations* Oxford: Blackwell.

Wright, Quincy (1942) *A Study of War* Chicago: University of Chicago Press.

Zinnes, Dina A. and Muncaster, Robert G. (1984) 'The dynamics of hostile activity and the prediction of war'. *Journal of Conflict Resolution*, 28(2): 187–229.

Index

Index

chromosomes 36
Churchill, Winston 69n
Cioffi-Revilla, C. 5, 23
civilization, Christian 67
claims, universalist 83
Clausewitz, C. 158, 192
cliometrician 145, 149n
cliometrics 110
Coase, R.W. 28
Cohen, John 192
Cold War 13, 21, 22
Collingwood, R.G. 4, 6, 59, 109, 110, 111, 113,
commodities 152
common understanding 127n
communication 44, 46ff, 107, 112
community, scientific 73
Compte, Auguste 189
computers 15, 42, 172
conceptual communities 105ff, 116
condition
    initial 34, 53n
    sufficient 49
conduct, altruistic 157
conflict 24, 151, 186
confusions 5
consciousness 58
consensus 127
consequences 30, 31
constants 182
content analysis 138
content, mathematical 175
context, intellectual 12ff
Copernicans 76
Copernicus, Nicolaus 196, 197
corporation, multinational 83
Correlates of War project 23
correlation 143ff, 146, 148
counter-instances 71, 72, 92
counting 130, 136
covering law 35, 36, 37, 50, 51, 53n
covering law model 48, 49
creationists 80
Crimean War 110
crises, international 7, 23, 24, 62, 63, 64, 65, 119,
    140, 143, 164, 187
Crisis, 1914 49, 64
Crisis, Bay of Pigs 64, 66
Crisis, Bosnian 1908 49
Crisis, Suez 92
critical theory 176ff
Crystal, David 134
Cuban Missile Crisis 24, 60, 64, 66, 164

Dardenelles 69n
Darwin, Charles 77
data 2, 5, 14, 19, 23, 37, 66, 135, 143, 145, 146,
    147, 148
Dawkins, Richard 77
deadly quarrels 23, 98
debates, epistemological 14
decision makers 139
decision-making 66, 91, 119, 187
decisions, irrational 164
deductions 150
definition 44ff, 96, 149
    nominal 44, 46
    ostensive 44, 47
    operational 96
democracies and war 129
determinism 51
deterrent, nuclear 21
Deutsch, Karl 7, 29n, 66
dichotomies 141
dictionary 44, 81, 138
Diehl, Paul 129

dilemma, methodological 3
dilemma, Quinean 101
Dimensionality of Nations 23
diplomacy 60
disagreement, rational 27
disputes 57, 142
Dray, W.H. 50
dreams 106, 107

earthquakes 35, 36, 68, 69
econometrician 145, 149n
econometrics 149n
economics 2, 10, 11, 13, 16, 31, 43, 73, 133, 135,
    150
    mathematical 10
    positive 190
economists 11, 119, 137
Edelson, M. 98
Einstein, Albert 116, 127n
elections 106
electromagnetic fields 46
electrons 46
élites 174, 176
Elster J. 170n
emancipation 177, 179
empathy 3, 6, 58, 67
empire 1, 140
empiricism 6, 160, 182, 190
empiricist 17, 18, 26, 69, 176
Enlightenment 17, 78
Enloe, Cynthia 175
entrepreneur 69, 91, 165
environment 121, 152, 153, 154, 155, 164
epicycles 76, 146, 195, 196
epistemology 7, 88, 161, 189
equation 182
    differential 165, 181, 182
    linear 182
    non-linear 182
    non-linear differential 184
equilibrium 193, 194
equilibrium , Nash 184, 186
ethics 179ff
evaluation 157
event 6, 55, 87n, 112, 143, 146,
event, necessary 50
events, historical 110
    mental 56, 58, 115, 116
    physical 56, 57, 62
    probabilistic 50
    similar 66
    social 4, 61
evidence 9, 22, 94, 102, 106, 148,
evolution 8, 78
expected utility 135, 136, 139
experience 44
    common 47, 48, 105
    human 113
    mystical 107
    other people's 108
    physical 105
    private 107
explanandum 33
explanans 33
explanation 3, 4, 22, 30ff, 49, 58, 125, 157
    causal 27, 33, 34, 58
    'how necessarily' 48ff
    'how possibly' 48ff
    ideological 83
    parsimonious 85
    scientific 8, 25, 38
    sketches 49
    sociobiological 83
    teleological 33
Eysenck, Hans 164

Index

Index

sentence, observation 104n
Sherwood, Michael 169n
Simon, Herbert 151
Singer, J. David 7, 23, 65, 104n, 110, 129, 149
Small, Melvin 23, 65, 104n, 110
Smith, Adam 13, 87, 188
Snow, C.P. 127n
social sciences 2, 3, 6, 7, 10, 13, 15, 16, 17, 22, 26,
    27, 49, 54ff, 63, 81, 93, 102, 103, 106, 108,
    109, 112, 120, 159, 172
social sciences, philosophy of 12, 55
societies 1, 67, 106, 109, 111, 156, 179
solar system 75, 195–7
solution (of game) 184
sophisticated methodological falsificationist 71
Spanish Civil War 57
stability, structural 118
Stalin, Joseph 158
standard of life 130, 137
Stanford University 24
star 44, 195
state 1, 11, 12, 19, 29n, 73, 82, 91, 92, 95, 131,
    139, 140, 150, 158, 162, 188, 189, 192
statements 18, 33, 44, 71, 88, 102, 165, 190
statistical inference 190
statisticians 135, 149
statistics 19, 134, 140, 143
Stewart, Ian 181
Stigler, G. 120
strategy 56, 57, 122
    maximin 184, 185, 187
    minimax 184, 186
    mixed 186
structuralism 82, 84, 192, 198
structure of beliefs 168
Sun 26, 72, 75, 79, 171, 195, 196, 197
survival 71, 162
symbols 45
system
    closed 37, 38, 53n
    complex 118
    deductive 117
    logical 31
    market 119, 150
    meteorological 42
    non-chaotic 38
    open 53n
    solar 27
    structural 91
    Waltzian 93, 99
    vulnerability 99ff

tautology, tautological 72, 88ff, 96, 148
Taylor, A.J.P. 69n, 158
technology 8, 9, 16, 35, 100
terrorism 169, 170n, 175
tests, testability 2, 3, 100, 129, 140.147
texts 75, 112
Thagard, Paul 74
theoretical concepts 46, 189
theories, theorists 2, 3, 7, 9, 10, 14, 22, 27, 30ff,
    44ff, 71, 74, 85, 88, 93ff, 97, 158, 162, 165,
    167, 171
theory
    androgynous 175
    chaos 35, 37ff, 122, 181
    Darwinian 77, 79
    drama 166
    Earth-centred 74, 77, 79
    goal-directed 152, 157
    heliocentric 27, 77
    international 5
    Keynsian 15
    Marxist 90, 91, 198
    monetarist 16

Nazi 180
Newtonian 94
probability 147, 189
rational choice 150ff, 164, 167, 168
relativity 72, 94, 104n
Third Reich 83
Thucydides 192
transitivity 149n
Trevor-Roper, Hugh 158
truth 2, 31, 32
typology 143

UK see Britain
UN operations 100
uncertainty 192
understanding 3, 6, 11, 58, 59ff, 105ff, 159ff, 169
    adults' 108
    children's 108
    common 105ff, 108
    hierarchic 123ff
unemployment 26, 27, 179
Universe 79, 196
urbanization 110
US Embassy, siege of in Iran 60
utility, expected 139, 150, 198–9
utility function see function, utility
utility functions of states 152

Valadez, J. 24, 66
values 28, 171ff
Van de Graaf, J. 178
variable 23, 71, 95, 118, 130, 144, 145, 182
Vasquez, John 19, 23, 81, 83, 84, 143, 152
velocity of circulation 97
verifiability 88, 89, 147, 148
Vienna Circle 25, 88, 189
violence 7, 100, 175
Von Neumann, J. 139, 187, 199
voting 54, 57, 106

Wagner, Harrison 151
Walker, R.B.J. 6, 109
Wallace, Michael 129, 142
Waltz, Kenneth 73, 91, 161, 162
Walzer, Michael 170n
war 1, 8, 9, 50, 56, 57, 59, 84, 90, 98, 139, 140,
    142, 143, 172
    bacteriological 180
    causes 1, 2
    incidence 133
    initiation 129
    likelihood 131, 132
    nuclear 180
war see names of specific wars
'warfinpersal' 137–8
weapons, nuclear 1
Weber, Max 4
weights, (in index numbers) 137
Wight, Martin 5, 12, 14, 17, 29n, 113, 132, 171
Winch, Peter 3, 4, 6, 10, 16, 28, 29n., 58, 59, 61,
    62, 105, 106, 111, 112, 113ff, 120, 129, 140,
    159, 160
Winchean, 3, 4, 59, 111, 129, 159, 160
Wittgenstein, Ludwig 3, 4, 59, 111, 159, 160
word 81
work, behavioural 122
world, external 26, 45
world, natural 105, 136
Wright, Quincy 23, 28n
World War I 1, 13, 49, 51, 63, 192
World War II 13, 14, 15, 69n, 119, 142, 158, 170n,
    172, 192

zebra principle 35ff, 51, 122
Zinnes, Dina 43